Richard Brevard Russell, Jr.
A Man of Consequence

This biography of Senator Russell was donated by the Richard B. Russell Foundation, Inc.

The Foundation serves to preserve Senator Russell's legacy of unparalleled service to Georgia and the United States.

December 2011

Richard B. Russell

Library for Political Research and Studies ~ University of Georgia Libraries

http://www.libs.uga.edu/russell

MERCER
UNIVERSITY PRESS

Endowed by
TOM WATSON BROWN
and
THE WATSON-BROWN FOUNDATION, INC.

RICHARD BREVARD RUSSELL, JR.

A LIFE OF CONSEQUENCE

Sally Russell

MERCER UNIVERSITY PRESS

MACON, GEORGIA

MUP/H834

© 2011 Mercer University Press
1400 Coleman Avenue
Macon, Georgia 31207

First Edition

Books published by Mercer University Press are printed on acid-free
paper that meets the requirements of American National Standard for
Information Sciences—Permanence of Paper for Printed Library
Materials.

Mercer University Press is a member of Green Press Initiative
(greenpressinitiative.org), a nonprofit organization working to help
publishers and printers increase their use of recycled paper and
decrease their use of fiber derived from endangered forests. This book
is printed on recycled paper.
Library of Congress Cataloging-in-Publication Data

Russell, Sally, 1942-
  Richard Brevard Russell, Jr. : a life of consequence / Sally Russell. --
1st ed.
    p. cm.
  Includes bibliographical references and index.
  ISBN 978-0-88146-259-3 (hardcover : acid-free paper)
  1. Russell, Richard B. (Richard Brevard), 1897-1971. 2. Legislators--
United States--Biography. 3. United States. Congress. Senate--
Biography. 4. United States--Politics and government--1933-1945. 5.
 United States--Politics and government--1945-1989. 6. Governors--
Georgia--Biography. 7. Georgia--Politics and government--1865-1950.
I. Title.
  E748.R944R87 2011
  328.73092--dc23
  [B]
                                        2011024688

In Memory of
Harriet Caroline Orr
Ina Russell Stacy
Mary Willie Russell Green
Patience Elizabeth Russell Peterson

and
dedicated to my husband,
Leslie Warrington,
again

Also by Sally Russell

Roots and Ever Green: The Selected Letters of Ina Dillard Russell

Shatter Me with Dawn: A Celebration of Country Life

A Heart for Any Fate: The Biography of Richard Brevard Russell Sr.

Latitude of Home: A Storytelling Journey

Contents

Acknowledgments

Acknowledgments are one of the most enjoyable and yet most worrisome parts of writing a book. It is a genuine pleasure to think back on the shared work and to recognize what it means to conceive such a creative project as a book and then to have so many befriend it on its way to completion. Acknowledgements are worrisome—because I always fear I'll leave someone out. Thus, let it be said here at the beginning that no one is omitted deliberately. Named or unnamed, many have helped bring this book to fruition, and I am grateful.

Let it also be confessed here that this story would never have been told without the inspiration and encouragement of Marc Jolley of Mercer University Press. It was his idea, following a surprising evening we spent at a meeting of the Georgia Democratic Party, and his faith and support have kept it alive. Without Marc's quiet wisdom and guidance, I would not have had either the idea or the courage to tell the story of the man Richard Russell from this particular and important standpoint. I have said in other books that every writer should hope and pray for an editor like Marc Jolley. Today that statement is truer than ever.

The people who work at Mercer University Press deserve, as always, a huge round of applause.

Since beginning work on Ina Dillard Russell's letters in 1994 (published in 1999 by UGA Press), I have spent countless hours in the Russell Library for Political Research and Studies, and these have been some of the happiest and most productive hours of my life. I thank all the staff, particularly Sheryl Vogt and Jill Severn, who became and have remained my friends in spite of the myriad and continuous questions I've fired at them over the years.

Again, I come up short trying to find a way to thank all my family members for their practical help. These include my two daughters, my five siblings, and straight through to my many cousins (there are more than 100 of us), and almost all these are accompanied by attachments who supported my helpers. I thank all my first cousins who shared with me their Uncle Dick memories. Though a specific story might not be part of the narrative, all helped me see the man in a clearer light. In particular

I will name only a few of the kin, those who met specific cries for help again and again. I am deeply indebted to William Don Russell, who shared so many intimate memories of working for his uncle in Washington throughout the fifties. Kate (Catherine Rose) Russell, granddaughter of Robert Lee Russell, Jr., literally saved my sanity by conducting research at the Russell library when I could not go myself. A busy graduate student at the University of Georgia, she brought youth, enthusiasm, and determination to a volunteer position (read, no pay) and did the job with exceptional skill and promptness. Kim Simon Reynolds, wife of my nephew John Fielding Reynolds, did her cheerful best up in Charlotte, North Carolina, to help me track down information on Harriet Orr, in spite of a busy schedule with grade-school children. To Kim and Kate, my heartfelt thanks.

Once again my friend Barbara McMichael read the manuscript in various stages and offered wise advice and much-needed encouragement. Betsy Russell DuBard did the initial copy editing, helping me get the manuscript off in style. Many thanks to both of these skilled linguists.

I am also indebted to President Jimmy Carter and Judges Herbert Phipps and Yvonne Miller of the Georgia Court of Appeals, all of whom I interviewed at the start of my work. These distinguished public servants gave me humbling insights into Russell's lasting influence in many areas, and I am grateful for their help.

Thanks also are due to Charles E. Campbell for several interviews that provided outstanding insights into Dick Russell's life and work. How I wish I could thank Proctor Jones for his insights, but he left us for a better place not long after I interviewed him.

Last, I again thank my husband Les Warrington for his continued support and encouragement. His faith in me and in my work keeps me writing in a figurative sense, and his technical skills keep me writing in the most practical sense. I have said before and now say again that I can never thank him enough, but I will keep trying.

Preface

Not far outside the city limits of Winder, on Georgia Highway 8, between Atlanta and Athens, travelers might notice a modest black-and-white sign pointing down a narrow, paved county road. Like so many rural roads, this road's name indicates what was once found, or might still be found, on the road. The green-and-white road marker reads *Russell Cemetery Road*, and the arrow on the lower sign points the way to the Russell Family Cemetery.

The spot is the final resting place of Richard Brevard Russell, Sr, and Richard Brevard Russell, Jr., men who each served the state of Georgia for fifty years in high public office. Although chronicling a significant period of Georgia history, the graveyard is worth a visit if for nothing else but a quiet pause in a journey. Shielded from the road by thick pine woods, starred with exuberant magnolia trees, and bordered by a few acres of wooded parkland to the east, the cemetery is a peaceful and well-tended spot. It has something of a church air about it, being clearly a place for prayer, reflection, and, oddly, celebration of life. I have been coming to this place for more than fifty years for just such activities.

A low granite wall, topped by a gray metal railing with two matching gates, surrounds most of the gravestones, though a few have spilled outside the walls. An imposing obelisk, likely fifteen feet tall, presides at the center of the enclosed space, and around it, similar gray granite headstones, about twenty of them, sit like church members in a hall. These headstones usually represent couples. Most have extended before them two long slabs of similar stone, which bear a brief record of the lives whose mortal remains have here found final rest. There are scripture verses on most of the stones: "Her children arise up and call her blessed; her husband also and he praiseth her." "The memory of the just is blessed." "Because Thy loving kindness is better than life, my lips shall praise Thee." "Be not forgetful to entertain strangers, for thereby some have entertained angels unawares." The scripture sources are not generally noted. This family thought you ought to know these without reminder.

These stones are called ledgers, a fitting word for the record of a person's life.

Summarizing any person's life on the brief page of a gravestone is one of life's chief challenges, and Russells have risen to the task. The obelisk was first erected to the memory of Richard B. Russell, Sr., and his wife, Ina Dillard Russell, so their record is lengthier, a tender commemoration by and of the prolific family they founded. The names of fifteen children fill one side of the obelisk, and thirteen of those grew to adulthood. The name Dick Russell, Jr., is fourth on the list, the first son. His monument, next to those of his parents, is somewhat bulky—the headstone and the ledger have been melded—so there's room for a few more words than ordinary mortals might hope for. That being said, it is only right to add that Dick Russell, Jr., considered himself the most ordinary of mortals. His marker, which he designed himself, gives the impression of someone who is asked to stand up for recognition but who hesitates because praise makes him uncomfortable. Dick Russell was a genuinely modest man, which is not to say he did not have a vigorous ego. The wise don't look for politicians without ego. Ego is part of the job description. What to hope for is a politician whose life illustrates a healthy equilibrium between self-worth and a sincere desire to serve others. Richard Brevard Russell, Jr., governor of Georgia and United States Senator for thirty-eight years, was such a man.

There are three distinct parts to Russell's ledger, all chosen by his family. The first covers public career; the second is a personal judgment; the third, going beyond either of those, cites a verse of scripture appropriate to the witness of a life that sought to have meaning beyond itself, a life of consequence.

The Ledger
Richard Brevard Russell, Jr.,
2 November 1897, Winder, Georgia–21 January 1971, Washington, D.C.
United States Naval Reserve, 1918
Georgia House of Representatives 1921–1931
Speaker, House of Representatives 1927–1931
Governor of Georgia 1931–1933
United States Senator from Georgia 1933–1971
President Pro Tempore 1969–1971

"When the security of the United States was the issue, six American Presidents leaned upon this great patriot. He never failed them."
—Richard M. Nixon, 1971.

"A noble desire to excel and to serve spurred him to vast achievements. Yet an innate modesty constrained him. His mind and his heart were large enough to serve and to love his state, his nation, and his family. A true noblesse oblige prompted his highest relations with all."

"He sought the good of his people and promoted the welfare of all their descendants."

The range of history in the dates of Richard Russell, Jr.—1897 to 1971—and the obvious differences between a Georgia country town and the nation's capital are immediately striking. In 1897 the world was beginning a dramatic swing into a century that would see more changes in religion, politics, society, science, technology, and war than almost all other centuries of human history combined. It would be a wild ride for a boy born to fulfill great expectations in the mercurial modern political arena, yet reared to venerate the worn and vanishing splendor of the American South. Russell would become one of the half dozen most powerful men in Washington for a period of almost twenty years, and it would be frequently admitted, most notably by President Harry Truman, that if Russell had not been from Georgia, if he had been from a state such as Indiana, Illinois, or Missouri, the presidency could not have been denied him. Such was Dick Russell's love of the South and his native state that when he heard about Truman's remark, his reply gave deep insight into the man: "I'd rather be from Georgia than be president." Another time, in a national broadcast, he said in response to this mention, "I am very proud of my Southern heritage, and I wouldn't have sacrificed it for any honor anywhere in the country."

Dick Russell lived in a time when to be Southern on the national stage was still to be something of a stepchild, yet all who knew him judged that he worked within that limitation with consummate grace. As his epitaph declares, "His heart and his mind were large enough to serve and to love his state, his nation and his family." Nothing in his life denies that statement.

Although Richard Brevard Russell, Jr., became an exemplary public servant at an early age and grew into a legend in his own time, respected by all who knew and worked with him on an astonishing range of national problems, his stand on civil rights has tainted his reputation in the years since his death. As a white Southerner and the man who understood the rules of Congress better than almost anyone else, he became the formidable head of the Southern bloc that for years fought successfully to defeat civil rights legislation. In many ways he was the General Lee of his time, a man respected nationally for his personal integrity and superior ability in his field, who inexplicably opposed human rights. It is hardly surprising that a man born in 1897 in Winder, Georgia, the son of Southern parents, who were themselves children of the social and economic horrors of the Reconstruction, would grow up believing in racial segregation. There were no radios or television broadcasts, only white Southern newspapers and histories presented to him until he was grown. In his family life he saw no abuse of the many black people who worked as servants and farm laborers around him. Instead, he learned a respect for them as human beings in a specific place within an ancient hierarchy. As a youth, he had the same attitudes towards women, white and black.

It is debatable whether those from later eras have the ability or even the right to judge those from earlier times, but because history and humankind are enormously complicated, it seems reasonable to consider that here is a case where we should judge not that we be not judged. From an early age I disagreed with my uncle on this question, but in our family disagreements were common and never a cause for condemnation. What I have tried to understand is how it is that my generation was able to change an age-old view of the black and white races, whereas our parents and grandparents were not. I have failed in arriving at any logical explanation except that humankind, in general, is slow to change. I know that a cataclysmic shift happened in my lifetime, but I am sure that this does not mean we are better than were our ancestors. How we live by our lights has been different, that is all.

As a child and young adult I knew Dick Russell as a beloved bachelor uncle, distant and reserved yet affectionate and attentive to his thirty-nine nieces and nephews. My family lived next door to him all my growing-up years, and he was specifically helpful to me at a critical time in my college education. As a young wife, I was privileged to live next door to him for three years and to have some small responsibilities for his homecomings. Therefore, I had no ambition that this story of his life would be objective in the academic sense, but I believe that it gives a true picture of a complex and fascinating personality, a man of contrasts.

An ardent segregationist who fought civil rights legislation, Richard B. Russell was also the father of the School Lunch Program and maintained the struggle for it to become a permanent feature of government for over ten years.

As a Georgia farm boy, Russell almost idolized the agricultural society from which America sprang, but he also came to embrace the nuclear age and space technology as he saw them become necessary for national security.

An intense family man, Dick Russell appreciated women, fell in love easily, and conducted numerous affairs, including one that lasted nearly thirty years. Yet he never married.

Deeply private, he lived his entire adult life in the public eye.

Harry Truman once defined a statesman as a politician who has been dead twenty years. A wise and vigorous politician in his youth, Dick Russell achieved statesman status in his own time.

Above all, in my study of Richard Brevard Russell, I have come to see a profoundly gifted and capable leader, uncommonly devoted to public service, who believed his work a calling. Contrary to many politicians' records, Russell's dedication seems peculiarly rooted in belief in the value of public service rather than in a love of or addiction to power. He was a member of the white, male, dominating class, but his record is not one of careless racism and abuse of power. Instead, it reflects his belief in hierarchy, an awareness of his place at the top, and, in his creed, the responsibility to care for those beneath him. That he felt deeply the plight of all humankind cannot be doubted. Nor can it be doubted that he believed sincerely his way of dealing with that plight the wisest course.

Allegiance to hierarchy has dominated the world's governments throughout most of the history of humankind until the establishment of the American state in the late eighteenth century. Even then, the Founding Fathers created the United States Senate as part of the governing mechanism to prevent democracy's potential to deteriorate into mob rule. Dick Russell became a member of this Senate at a young age, and from his earliest time there, he studied its inspiration and its methods. Hierarchy was a way of life to him.

At the end of his long and distinguished career in the United States Senate, Dick Russell was often asked to write a book. He answered that he doubted he would get around to reviewing his part in "...the most thrilling fifty years in the life of the human family," and he did not. From another age and time, I have strong links to the earlier one from which Richard Brevard Russell, Jr., came. In addition to knowing him and his twelve siblings, the work I have done on his mother's and father's lives gives me assurance that I have important credentials to consider his view in a way that has not been done. Having discovered in my work a fascinating and sympathetic man, wiser, more thoughtful in some ways than many, and as flawed as most, I have chosen to write his story from the standpoint of those who knew him rather than from historical research surrounding the stunning epoch in which he lived and rose to such heights of human power. It is with pleasure that I invite the reader to meet, in these pages, an extraordinary American, who lived his belief in public service to an extent of self-sacrifice hard to fathom.

PART I

1897–1920

As the Twig Is Bent

Sleet was pinging the windowpanes of the Jackson County courthouse on 2 November 1897, when an excited courier arrived with a telegram for Richard Russell, who was arguing a case. Everyone in the little town of Jefferson, Georgia, knew that the popular young lawyer and his wife, Ina, were expecting their fourth child, openly hoping for a boy after three daughters. Although the Russells lived sixteen miles away in tiny Winder, Ina Dillard had been known in Jefferson since her marriage in 1891 to Richard Russell. Before their children began to arrive in 1893, she often accompanied her husband and acted as his secretary. Mary Willie, Ina junior, and "Dicksie" sometimes came to Jefferson with their mother during the summer, and the town's social circle valued Ina's amenable company. Today, the courtroom could not help watching as Russell tore open the telegram and read, *Mother and son doing well. Come tonight.* When he looked up, grinning enough for half a dozen fathers, everyone knew that he was now Richard Brevard Russell, Sr. Judge N. L. Hutchins had to call for order in the court.

Richard Russell, Sr., had worked with Judge Hutchins for many years, and that day the older man adjourned court early so that the new father could reach home before dark. Through sleet and rain, over fifteen miles of muddy and icy roads, Russell drove as fast as he dared and rushed into the house to find the doctor there with mother and baby. As Dr. Charles Almond held the swaddled child for the father to see, unable to express himself in words—uncharacteristic behavior for Richard B. Russell, Sr.—the delighted father slapped Dr. Almond on the back so hard that he almost dropped the baby. When Ina cried out in alarm, Richard, still speechless, grabbed his shotgun from a corner and ran into the back yard, where he fired off volley after volley into the night sky. Winder had earlier been named Jug Tavern after its principal business[1],

---

[1] The town's name was changed, as was its frontier crossroads village character, around 1894 when the railroad came through and it became a farming and industrial community. It was renamed for John Winder, a railroad executive.

and no doubt gunfire in town was a familiar occurrence. On this night, however, the entire town guessed that the Russell baby was a boy.

To Ina Dillard and Richard Russell, Sr., this longed-for son had seemed slow in coming. To greet his arrival with loud rejoicing was no insult to his three sisters, but in the patriarchal Southern United States, there was no question but that the heir apparent, the favored son, had arrived. When he was two days old, he received a postcard from his Russell grandmother in Athens, who was grieving the recent death of her husband. Harriette quoted 1 Colossians 11:22 to invoke prosperity for this new grandson (the Russells and the Dillards were talented at quoting scripture for almost any occasion) and added her own prayer that he would be a source of help and strength for his sisters. In Russell and Dillard creeds, the role of patriarch, while deserving high honor, also included a serious duty to care for others. A Dillard uncle wrote a few days later to "the future governor of Georgia, R. B. Russell, Jr." To say expectations were high for male achievement in the Russell family, especially for the eldest son, hardly states the case.

Richard Brevard Russell, Jr., who would be called R. B. for the first twenty-one years of his life, might well have become the only son if his father had had his way. A few months after the boy's birth, Richard senior came home with a novel idea. He was satisfied, he said, with three beautiful daughters and a robust son to carry on his name. Then he explained to Ina that it was possible in modern times, with a certain device, to enjoy their conjugal bliss and yet limit the number of children born of that bliss. He had, in fact, such a device in his possession for their immediate use.

Ina was not impressed. As her own mother's thirteenth child, she had been reared to believe that the work of Christian wife and mother was one of life's highest callings. Now in her maternal glory of a son and three daughters, she saw no reason to limit her family.

"I intend to have all the children God wants me to have," she said, "and you might as well bury that thing in one of the post holes that the hired man dug this afternoon in the backyard."

God's intentions as to the ultimate count of little Russells would remain mysterious for many years, but Ina Dillard and her firstborn son formed a loving bond that deepened even as new siblings arrived at a steady rate. Sister Harriette Brumby, named for her paternal grandmother, arrived in spring 1899, and in August 1900, a little brother "discovered America," as the older family members liked to say with a broad, congratulatory smile. The two boys were destined to become best friends, as their father and his brother Robert Lee had been. The new baby was called Robert Lee for this handsome uncle, an officer in the United States Navy who sent exciting letters home from around the globe. Family as fortress was a Russell and Dillard tradition.

As usual for the births of her babies, in summer 1900 Ina called upon her maiden sister Pipey (Patience) to come from the Dillard family farm in Oglethorpe County to assist with the new arrival. Sometimes her widowed sister Annie Launius also came. All the Russell children loved Pipey and Aunt Annie and understood that the two women had maternal authority equal to their mother's and were due the utmost respect. Shortly before Rob's birth, Ina hired Hettie Bell Bearden, a young white girl, about fourteen, from nearby Walton County. Hettie, whose family was numerous and poor, had had to leave school, but while living in Winder with the Russells she welcomed a chance to benefit from Ina's tutelage. In large families, children had to learn to attach readily to various maternal authority figures, and a child's ability to do this naturally was an important survival skill. Hettie proved a faithful maternal authority, warmhearted and generous, who adored "Miz Russell" and paid attention to her mentoring. Soon R. B. and the other children adored Miss Hettie. R. B. did not know a time when he was not surrounded with capable and faithful women who had as their deepest concern his welfare and that of his siblings.

By early 1902, Patience Elizabeth, named for Pipey and Annie, had arrived. Also by this time Richard senior had been elected superior court judge of the Western Circuit, one of the largest in land area in the entire state. Because Winder was situated on the line of three counties— Jackson, Walton and Gwinnett—Richard senior often travelled to court as a lawyer in those three counties, as well as to nearby Clarke County, his former residence. As judge he was away from home even more frequently and for longer periods of time as he held court in the counties of Clarke, Oconee, Jackson, Walton, Gwinnett, Banks, and Franklin. R. B. heard from his mother and from his aunts about the importance of his father's work and about how hard he worked to provide for his family.

By summer 1902, before he was five years old, R. B. had the thrill of going to "court week" in the mountain counties of Banks and Franklin. His father liked for his wife to join him, usually with one or two of the children, during the busy summer court weeks away from home, in the cooler northern counties, at watering places such as Franklin Springs or at tourist-attracting Tallulah Falls, a little farther north. R. B., who called his mother "Dear," was proud even as a four-year-old to be her escort, assimilating early that there were responsibilities unique to the male of the species that he could uphold. It was indeed pleasant to sit with his mother on the train watching the piedmont hills turn to mountainsides, and then to arrive at a white clapboard hotel in a picturesque community where he was something of a celebrity as "the judge's son." The little boy was recognized by many citizens on the street as he tripped along in the company of the most beautiful woman in the world. The town was in a festive mood from increased business and the social activity associated with court week. Both his father and mother had a genius for friendship, and their friends in all these places welcomed them warmly, giving parties in their honor, exclaiming over the growing family, and predicting success for his father in future political endeavors. R. B. listened and looked, impressed by how his parents and their work were regarded as important and necessary.

In addition to his father as a strong male role model, the little boy looked up to his uncle Lewis, who had come to live with the family about 1898. Lewis Carolyn Russell was the youngest of five sons of Harriette Brumby and William John Russell. A bachelor, Lewis became Richard senior's stenographer in his law office while studying law, and the younger man proved capable, loyal, and hardworking. Soon admitted to the bar himself, Lewis continued the practice of law after his brother became judge. When Harriette Brumby Russell began to have health problems about 1900, Lewis moved her and sister Mary, the only Russell daughter, from Athens to Winder and lived with them in a bungalow across the street from R. B.'s home. Mary had serious health issues and had given up her teaching job, so she and Lewis shared the care of their mother, but Lewis often had the caretaking role for both of these women. Lewis was not always benign about his filial duties—he had a sharp, sarcastic wit, and he suffered from occasional bouts of depression—but he was ever faithful in them.

The Russell bungalows were only two blocks off the main street of Winder, where houses had been built on cleared acre lots as the town grew. R. B. early loved to follow his mother around in the yard as she planted flowers, worked her vegetable garden, and fed her chickens and pigs. She was a woman of an extraordinary energy and cheerfulness, and people simply enjoyed being with her in spite of the inevitable fact that to be around her meant work. She involved all members of the family in the chores of daily living, assuming that the children were capable at an early age of hauling water from the well, plucking a chicken, or weeding the garden. An idle mind is the devil's workshop, and she was not going to give any of her children over to the devil. Ina sent them across to Grandmother Harriette's house to offer help there as well. R. B. much preferred the treat of going downtown to Uncle Lewis's law office, where he was allowed to type on the typewriter or sit at the desk and "read" the newspaper.

Russells and Dillards were avid readers. R. B.'s grandmother assured the little boy that his father was reading by the time he was three and had memorized the Gospel of Mark in Latin before he was seven. Harriette's eldest son had, after all, been taught by her father, the brilliant Professor Richard Brumby of the Universities of Alabama and South Carolina. Russells had to be learners. Mary Willie, called Sister, and Ina junior had been in school in Winder for several years, and with his sisters and his uncle coaching him, R. B. learned to read almost without realizing it. Being able to read was also a surefire way to get his father's attention when Papa was at home.

By summer 1902, R. B.'s comfortable little universe of Winder was heading for major disruption. His father was up for reelection, and during the campaigning, someone started a rumor that Richard Russell, Sr., was not eligible to be judge because he did not live in Jackson County. Winder's situation on the lines of three counties gave the rumor credence. Furious at such groundless gossip, Richard Russell went a mile out of town along the railroad and purchased a 200-acre farm that no one could dispute was located in Jackson County. He was going to start his own town. Because he had served three terms in the state legislature in the 1880s and still had many friends in state government, Russell managed to get the city of Russell incorporated, slicing off a piece of

Winder that was on his property in the process. Winder city fathers were enraged.

Richard Russell wanted nothing else to do with Winder and proposed that they build a house and move immediately, but Ina would not budge. The older girls had only the Winder school to attend, she said, and, no, she and Pipey (who had both been teachers) were not prepared to follow her husband's suggestion that they homeschool.

During this critical time, with the house and the streets of Winder buzzing with campaign furor for the 1902 elections, Harriette Brumby Russell died, following several months of illness. R. B. saw the family united in grief as all the Russell brothers came home to bury their mother. To be near his Uncle Rob, resplendent in his Navy uniform, made the boy's heart beat faster, and he announced that he would go to Annapolis when he was grown up. Rob was a good-natured fellow, still a bachelor, and he was flattered by R. B.'s adoration. The boy stayed near this uncle as the five men, Richard, Rob, Edward, John, and Lewis, discussed this development in the family fortune. Or lack thereof. There was little money or property left in William John Russell's estate, and how was Mary to be cared for? R. B. saw that his uncles deferred to their eldest brother and that his father accepted the leadership position without question. It was a man's responsibility to take leadership, to know how to take care of things. So there was little money? Russells had come through hard times after the war. They would do so now. Thanks to Harriette's homeschooling and determination that her sons go on to the University of Georgia when they were old enough, they all had good educations and respectable work. Thanks also to her insistence that they love and support each other, no one questioned his duty to contribute. They were a true band of brothers.

This grieving time was hardly the first time R. B. had heard stories about Harriette Brumby Russell, for a favorite Russell pastime involved thoroughly discussing relatives and friends, their foibles, their strong character traits, their triumphs, and their failures. And the why of all of it. But this time of Harriette's crossing the Great Divide just might have been the first time R. B. and his siblings heard all of Harriette's children together talking about their mother.

The night of Harriette's wake, as the guests cleared the house and the family was alone, this team of uncles and their father gave the older girls the opportunity to kiss their grandmother, lying posed on her bed, with her hands clasped, good-bye. Mary Willie, the undisputed leader of this growing Russell brood, observed the dead woman solemnly. Harriette had been a difficult grandmother, demanding and stern in her last years, not gentle and full of laughter as were Pipey and Grandmother Mec in Oglethorpe County. Mary Willie thought that she loved her Grandmother Harriette, for her mother's attitude towards life made it clear that love was much more than a feel-good sensation. Yet Mary Willie did not want to kiss a dead person. She slowly shook her head, fearing she might be censured, but determined to say what she believed. Her aunt Mary took her hand and led her and Ina junior and Margo away without a word.

To escape the heat of the house and to wind down after an emotional day, the adults sat in the oak rockers on the front porch. Mary Willie sat with little Rob, who had become her special baby at birth while his mother struggled with mastitis. R. B., still small enough to sit in his lap, climbed in with Uncle Rob. Ina junior chose to sit beside Uncle Lewis, who favored the girls. Margo was fond of Uncle Lewis, too, but she did not get to see Uncle John often, and she had taken to him from an early age. She squeezed in beside him. Uncle Ed, who worked in Washington, DC, was not very well known to the children, and he and Mary and Richard senior sat alone. Little Patience, the baby, was in bed in the dark house across the street. Harriette's namesake was living at Farm Hill in Oglethorpe County with Pipey and Grandmother "Mec," where she had been sent when Ina was desperately ill after Rob's birth. Little Harriette had not come home after her mother's health improved because the child had contracted rheumatic fever and needed more attention than she could get in Winder.

Rocking and talking softly on the cool porch that hot July night, the adults recalled cherished memories of their mother. Front and center was the story of how Harriette Brumby had been so determined to go to school that she petitioned the faculty at the University of South Carolina to be allowed to attend her father's chemistry class. The girl pestered them so thoroughly that they finally agreed. Of course, she had to sit behind a screen so that her presence would not disturb the all-male class, Uncle Rob finished, slapping his knee with uproarious laughter. R. B. did not have to understand to laugh along with his uncles.

Aunt Mary, whose wit could be as ascerbic as her brothers', did not fail to point out that any man worth his salt would have been disturbed by Harriette's presence, as another story proved. About 1848, when Harriette was nineteen and attending a prestigious social event in Charleston honoring the famous South Carolina statesman John C. Calhoun, Calhoun presented her with the bloom of a century plant to honor her as the most brilliant and gracious woman at the party. Among those present, this moment proved so memorable that fifty years later the story appeared in the obituary of a fellow party guest who, while not receiving a century bloom herself, had been present to see Harriette receive hers.

In these stories, the children that evening saw not their withered and embittered old grandmother, but a vital, courageous, handsome young woman, equal to astonishing challenges. R. B.'s favorite story proved indisputably her worthiness to rank high among the flowers of Southern womanhood; he never tired of hearing how she behaved during the devastation that came when the Union army invaded Georgia.

"Your grandfather, William John Russell," his father would begin the story—he always repeated the entire name, with relish—"was co-owner, with your grandmother's brother, Arnoldus Brumby, of one of the largest textile mills in north Georgia. Built by former Georgia governor Charles McDonald, with young William John Russell as his assistant—your grandfather actually planned and laid out the streets of the town for the mill workers—the five-story brick building was located on Sweetwater Creek, in Cobb County,[2] and employed a hundred workers. Charles McDonald named the site Sweetwater Mill, but when they bought it, our kin renamed it New Manchester Mill, after the English home city from which Brumbys hail, a famed place of industrial manufacture. During the war New Manchester Mill on Sweetwater Creek made coarse osnaburg cloth for uniforms, tents, and blankets for the Confederacy. As the war raged on, and more and more Confederate soldiers were required, most of the mill's employees became women and children."

---

[2] Today the ruins of the mill can be seen at Sweetwater Creek State Park, off Interstate 20.

This part of the story, while not directly concerning Harriette, inevitably took precedence, for it was history as well as family history. It picked up speed that night, as others chimed in with details they remembered of that faraway time that yet seemed so near.

In July 1864, when Sherman's army was battering at the gates of Atlanta, the Union general sent troops into the countryside specifically to destroy such mills.[3] On 9 July 1864, Union troops gained control of the mill, soaked it with kerosene, torched it, and took all workers prisoner. In an unprecedented move—even if war were not hell, Sherman made it hell—the general ordered these prisoners sent north into Indiana. They were housed briefly near Arnoldus Brumby's home in Marietta, which was being used to stable Yankee horses. When they left this fine home they'd used as a barn, the Yankees burned it.

Hearing these stories, young R. B. was filled with sympathy for the victims of this diaspora, and he heard something else—shame?—for the family's humiliation. In 1902 no one knew exactly what had happened to the residents of Sweetwater, only that they were gone, and the mill and village left in rubble. It would be thirty years before his Uncle Lewis met a survivor and learned that the factory workers, herded like cattle onto boxcars, were indeed sent north and across the Ohio River at Louisville, Kentucky. For a boy who loved home so much, it was heart-wrenching to learn that some of them were never able to find their way home.

Equally as dramatic and tragic as that of the millworkers, Harriette's story continued. William John and Harriette did not live at Sweetwater, but in Marietta town, where they had a lovely home, once the property of a judge, and a small shoe factory with attendant servants' and workers' quarters. Although forty years old, William John Russell had joined the state militia in the early part of 1864, leaving Harriette at home with two little boys and a third baby on the way. Fleeing her home in summer 1864, Harriette headed for middle Georgia, hoping to be near Augusta, where John was stationed. In November, just as Sherman's

---

[3] Although it isn't likely that the Russell family knew at that time that William Tecumseh Sherman had worked as a geological surveyor in Georgia during his early Army career and was, as a result, aware that the area was suitable to support many kinds of mills, the family's sense of the importance of the mill made it logical that Union troops would seek it out.

armies were leaving Atlanta on their infamous "March to the Sea," Harriette, still trying to get to Augusta, gave birth to a third son, somewhere on the sand flats of Edgefield County, South Carolina. This was the son who would become R. B.'s adored Uncle Rob. Mary Willie and Ina junior had read about this birth in the family Bible, and read there also about the loss of William Edward, known as "Little Willie," a few months later. A painful and never-forgotten detail told how the two-year-old boy had to be buried in a dresser drawer. Little Willie's burial came only a day or two after Lee surrendered at Appomattox Court House. In the family Bible, the heartbroken mother recorded the hour of death and the years, months, and days of her child's life.

None of the children would ever forget the sorrow and loss in the voices of their kin as this story was told, nor the underlying respect for their grandmother's bravery.

For a while, the story continued, Harriette was able to stay near Augusta, where John was trying to sell cloth they had salvaged before the mill's destruction. She was with the William Northen family in Hancock County, Georgia, helping to teach in a boys' school there. Paper was so scarce that when John wrote to Harriette, she had to write back between the lines of his letter. John reported that everything in Marietta—house, barns, slave quarters—had been burned to the ground and the mill as well. It was start-over time.

Harriette had managed to get away from Marietta with some cash, money she had been saving to ensure that her eldest son could go to Princeton Theological Seminary in New Jersey to become a Presbyterian minister. Yielding to her husband's pleas that they use this money to invest in a business sure to succeed, she turned her cash over to John, who went to Florida with a partner to start a lumber business. Everyone agreed this was a sound idea in that era of massive rebuilding. Harriette stayed with her sister in Marietta, waiting for John to send for her and the children.

The business did indeed prosper, but the partnership did not. Alas, one dark night the partner absconded to a foreign country with the phenomenal sum of $10,000—everything—and another man's wife. Richard senior liked to add here that there was no treaty of extradition with the country to which the partner fled, as if to excuse the hard and understandable fact that there was no money or heart with which to pursue the traitor.

William John Russell came home to Marietta and took a job managing a textile mill at Princeton, Georgia, a village on the outskirts of Athens. The family lived in the three-story manager's house, which was comfortable and roomy enough for them as the family grew, and even provided the place where Harriette's professor father and her mother, Mary, would spend their final days. Nevertheless, the family would never regain the property and prestige of their place in Marietta before the war. The night of Harriette's wake, her children recalled these hard times as an explanation of why she sometimes seemed so harsh and bitter, becoming rigid and controlling as she tried to protect and promote her children in old and aristocratic Athens society.

Harriette was buried the next day from the First Presbyterian Church of Athens in the family plot at Oconee Hill Cemetery. Mary let her brothers know that she was going to take care of herself by moving back to Athens to the house her father owned there in order to take up teaching again. When this plan did not succeed because of her health, she and Lewis sold the Athens house and kept house together in the Winder home. The other brothers sent money from time to time to help Mary.

While brother Rob was visiting, he and Lewis decided to buy a farm near Richard's. Lewis would supervise tenant farming on it. Uncle Rob joked that he was indeed pleased to "owe" a farm with his baby brother. R. B. might not have understood the joke, but he learned early that his kin enjoyed playing with words. Uncle John said he was looking to buy a farm nearby as well, and did so, but in Oconee County. R. B. early got the message that a man ought to own property.

Walter Dillard was born on 19 June 1903, named for Ina's brother, who was minister of the Methodist church in Winder. Walter and his wife, Mary, also were engaged in raising a large family, and the Russell and Dillard children enjoyed playing together. Unfortunately for playmates, shortly after Walter's birth, a black man with a high-sided wagon and a two-mule team pulled up to the Russell house in Winder, went to the back door, removed his sweat-stained hat, and knocked.

When Ina came to the door, the man said that the judge had sent him to take the family and furniture out to "the Gresham house."

This was the first news Ina had that her husband had not forgotten his vow to get out of Winder. Sighing, she directed the loading of chairs, a table, and the excited children into the wagon. As the eldest son, R. B., age six, got the seat beside the driver. Sitting in a chair, Mary Willie, ten years old, held tiny Walter Dillard in her lap and kept a steadying hand on twenty-month-old Patience on the wagon floor beside her. Ina junior, 9, Margo, 8, and Rob, 3, piled in. Ina stayed behind to pack.

By nightfall the Russells were at home in Russell, Georgia. No one ever remembered their mother's complaining about this sudden upheaval, but soon Richard senior had a spacious room added to the house, one known from the first as "Mama's room," with her own door opening onto the deep, cool porch.

R. B. might have missed his playmates, but he gloried in living out of town, where he had woods to explore and open fields in which to play. Besides, there was his sister Ina, a tomboy, with whom he adored finding young beech or birch trees to climb. They would swing them towards each other until they could touch, whipping back and forth with uproarious glee, unaware of any danger. The family now had a horse, a shed to shelter it and the buggy, and plenty of room for a sizable flock of chickens and several pigs. R. B. watched the life of the chickens, and with characteristic Russell/Dillard interest in personalities, he named one of the roosters Napoleon Bonaparte. The boy quickly learned the food value of these animals and would guess a pig's weight and how many sausages it might produce. Helping to butcher hogs in the late autumn was a normal chore for a little boy. The smell of his mother's sausage cooking on an autumn morning was one of his favorite pleasures throughout his youth.

The City of Russell did not have an identifiable main street, its few houses being scattered about, with homes for both the black and the white citizens near each other, attached to farms, not to sections of a true town. Several of the houses were near the railroad, and although there was no station at Russell, the engineer would slow down just enough for Papa to jump from the moving train. After the quarrel about the city limits, Richard senior preferred not to use the station at Winder. As the train loomed noisy and powerful in the distance, the children stood by the tracks, waiting eagerly to greet their father. Heeding both their mother's and Pipey's instructions, the little ones wanted to make Papa's homecomings happy, and they did so, gathering around him for hugs and kisses and sometimes a sack of pig's feet he would bring for a treat.

That Papa had missed his family and his home was never in doubt, and the nights he spent with them were joyful. Richard senior was a good-looking man, tall and fit, a talented and eloquent storyteller of his weekly adventures—his vocabulary was astonishing—or of interesting cases. Their father could dance and would dance. Ina senior and later Mary Willie played the piano, and Richard danced with his older daughters, and the little boys soon learned to dance as well.

About 1904, Richard senior was asked to hold court in Blairsville, Georgia, in the absence of the judge of that circuit, and the visiting judge decided to take his eldest son with him. There was no train to Blairsville, and so R. B. crossed into the rugged north Georgia mountains on an unforgettable buggy ride. Sometimes the roads were barely discernible. The buggy bounced and jostled and jerked. The seven-year-old clung to the sides of the buggy and stared at a precipice inches from the road. He prayed that the horse would not stumble or shy or—may the Good Lord forbid it—bolt. Yet it was thrilling to be with his father, who stopped often to speak with those whose paths they crossed. Richard senior was eternally campaigning, but the boy sensed more: his father had a genuine affection and respect for the country folk they met, and they appreciated him. It was fine, a privilege even, to be a Georgian, and to serve one's state, one's native land.

When Lewis Russell was elected mayor of Winder in 1902, it must have been hoped that the feud with the town would die out. Alas, in 1905 the town fathers, Lewis now among them, decided to try to form a county with Winder as the county seat, taking land off Walton, Jackson, and Gwinnett to do so. This new county seemed a logical move because of the legal difficulties presented by the town's location. A legendary case reported that two men had quarreled on the streets of Winder, and one, standing in Jackson county, shot the other, who was standing in Gwinnett. The wounded man then staggered over into Walton County and died there. Where, in the name of heaven, should the case be tried? Although this case is likely mythological, the creation of a new county seemed a wise solution to less dramatic legal tangles resulting from Winder's location. Even more importantly, if Winder became a county seat, the community would gain in business and prestige. Winderites were going for it.

Inexplicably, Richard senior was opposed to a new county, even though it was to be called Stephens County after his childhood hero Alexander H. Stephens, vice president of the Confederacy. In 1905 Judge Russell rallied his friends in the General Assembly and the new county never came to a vote. Once more, the town fathers raged that Russell had the power to thwart them. They raged again a year or so later when Toccoa, in north Georgia, succeeded in forming Stephens County, with Toccoa as the county seat.

R. B. started school in Winder, walking the mile into town with his sisters, but as the feud heated up again, Richard senior took his children out of the Winder school and hired Miss Nita Stroud as a live-in teacher for them. Nine children and several adults were living in the four-bedroom bungalow. Pipey and Lewis were often there in various helping capacities, Hettie remained a valiant and loyal helper, and then Susan Way, baby number nine, was born on 15 April 1905. Yet in Ina's home there was always room for one more.

At first Miss Stroud, who was about forty-five, shared a room with Mary Willie, Ina junior, Margo, and Patience; later she boarded with another family in the settlement. Nita Stroud was a talented teacher, and throughout his life, R. B. credited her with awakening in him the love of reading and history. He might have felt himself quite the little prince with his own teacher, but neither Miss Stroud nor Ina encouraged such sentiments. Their emphasis was on learning, helping the younger scholars, and making the most of the chance for an education. A few other white children went to the Russell school at this time, which, as it grew, was held in a vacant tenant house on the Russell farm, where bales of cotton were stored on the porch. The message was clear: school was one of life's important endeavors and must be carried on in spite of other work.

In summer 1905 Susan Way, named for Richard senior's grand-mother, was taken ill and died of a digestive upset believed to have been caused by tainted evaporated milk. The family reeled at the blow. Most of the children had been at their Dillard grandmother's farm when the baby died, and the family was reunited at the graveside at the Russell plot in the Oconee Hill Cemetery in Athens. The tiny casket was opened for the children to say good-bye to their little sister. Not quite eight years old, R. B. watched his mother weep for perhaps the first time; his father was more likely to weep than was his mother. This grief, however, was more than she could contain.

Life went on in spite of sorrow. Ina still worked in her garden and among her flowers, perhaps more so than usual, and Pipey came to help put up quarts and quarts and quarts of pickles, tomatoes, jams, peaches, and beans, necessaries for the winter table. They also cooked up fresh peas, beans, squash, and potatoes from the garden, and they killed, cleaned, and fried chickens or made chicken and dumplings. R. B. and Rob had to carry water from the well, and the children helped weed, hoe, and gather everything from wild blackberries to cultivated Concord grapes, as well as the garden vegetables. Richard senior insisted that Harriette come home from Farm Hill during this period, fearing the little girl would not know her brothers and sisters. He wanted all his children under one roof. For R. B. and the others, it was clear that death should lead to more emphasis and energy on life.

Richard senior had had his heart set on the 1906 gubernatorial race for two years. Although most Georgia campaigns in those days took place over a sixty-day period in the summer before a late August or early September election day, in this race the front-running candidate, Hoke Smith, was already campaigning in fall 1905. Smith had collected a weighty campaign chest, and he meant to leave nothing to chance in his bid to become Georgia's fifty-fifth governor since colonial times. Although still grieving his daughter's death, Richard senior reacted to grief in typical fashion for him: he went to work harder than ever. He had done this when his first wife died in 1886 and when his father died in 1897. Ina was not surprised when her husband decided that he, too, would make campaign speeches in the fall and began traveling to places he could reach easily when court was not in session. At Richard's request, Ina travelled occasionally with him while Pipey minded the children at home. Richard senior was always comforted by Ina's presence, and by Christmas she was expecting another baby.

On 20 October, Richard senior took R. B. and the elder three girls to Atlanta to try to catch a glimpse of President Theodore Roosevelt, who had come to visit his first wife's home, Bulloch Hall, in Roswell, Georgia, and to speak at Georgia Tech. Southerners were proud of Roosevelt's connection to the wealthy and influential Bulloch family, who owned textile mills in Roswell. Richard senior recounted how Roswell mill workers were taken prisoner at the same time as those from Sweetwater/New Manchester Mill and were also shipped north and dispersed.

In 1906 R. B. became old enough to remember his first taste of a political battle, and it was not a pleasing sample. Legal and political discussions were common in the household, with Lewis, Papa, and constant visitors intently discussing cases and races. Now a race was coming home, a race that represented one of his father's most intense desires and long-term goals. The youngster knew that from the age of twenty-one, when his father first entered the political arena in a race for the General Assembly seat from Clarke County, Richard B. Russell, Sr., had longed to serve as governor of Georgia. R. B. had heard many times the story about his father being carefully tutored to become a Presbyterian minister by Harriette Brumby Russell. Pursuing his mother's dream, Richard had learned the shorter and longer versions of the Presbyterian catechism from memory by the time he was twelve. R.B. could not help giving thanks that the family now attended his mother's church, the Methodist, which had no such lengthy questions and answers to be learned.

Then at the age of fourteen, the young Richard was invited to visit Alexander H. Stephens in Crawfordville to recite the catechisms for the elderly statesman. Richard Russell came home from his time with Stephens with a fire in his heart to study law and serve his fellowmen in public office. With the vigor and blind ignorance of youth, by the time he was twenty-one he had vowed to become governor of Georgia, chief justice of her Supreme Court, and a United States senator.

Still possessed at age forty-five of a healthy portion of commendable idealism, but apparently not shed of blind ignorance, Richard senior believed he could beat the steamrolling political machine assembled by the wealthy and experienced Hoke Smith. By summer 1906, three other candidates had entered the fray as well, but none of the candidates were considered close rivals of Smith.[4] The closest contender was thought to be Clarke Howell, owner of the *Atlanta Constitution*. Smith had owned the *Atlanta Journal*, selling a few years earlier for an enviable profit as he stockpiled campaign money, and both papers were filled with political news that summer, obviously favoring their respective candidates of Howell and Smith.

Reading the newspaper was considered a virtue in the Russell household—it was practically a civic duty to keep up with current events—and R. B. took every opportunity to read the paper. Although he truly enjoyed reading, the youngster discovered that reading the newspaper was sometimes considered an acceptable alternative to weeding the garden or hoeing the cotton, and this fact might have also influenced his penchant to keep his nose buried in any paper which his father or uncle Lewis brought home. That summer, in 1906, there were no favorable stories in the two major Atlanta papers about his father (quite the contrary), but the *Georgian,* a weekly Atlanta-based paper, sometimes featured less biased articles on the governor's campaign.

Not that R. B. spent all his time reading the papers. There was also time for little lads to build a fort in the woods. The fort could be called nothing but Fort Lee, and from it R. B. and Rob fought many battles against Yankee hordes. Little Walter tried to join them, but he was too young to understand how serious fighting Yankees could be and would most often run back to the house in hopes of getting a few sugared peaches or a handful of peanuts from the women processing foods in the kitchen and on the porch. Walter was going to be his own kind of rebel.

At eight years old, R. B. was less interested in political battles than he was enamored of fighting the American Civil War, which, in the best Southern parlance, was known as the War Between the States. When he could not seduce, badger, or boss Rob and Walter into playing war with him, he liked to run between cotton rows or pea rows, firing a rifle-length stick at the enemy, ducking for cover, and rising to dash forward again and again. Sometimes he would fling himself writhing in wounded agony onto the ground. A farmer/voter visiting with Judge Russell and walking over the farm saw R. B. appear in a far-off row and

---

[4] Candidates were Hoke Smith, Clarke Howell, Richard Russell, John H. Estill, and James M. Smith.

fling himself moaning and turning on the ground. The visitor said sympathetically, "Lots of folks got a child that has fits, Judge. Don't let it worry you none. He might grow out of 'em." Papa first told that story with great relish that night at the supper table, and it became one that R.B. would never live down.

A major problem for the Russell political endeavor was lack of money. Richard senior had started a small textile business in Russell, one which did not prosper because he was rarely on hand to supervise the making of socks, and he had mortgaged this project to fund a small campaign chest. The only staff he could afford was composed of Lewis, Ina, and the older children, who were already on the payroll. Ina was mothering eight children and expecting another while Lewis had his law practice and, in addition, was farming peaches and grain on the 400-acre farm that he and Robert "owed" together. In spite of these numerous responsibilities, Ina and Lewis worked hard on Richard's campaign. Lewis set up the speaking schedule, arranging train rides so that the candidate could sleep on the train, thus avoiding a hotel bill. Notified by postcards from Lewis, friends in various counties, aware of the shoestring budget, offered to take Richard in for breakfast and a wash before he was to speak. Lewis managed what few funds they had and tried to put ads they could afford in newspapers statewide. As Lewis worked side by side with Ina, he grew to respect and love her more and more for her steadfastness, her cheerful attitude, her energy, and her faith in her husband. He was fond of reminding his brother that the best day of work that Richard Russell ever had was the day he married Ina Dillard.

R. B., like most children, was not particularly aware of his mother's skill at running her busy home. Family and other visitors came and went constantly. Even without campaign duties, her list of chores included tenant farmers needing supplies from the storerooms, help with sick children, or repairs to the tenant houses. The garden had to be tended, foodstuffs preserved, and meals cooked. There was ever a new baby to nurse, other children to supervise, and spats to referee. In addition, Ina sewed most of their clothes, including their underwear. These ten thousand things were simply a mother's work. That particular summer was the first time in his life that R. B. saw his mother asleep. When he did, a cold fear gripped his heart because he thought she must be sick.

The campaign brought duties to usurp the children's carefree summer days. Campaign letters, typed by Uncle Lewis, had to be put into envelopes and addressed, with help from Ina, Pipey, and Aunt Mary. R. B. and Sister (Mary Willie) then had the chore of taking the letters each day to the post office in Winder, a mile away, to be stamped and mailed.

In June, a fine baby boy was born and named for Uncle Lewis because Richard and Ina wanted to show their appreciation for his unstinting loyalty to Richard, especially concerning his political ambitions. Richard senior had two other brothers—John and Edward—who came before Lewis in birth order, and by tradition had prior claim to babies' names (Robert Lee having already been honored), but no one in the family could dispute that Lewis deserved to move to the front of the line. The baby was healthy and bright. When a reporter came in August to do an article on the candidate for the *Georgian* newspaper and photographed the entire family, at less than two months old, Lewis was already sitting up straight in his mother's arms, watching the proceedings alertly. For the photograph, R. B. stood straight and solemn in dress shirt and tie, a confident lad with prominent ears, not smiling but wearing a benign expression. Rob, standing in front of R. B., not yet old enough to wear a tie, frowned at the intruding photographer. The older boys were barefoot, while someone had managed to get shoes on Walter, who was still young enough to be wearing a skirt. All the girls—Mary Willie, Ina junior, Margo, Harriette and Patience—were dressed in their light-colored Sunday frocks, all wearing shoes.

The day of the photograph was exciting to the family because there was a rally in Winder for Richard Russell, Sr. Hoke Smith had a system of going from town to town making speeches, traveling on his own train with a band to strike up a festive note when the train arrived. Often the same passengers were herded from town to town, giving the impression of numerous supporters in all places. Friends in Winder and Atlanta decided they could at least get up such a show for Richard senior in his hometown district.

This action seemed especially appropriate because another Winder group had started the rumor (and even published it in some papers) that

Richard senior was a heavy drinker, the implication being he was not fit for public office. They cited as proof the fact that the City of Russell was chartered to allow the sale of alcoholic beverages. The subject of alcohol consumption was frequently discussed in the Russell household. Richard senior told his eldest son that his mother, Harriette Brumby, was so vehemently against alcohol that she would rather see a child of hers die of a rattlesnake bite than accept the drink of alcohol that was thought to cure snakebite. R. B.'s mother was a teetotaler, on the grounds that much evil resulted from drinking, and thus it was not worth the risk to drink, whereas Richard senior was not against alcohol consumption on moral grounds. He would take the "risk" of a drink with the fellows, but was careful in his consumption. Richard had grown up hearing increasingly horrific stories about his mother's two brothers in Athens, who were both alcoholics and ran a drugstore where a questionable "medicine" could be obtained. In fact, the Brumby name became so tainted in Athens that Richard senior had changed his name from Richard Brumby to Richard Brevard when he was twenty-one so that he would not be associated with this evil. Considering these two sides of the question, R.B. was no doubt reassured to see a large crowd assembled to greet his father on the day the Russell campaign steamed into Winder.

Excitement was high in town as the train pulled in. Having walked in from Russell, the children, with Miss Stroud and Miss Hettie shepherding them, gathered with the crowd at the station awaiting the regular train from Lawrenceville. There was no possibility of affording a Russell Special. The local band blared willingly on the platform as the train pulled in. R. B. and Rob scuffled, paying no attention to Miss Hettie's warnings not to spoil their clothes. They were still barefoot. The celebratory feeling was gradually overshadowed by heavy thunder-clouds amassing. Just as the band quieted and his father started to speak, R. B. felt the first drops of rain. The boys looked at each other with bright eyes, anticipating the chance to play in the rain, but it was quickly decided to move the throng into the schoolhouse. As Richard senior thundered in his best campaign style, Mother Nature also thundered and lightning flashed. Jokes abounded about the judge's oratorical ability, which apparently could bring down fire and brimstone. His eldest son was all ears.[5]

Such enthusiasm was catching, and the children, eager to do more to help their father, decided to make campaign posters to put along the road between Winder and Russell. They knew that their Uncle John was putting up campaign posters in south Georgia, accomplishing his task on a bicycle. Eagerly, they set out to draw big signs instructing people to vote for Plain Dick Russell, for the campaign could finance only a few ready-made posters. Sister (Mary Willie) and Ina junior organized and instructed, with Margo not far behind. R. B. did not take instruction especially well from his older sisters, but everyone was involved and excited. R. B. thought he could make stakes, sharpened on one end, upon which to fasten the posters. Rob, not quite six, struggled to help both his sisters and his brother.

The summer was hot and sticky, and the task, entered so willingly, began to drag. The posters were not finished by nightfall, but the children resolved to complete construction and put them up the next day. Uncle Lewis brought in an *Atlanta Journal* that evening, and little Rob looked through some of the pages, eager to learn to read. A special bond existed between him and Mary Willie, and she often read to him. Mary Willie showed him a picture of Hoke Smith and read the caption beneath it, identifying their father's portly rival.

"*That's* Hoke Smith?" Rob asked, incredulous. Sister assured him that it was.

"Well, we can stop worrying about those posters," the little boy said, obviously relieved. "Our daddy won't have any trouble beating that big ol' fat man in the race."

Of course, all the adults and the older children, including R. B., laughed uproariously at this comment. R. B. explained to his little brother that this wasn't a footrace. Their lean and fit daddy, fond of

---

[5] After Dick Russell, Jr., became a US senator, he heard from E. Merton Coulter, a well-known Georgia historian, that his father had challenged Smith and Howell to debate, but that after one such debate, these two men refused to participate in any other sessions because they had appeared weak and ineffective opposite Russell's oratory. This report made the son proud all over again.

digging dirt and hauling it around in the wheelbarrow, would not have any advantage against the rotund Hoke Smith.

Nevertheless, as Election Day, 22 August, drew near, optimism in the Russell camp soared. Those close to the candidate saw the way people welcomed him and were moved by his oratory. They reported these reactions to the home base, which did not receive any other information besides the biased Atlanta paper reports. Richard senior himself felt, as he travelled throughout the state, that the voters were happy to choose someone free of all political "ring" influence, a choice rare in Georgia politics. He suffered mightily when Smith accused him of being funded by the railroads and lying about it. Richard felt that if voters could believe that of him, his life was a failure, but he held up his shoestring campaign as proof enough that he was bought by no man or interest group. He was free to do the will of all the people. R. B. understood from an early age that honesty and frugality were basic to his father's creed, basic to a real man's creed.

When the votes were counted and Election Day dust had cleared, Hoke Smith walked away with a landslide victory.[6] When Papa came from Atlanta to deliver the bleak news, he broke down and wept. He had not succeeded in making them the First Family of Georgia, he said. They would not be moving to the Governor's Mansion as he had promised in gleeful moments. Neither Ina nor the children understood why this was important to him. He was the best papa in the world, they were his family, and that was all that mattered. Seeing her husband defeated and brokenhearted, Ina turned away and stepped into her room, where she collapsed weeping onto the chair at her sewing machine. R. B., puzzled and troubled, followed her. To see his usually serene mother sobbing so made his heart ache. He put his hand on her shoulder and said, "Don't cry, Dear, please don't cry. When I am grown up, I will be elected governor, and you can come and live in the Governor's Mansion with me."

Ina Dillard Russell was a woman whose affections for all those she loved ran deeply rooted and strong, but she was not as openly affectionate as her husband. That day, she mastered her tears, straightened

---

[6] To almost everyone's surprise, Russell came in second (not Clarke Howell) but still many votes behind Smith.

herself, and said, "There are many things in the world more important than living in the Governor's Mansion, dear boy. It just hurts me to see Papa so unhappy."

Just how unimportant being governor was became even clearer only two weeks later when little Lewis was taken suddenly and dangerously ill. Suffering from what was likely an intestinal blockage, the little boy died on 9 September, leaving an aching void in the family. Lewis had quickly become the prince of his brothers and sisters. Pipey had felt proud of how eagerly they had pitched in to care for him. The day Lewis was laid to rest beside his sister in Oconee Hill Cemetery was one of the bleakest of the family's life.

When they returned home to Russell, Richard senior sank into a dark despair. His life seemed a failure both as a public servant and as a father. Bereft of his dreams, his hopes, his ambition, he wondered if in burying this son, he was also burying everything he had lived for. Having resigned from the bench in June, he was out of a job, in debt from the campaign, and needed months to build up a law practice. His textile business was in trouble, and the farming operation had never done much more than pay the land taxes. No wonder depression set in. He dug a lot of dirt in the early days following the election and the baby's death.

One afternoon, contemplating his fortunes and misfortunes, Richard senior saw R. B. out in the woods near the house, not too far from Fort Lee, playing with a stick longer than he was. The distraught father wandered out to this sturdy, healthy boy and sat down on a log, watching the child lift his rifle stick and fire at a doomed target. This carefree childhood innocence made him weep, and he called R. B. to him.

Unlike Ina, who was careful not to burden her children with what she considered adult matters, Richard senior was known to bare his soul to them in emotional moments. "Dear boy," he said, tears streaming down his cheeks, "I have failed in my dream of becoming governor. You are not only my boy, but you bear my name. It is my prayer that you will one day do what I failed to do."

Papa's sobs did not disconcert R. B., and he had heard all his life about his responsibility in bearing his father's name. He knew what he had to say. "I will run for governor and I will be elected," he blithely assured his downcast father.

Late in 1906 a special statewide election was held to elect three judges to serve on the newly formed Georgia Court of Appeals. Weary and impoverished, Richard senior had not thought of running for this office. His friends, however, believing him eminently suited in temperament and experience for the job, had other ideas. They entered his name in the race, paying the qualifying fee of $100 out of their own pockets. Without money with which to campaign, Richard did not ask for a single vote, but when the votes were in, Richard Brevard Russell, Sr., led the list of sixteen candidates. He could not but be pleased that the people had called him back into service.

Young R. B. had seen in a short and action-packed six months just how fickle and how faithful the electorate could be.

Early in the new year, the new judge invited his wife to come to Atlanta to spend the night and consider where to buy a house in the city. As was their custom, the couple took along one or two of the children on such outings. R. B. was pleased to go to Atlanta any time, and for this house-hunting expedition, he was included along with Ina junior and Margo. The judge had arranged for the family to see several houses, much roomier than their Russell bungalow, but situated on mere scraps of land. Ina considered several houses, but she knew immediately that a larger house would not contain her eight children. They needed room to roam.

As the family returned to the hotel after exploring several houses, Ina shocked the children in the car by pointing to a large house on Peachtree Street, nestled among trees on a three-acre lot. "Papa," she said, "when that house is for sale and you can afford it, we will move to Atlanta."

The judge lived in Atlanta at the Kimball Hotel during the week and was home on Saturday afternoon and Sunday.

Soon another exciting invitation to visit Atlanta arrived. Richard senior's good friend from early legislative service, Joe Terrell was the outgoing governor, and Governor and Mrs. Terrell invited Richard, Ina, and R. B. to spend an evening with them at the Governor's Mansion before the end of Terrell's term in June 1907. In March, Ina and her eldest son came to Atlanta on the train to visit Papa's chambers and to see the governor's office. R. B. was allowed to sit in the governor's chair for, he estimated, about three minutes. The highlight of the trip, recorded in a journal—part of all the children's schooling was to keep journals—was spending the night in the Governor's Mansion. R. B. woke before the rest of the household and enjoyed wandering around in the yard before breakfast.

As judges on a brand-new court, Richard senior and his two colleagues, Arthur Powell and Benjamin Hill, were given more publicity than judges generally received. R. B., still reading the paper avidly, kept up with his father's vote for the first woman stenographer of a Georgia court of last resort, his rendering of an opinion in rhyme, and other articles about the work of the court that appeared in the Atlanta papers. Here, indeed, was public service, for the work involved long hours and, as time went on, little recognition.

Going to church was an assumed Sunday activity in R. B.'s household, and with his mother's brother preaching at the Winder Methodist Church, this was the church the Russells attended. In late spring 1907, a special revival was held in Winder, and R. B., now age nine, was moved to go up to the altar at the end of the service and "give his heart to God." Having heard many times that his mother had joined the church at the age of nine, this seemed the right time for his own conversion. He wrote in his journal, "I am going to always try to be right with God." On 26 May 1907, he formally joined the Methodist Church in Winder.

One August morning, R. B. woke up to hear Dr. Almond's deep voice in the house. He jumped out of bed, knowing a new baby must have discovered America. Indeed, when the children were allowed into their mother's room, they saw her propped up in bed, holding not one but two baby brothers, one in each arm. In a front page story, the Atlanta papers announced the arrival of William John and Fielding Dillard Russell on 21 August 1907, twins born to Richard B. Russell, Sr., distinguished judge of the Georgia Court of Appeals, who was already father to ten children.

Ina was enormously pleased that she had at last produced the twins she had longed for since before she and Richard married. The boys were named, as had been planned more than twenty years earlier, for Richard's father and for hers. Ina felt the twins had come to replace the two children she and Richard had lost, and at last she prayed this would be all the children the Lord intended her to have.

Ina continued to involve all the children in the running of the home. She had developed the custom of "giving" a baby to one of her older daughters. Ina junior was Walter's sponsor, and Margo was proud to have Fielding as her special boy. Ina junior also volunteered to take on the smallest of the twins, William. As the eldest son, R. B. learned that his mother expected him to help all the children, for they were weaker than he, and to help older people, such as his grandmother Mec. While they were visiting the farm at Oglethorpe County in summer 1908, Ina was called to Atlanta to nurse Richard senior, who was suffering from an attack of pneumonia. Although Ina and Pipey were both skilled at home medicines, Ina brought Margo, ill with a recurring throat infection, for treatment by an Atlanta doctor. While there, Ina received a letter from Pipey commending R. B.'s efforts to help on the home front, and Ina wrote a card to the ten-year-old to say how proud that report made his mother. It was always the duty of the strong to help the weak.

When the family needed a new milk cow, Richard's brother John offered one, but his farm near Athens was nearly twenty miles away from the Russell farm. A cow could have been purchased that was closer to home, but this one was free. How could they get it to the City of Russell? The only sensible (and cheap) solution was to walk the cow to Winder. Eleven-year-old R. B. got the job. On a hot summer day, the lad walked, maneuvered, pushed, prodded, and prayed that cow for more than eighteen miles. Often when the cow stopped to graze again and again, he despaired of success. There was little traffic. One or two new-fangled motor cars sailed by, frightening the cow into the ditch. Drivers of mule teams and wagons offered encouragement, but no one offered to tie the cow to the back of a wagon and let the boy ride.

R. B. stuck to the job, taking one step at a time, refusing to be too discouraged if sometimes they seemed to be going backwards. By nightfall, his family had a new milk cow in the shed behind the house, and R. B. had learned lessons of patience and perseverance that would propel his political career.

Ina's prayer for a completed family was not answered in the affirmative. Two years after the twins, Henry Edward arrived, and this time the birth made not only the state papers but national ones as well. Henry Edward was the thirteenth child of his mother, who was herself a thirteenth child, a fact noted in a front-page story in the Atlanta paper. Washington and New York papers picked up this human interest article, and the family received clippings of the news from far-flung friends and relatives. Harriette was given Henry Edward as her special boy.

Scarcely a year later on 19 October 1910, another son was born. Although they had waited a long time for their first son, Ina and Richard now had so many that they could not settle on a family name for the most recent. They had their RBR junior and had named sons for their fathers, all of Richard's brothers, and one of Ina's. Bemused, Richard senior decided to call this boy simply "Dickson," that is, Dick's son, enjoying the play on his own name. In the 1906 gubernatorial race, he had been called Plain Dick Russell, and he liked this image. With his junior known as R. B., no one thought duplication of names would be a problem.[7] Patience Elizabeth, nine years old, received Dickson as her special boy.

Work viewed as a calling is easier than less divine interpretation of such activity. Ina managed, thanks to a serene nature, a calm philosophy of life, and her deep religious faith, to keep the Russell home a happy one. With so many siblings, there was no lack of sibling rivalry, but family love and loyalty decreed that they make their peace and stand by each other. Everything had to be shared fairly, and common courtesy was essential to communal living. When one of the children, feeling deprived and pitiful, protested that "we are too many," Ina said, "Too many? We are too many? Well, let's just all line up here on the porch." She made them all line up, and as they stood wondering, she said, "Now, who shall we send back?" Everyone laughed, but the lesson was not forgotten.

The family continued during this time to benefit from the help of Pipey and Annie. Sometimes black servants helped with cooking and cleaning, but most black workers avoided the crowded Russell

---

[7] Dicksie's name had been changed about 1900 to Frances Marguerite, but her father continued to call her "Dicksie" while others called her Margo. Pipey once wrote to a friend that she thought Richard would have been happy for all the children to be named for him.

household, and Ina seems to have understood this without rancor. Ina made a point of having the family welcome back a former house servant named Belle when she returned to the household. Belle was needed and valued. Another black woman, called Doscia, figured in Ina's frequent correspondence with her children, and she stayed with the family for many years, but she was slow-moving and wasteful. She missed work often, suffering from nameless illnesses that Ina said could have been called "do nothingness." Nevertheless, Ina was as patient and tolerant with Doscia as she was with every member of her household. Watching his mother, R. B. learned to respect even the weakest member of a team. The team, however, had a strict but comforting hierarchy that should also be respected. Under Ina Russell's tutelage, her children learned to respect others and to take responsibility as leaders.

A black woman named Jinsey from Russell did most of the family washing, and it was the duty of the children to push wheelbarrow-loads of dirty clothes to Jinsey's house and to collect them after they were washed. Sometimes Jinsey ironed clothes, but Ina, Pipey, and the older girls also ironed. Ina was a person to turn her hand to whatever task needed doing, and she cultivated the same attitude in her children.

Black and white children played together, and they were in and out of each other's houses on a daily basis. The boys loved to get up a baseball game, and while the game was an informal one, it was the best players that counted, not the color of skin. At this stage, the boys of both races hunted together, too, in the company of adult hunters of both races. R. B. gloried in these hunts and the feeling of male camaraderie that they fostered. The hierarchy was clear among the adult males, of course, yet also clear was a mutual feeling of respect. The game would be fairly divided at the end of a hunt so that all went home with birds or rabbits for the pot.

There were only about a dozen or so houses in the settlement of Russell, with no distinct separation between those belonging to white families and those belonging to black families. The entire community was frayed and unkempt. Some of the homes for white families had been painted, while many homes belonging to the black families were left graying and weather-worn. The only church was a Baptist one, built of lumber that had been salvaged when a twister tore down several houses. There was one brick building that had served to store cotton at an earlier time and continued to serve as storage area for various implements and crops. A family named Huff ran a small store in the settlement for a while. There was little wealth in evidence within this community. While the Russells were the leading family, they certainly did not consider themselves wealthy. Everyone lived simply and shared with those around them.

R. B. adored baseball, and there was a heated rivalry with the Winder boys. While stories are not clear as to whether the town teams were biracial or not, what is clear is that a Sunday afternoon game with Winder frequently led to fistfights. Richard senior encouraged his boys not to start fights, but once in, they were to give as good as they got. They had heard tales of their father's scuffles, both in and out of courtrooms before he became a judge, and the girls were old enough to remember his coming home with a black eye or skinned knuckles. Knowing how to avoid a fight must be balanced, for Russell men, with knowing how to fight.

By 1910, with the birth of Dickson, Ina found herself more and more in need of regular help with her brood, because Hettie had married, Anita Stroud had left, and the older girls had been sent off to school. Nothing was more important to Ina than a good education for her children, both girls and boys. Mary Willie was at Georgia Normal and Industrial College, and Ina junior and Margo were living with Ina's sister Hattie Arnold, recently widowed, in Washington, Georgia, in order to attend the public school there. The continuing county-question feud with Winder meant that Richard senior would not allow his children to attend a Winder school.

Ina and Pipey soldiered on with homeschooling the younger children, but keeping up with household tasks, gardening, and cooking meant that one of the spheres inevitably suffered. Into this messy scene came Laura Glenn a few months after Dickson's birth. Laura, an older black woman, perhaps the wife or mother of one of the tenant farmers, was a talented cook, and she wasn't afraid of crowds. Laura and Ina became friends as they united in Ina's household to rear her rambunctious brood. Ina found that Laura was quick yet steady and brought her own sense of order and creativity to the kitchen, releasing Ina for other household tasks and mothering roles. For a time, Laura was lured away to cook at the Winder Hotel—she was skilled at cooking for a crowd—but she was soon back with Ina, in a place where she admired her boss and felt appreciated. Ina gave thanks daily and in the hearing of her children for this fine soul, who had come to their rescue just when their mother felt she could not hold up.

When Papa had business trips or travel for other reasons, he often took Ina and one or two of the children. In 1908 R. B. and Ina junior went with Papa to Savannah for several days, just the two of them, having a berth on the train and staying at the grand Desoto Hotel, where they ordered what they wanted in the dining room even when Papa was out. Ordering four desserts instead of a regular meal was a plan they carried out with glee. They saved fresh fruit brought to the table to take home to the other children. Trips to Washington, DC, were fairly common, since Richard's brothers Edward and Robert lived there during the early part of the twentieth century, and brother John worked there for a few years. The Russell men were close and made yearly visits to each other's homes whenever possible.

As a career naval officer, Richard's brother Robert Lee was often at sea. He had travelled, literally, all over the world, and his letters served as geography lessons of the most relevant kind. R. B. did not abandon his dreams of following Uncle Rob's example in attending the Naval Academy when he grew up. It was frequently quoted in family circles that Uncle Rob was the first Georgian to graduate from the United States Naval Academy following the Civil War. Richard senior was adept at finding marks of public distinction among his kin, going back into the night of Time. Ina, on the other hand, was likely to emphasize character as the most distinguishing mark of achievement, and Richard was quick to support her in this observation. He often told his seven sons that while perhaps not all of them would be brilliant, nor all of them successful, every one of them could be honorable. From early youth, R. B. took his father's words to heart and tried to follow them.[8]

Both the Russell and the Dillard families were strong on telling family stories, not only to verify the respectable stock from which the families came but also to inspire the young to like achievement or warn

---

[8] It should perhaps be noted here that all seven of those sons were successful, honorable, and likely brilliant, though the younger ones were overshadowed by the achievements of their elder brother.

them against falling into the same regrettable behavior. An eager listener for almost any kind of story, R. B. adored those dealing with the Civil War. In spite of the sad ending to his Russell grandparents' war story, he begged to hear it over and over.

The Dillards at Farm Hill also recounted a dramatic and nerve-wracking war tale of escaping a roaming band of Yankee soldiers one August morning in 1864. The boy trembled as if he had been in the farm house, had heard the soldiers marching down the road, closer, closer, ready to pillage and burn. But because the land was shrouded in thick fog, and no cock crowed, no horse neighed, no cow mooed, nor any other farm animal made the slightest sound, the soldiers remained ignorant of the prosperous farm worth plundering that sat off the road in a grove of oak trees. While Grandmother and Grandfather Dillard sat rigid in their living room, preparing for the worst but praying for delivery, the soldiers marched past, thanks to that heaven-sent fog.

These stories thrilled and saddened R. B. He was proud of his family's courage and endurance, but he did not understand how Yankees could have been so cruel and vindictive. According to a Southerners' way of thinking, the war was, after all, a family quarrel and ought to have been conducted more in that spirit. Like all white Southerners of this time, R. B. had to live with the painful knowledge that his people had lost the most important fight in America's history as an independent country. The lad absorbed the essential sense of tragedy and loss that marked the South and the bitterness that tragedy had engendered.

Richard Russell, Sr., was a member of the Royal Arcanum, an organization similar to Woodmen of the World or the Masons. Such groups in the postwar South provided a venue for male bonding and the practice of leadership roles. Royal Arcanum sold insurance, and in exchange for legal work he did for the organization, Richard senior was often elected to go to national gatherings at the company's expense. He could usually afford to take Ina and one or two of the older children along while Pipey and Annie stayed with the other children.

In 1910 R. B. and Rob had the good fortune to attend a Royal Arcanum meeting in Montreal with their father and mother. After stops in Washington and New York for sightseeing, the family arrived in

Montreal to find Canada in mourning for the death of King Edward. Royal Arcanum business was suspended, and they all had the opportunity to see military parades and attend stirring ceremonies that included 101-gun salutes. R. B. and Rob were beside themselves at their good fortune. R. B. went out to meetings later to hear his father speak, while Rob stayed home with Mother to have a bath in a large white tub with running hot water. When they met Catholic priests wearing skirts like a woman on the street, the boys stared in amazement. During a visit with his mother to an institution where nuns gave their lives to caring for orphaned children and old people whose families were unable to care for them, Ina was impressed by the cleanliness and order of the place, but after a little while, R. B. burst into tears. He begged his mother to abandon the tour. The contrast between his own happy home—where young and old lived side by side, caring for each other in camaraderie—and this institutionalized family full of loneliness and distance, no matter how hygienic, was too much for his young heart to bear.

Long Pants at Last

By 1911 R. B. began to hear his parents discussing sending him away to school, and sometimes these were energetic and loud discussions. It was clear to Ina that in order to challenge his intellectual abilities, this eldest son must study at a reputable school. Richard Russell, Sr., however, was eyeing another run at the governor's chair and thus facing campaign expenses that would make school tuition difficult to pay. His wife thought if he could afford to run for governor, he could afford to educate his children, but if one or the other had to be chosen, education trumped political ambition. Although Ina had for twenty years scrimped and saved to help her husband's career—sewing most of her children's clothes, cooking and cleaning without regular house servants, ironing until her hands would blister, growing much of their food, wearing out her shoes and dresses—she would not back down on schooling for their children. Richard might grumble that this was the last thing he needed right now, but he knew Ina was right. Accordingly, it was decided that in fall 1911, R. B. would attend the Gordon Military Institute in Barnesville, Georgia.

Richard's first wife had come from Barnesville, and he was well acquainted with the respected school, which had been in existence there since 1852. Named in 1872 for popular Confederate general John B. Gordon, it had become a military institute in 1890. Georgians were proud that Gordon, an Atlanta attorney turned soldier, had become a trusted corps commander under General Lee. Any catalogue of Gordon's many battles made R. B.'s heart swell with pride: First Bull Run, Williamsburg, Seven Pines, and Antietam, where Gordon almost died from a head wound but recovered to fight again at Chancellorsville and Gettysburg. Later he led men at Spotsylvania and in the Shenandoah Valley Campaign before rejoining Lee in the trenches at Petersburg. At Appomattox, his men made the last charge of the Army of Northern Virginia. That this soldier then went on to serve Georgia as governor and United States senator made him hero *par excellence* for R. B. Russell, Jr.

In addition to the exciting idea of boarding school, summer 1911 contained other stirring elements. Pipey and Annie had moved from the farm in Oglethorpe County to Russell to live in one of Papa's houses about a year after the death of their mother, America Chaffin Dillard, in order to care for the three children of their brother Ben Dillard, a traveling salesman. Rowena, Frank, and James, whose mother had been killed in a buggy accident, were about the ages of R. B., Ina junior, and Margo, and with their arrival in 1911, the Russell community rang with even more shouts of children at play, arguing, squabbling, laughing, singing, shouting, and firing pretend weapons. There was a new order to be worked out, because Pipey and Annie were now the principal caretakers of the Dillard children, and the Russell crew would have to take second place. Once again, Ina's skill at compromise and her patience with all situations eased the transition. Pipey, too, was patient and kind. Annie was the fiery one, and the children did all they could to please her and avoid her stern discipline.

The education of R. B.'s sisters was not to be neglected. Mary Willie and Margo would attend Georgia Normal and Industrial College in Milledgeville, and Ina junior, who suffered from severe asthma attacks, was to attend Lucy Cobb Institute in Athens, because her parents wanted her closer to home. These four older children talked all summer of their upcoming school lives, but when Mary Willie saw R. B. in his school uniform for the first time, she felt a rush of nostalgia. He was wearing his first long pants, a soldier's clothes. That he was growing up somehow came as a shock.

Having their hands and hearts full with more immediate and daily matters, the women and children were not concerned with the chaos in the Georgia political scene at this time. Richard senior, however, had been watching developments since Hoke Smith's election in '06 with keen interest. A recession in 1907 had enabled conservative Joe Brown, son of Civil War governor Joe Brown, to blame economic woes on the liberal Hoke Smith in 1908, and although Brown had no political experience whatsoever, the former railroad executive bested Smith in a bitter election. Smith was again elected to the office in 1910—another bitter fight—ousting Brown. In a bizarre development, at the death of Georgia's United States senator Alexander Clay, Smith was then elected to the Senate by the state legislature. Because the Senate was adjourned for the summer, Smith went right on being governor. When the Senate resumed its session, he went to Washington, and a special election was held to choose a new governor. Richard Russell, Sr., felt sure his time had come to be elected governor of Georgia. Georgians were bound to be tired of this feud between Smith and Brown, bound to want a new voice, but one with experience. All he had to do was get to the voters and tell them about his ability and his desire to serve them. Even before the date was announced for the special election, Papa's hat was in the ring as he travelled from place to place in summer 1911, hoping to convince Georgians to elect Russell their next governor.

In early September, R. B. saw Mary Willie and Margo pack up their trunks and board the train for Milledgeville, familiar territory to Mary Willie, now in her senior year. In the afternoon of the same day, Richard went with Ina to deliver Ina junior to Lucy Cobb Institute. They carried the twins, now four years old, and basked in the attention the handsome little fellows attracted. Richard senior shook hands with other passengers, introduced himself. Campaigning was constant.

R. B. packed his trunk with his mother's help, and stored personal items he did not want his little brothers to interfere with in another trunk to be left at home. These included his baseball glove, baseball cards, his rifle, and a few books. Ina was amused at his concerns. He was to go with his parents a few days later to Barnesville, where they would see that he was registered and settled in a boarding house in town, which is how Barnesville cadets were housed. With many friends in Barnesville, Richard senior had several recommendations for suitable accommodation.

On the day they were to leave, Papa sent word that he had a chance to speak in Oxford, Georgia, and he wanted R. B. and Ina to go with him for the engagement. The most memorable thing about the election for R.B. was seeing his father sail into the yard in a fine automobile, complete with driver, rented for the trip. The Russells did not own a car, and apparently Papa had no interest in owning one. As a youth Richard senior had hauled wood with a mule and wagon, driven a horse and buggy, and ridden horseback as a matter of course, but in a time when trains could take him almost everywhere he wanted or needed to go, he exhibited little interest in other modes of transportation. The family had Toler, an old horse, who had hauled them to church on Sundays for more than ten years, but Papa no longer rode or drove. He enjoyed a long walk. He often chose to walk from his hotel to the capitol in Atlanta rather than take a street car. Richard's younger brothers, Lewis and John, had each gone the way of the automobile, and their nieces and nephews enjoyed rides with them whenever the men came for visits. For R. B., an open-air ride to Oxford through Georgia farms and towns, sitting up front beside the driver with his parents behind, a happy, royal couple, was a time of unexpected grandeur.

On the way to Oxford, the family stopped to visit Lella Dillard, Ina's sister-in-law and widow of her brother Miles, a Methodist minister who had died in 1898. Ina had lived with Miles and Lella when they were a young couple while she attended school in Oxford and helped them with their young children. Like-minded women of faith, Ina and Lella had been close friends ever since, but Ina was nervous about this visit. Lella, with her children now grown, had become active in the Women's Christian Temperance Union during this historical period of the determined push toward Prohibition. For this cause, Lella had become a crusader. Richard, on the other hand, stood for local option, which supported the view that each community or county ought to choose for itself whether it would sell alcoholic beverages. In 1906 this had been the official stance of the Democratic (and only) party in Georgia, but by 1911, Prohibition forces were growing increasingly persuasive, and more and more people were getting on the teetotaler bandwagon. Knowing how fanatic Prohibition supporters could be, Ina feared that Papa and Lella would not speak to each other. She dared not ask Papa how he felt about it, for there was R. B., delighted to be sitting up in the car watching the world sail by, unaware of prohibitions or options.

When they pulled into the yard, Lella welcomed them warmly and insisted, as she always had, on serving them a delicious country dinner. Ina ended up enjoying the visit. She trembled when Lella told Richard, as they were leaving, that he had broken her heart by the stand he was taking, but Richard replied easily that he was sure that they could respect each other's right to differ. R. B. saw that his mother felt no need to defend either of her loved ones. The lesson was not forgotten: one must be able to disagree without seeking to force others to change. "Judge not, that ye be not judged" was a teaching of Jesus' that Ina quoted often to her children. The other part of the lesson was seeing his father stand by his own convictions, even before the righteous onslaught of an admirable woman like Lella, backed by the religious and moral forces of the day.

On 22 September 1911, Ina and her eldest son boarded the Central of Georgia in Atlanta, bound for Barnesville, without Papa. Another chance to speak had come up, and the candidate could not miss the opportunity. So far Richard Russell, Sr., was the only announced candidate, but they expected Joe Brown to enter any day. Ina felt timid without her husband, who knew the Barnesville folk much better than she did, but she was determined to get R. B. settled to her satisfaction. She hated to give him up but knew it was time. R. B. had perfect confidence in his mother. He was relaxed and eager on the train, holding onto a big "Russell for Governor" poster that he had taken from the campaign headquarters in Atlanta to put up in his room.

In Barnesville Ina saw her son registered at the institute and then found him a room in town with the Ely family, whose mother seemed capable of handling teen-aged boys. R. B. would room with two other cadets; accustomed to a room full of brothers, R. B. would not feel lonely. His mother urged him to be sweet and good to the small children in the house and to be a big brother to them. She would not let herself feel sad that he was leaving home, but focused instead on feeling satisfied that the changes would be good for him.

R. B. took to life at the military school as long as drills and studies were not involved. He was pleased to be able to wander around town in his free time, buy soft drinks and candy at the drugstore, laugh and joke with schoolmates on the street corners. He was less pleased with studies in algebra and Latin and with marching for hours up and down the school quadrangle with a rifle, and certainly not pleased at all with extra guard duty spent working off demerits he'd been awarded for being late to class or drill.

At mail call, one of the brightest spots in life at boarding school, R.B. received letters frequently from his mother and sisters. Everyone admonished him to write, and he tried, but he was not as faithful or prompt a correspondent as the others longed for. His mother urged him to write descriptive letters, giving interesting details. His father seldom wrote unless to send much-needed funds (they were more often late than not), but he stopped in to see him in October, as the judge whirled around the state making speeches.

Only a few days after R. B. started school, Mama sent the all-important news that "Joe Brown has announced & now it is up to us *all* to *beat him* & to stand up for our side with *perfect* good nature, *good* judgement & great *composure*."[1] Ina Russell had been through quite a few political campaigns by this point, and she understood that essentially politics is a fight. She wanted her son to learn to fight with an emphasis on civility. She also wrote to her girls and R. B. not to forget that she was counting on all of them to keep up the family reputation. Even Mary Willie wrote to her brother not to forget where he came from and how much his parents were counting on him.

Then a few weeks later some shocking news arrived: Pipey's house had burned to the ground in the early morning hours of 14 October 1911. R. B.'s mother painted a vivid scene of the neighbors, black and white, pouring out of their homes, families standing in their nightclothes, watching Pipey's home go up in flames. Two-year-old brother Edward, called Jeb by almost everyone but Pipey and Ina, often stayed with his aunt, and it was the baby who had awakened her early, refusing to go back to sleep, patting her face and saying, "Hot, burny hand, hot, burny hand." He had learned this phrase when he tried to touch the stove, and they all said it to him when he got too close to any fire. It was a few minutes before Pipey realized the house was on fire, and by the time she had sent Rowena out to shout for help, it was too late to save much of anything but their own skins. Everything they had except a week's washing, which had not yet been brought home from Jinsey's, was destroyed.

Ina Russell described, too, the kindness of neighbors who brought clothes and gave money. As the house was still burning, Doscia gave Rowena a dollar, and Laura, tears streaming down her face, gave Pipey a dollar. Others in Winder sent aid as well, but the question of where Rowena, Frank, James and Pipey would live remained a worry. They were staying with Ina for the moment. Ina knew R. B. would be happy to know that James could wear some of R. B.'s clothes left at home.

---

[1] Italics Ina's.

There was no time to stand around feeling sorry for oneself, however, as the gubernatorial campaign heated up. On his fourteenth birthday, 2 November 1911, R. B. was allowed to leave school and come to Atlanta to see his parents. They stayed in Papa's hotel and talked late into the night. Ina thought her boy looked handsome in his khaki uniform. She was relieved to hear that his roommate, Tom Thrash, was good in algebra and didn't mind helping R. B. More interested in football than math, R. B. begged to be given permission to attend games in Atlanta and Milledgeville.

If political polls had been taken in these days, they would have shown that the majority of Georgians felt Joe Brown had been cheated out of his second term as governor and they planned to vote for him. Brown was not an avid campaigner, and because he had no skill in oratory, he made only one ten-minute speech during the campaign. Richard Russell, on the other hand, was speaking frequently and feeling supportive response. How could the electorate be gathering behind such a lackluster man as Joe Brown? Hopes of a Governor Russell soared.

A surprise issue surfaced, however, that would prove fatal to Richard senior's dreams of victory. The candidate could hardly believe that anyone would get upset about the reasonable position of whether or not the sale of liquor should be sanctioned locally. Yet as the Prohibition movement gained strength, and the evils of alcohol consumption were magnified to highlight ruined lives, local option did, in fact, become a touchstone for voters. The Women's Christian Temperance Union and the clergy from Baptist and Methodist churches in particular became highly vocal. Mary Harris Armour, a celebrated and outspoken WCTU crusader, followed Richard sometimes and spoke on the courthouse steps following the candidate's presentation. When word came in November that a Methodist bishop had said from the pulpit that Richard Russell ought to be tied to a whipping post and every voter in Georgia be allowed to take a whack at him, the family was astonished. Ina could not resist writing to R. B. to ask whether he went to church on Sundays and "what does the preacher say about papa?"

Richard senior had been reared in the Presbyterian church but had begun attending the Methodist church with his first wife. Because Ina was Methodist and had two brothers and a brother-in-law who were Methodist ministers, he had had no objection to continuing in this denomination after they married. When the rumor got out in Winder, however, that the Methodists there were going to ask Richard Russell to leave their congregation, he was quick to quit his membership before being asked. Ina, brokenhearted, could not remain in a church that did not accept her husband.

Georgians went to the polls on 7 December 1911, and excitement was so high in the Russell camp that Ina wrote her children not to expect letters for several days if they won. She would be too busy celebrating. Sadly, there were no fireworks for Governor Russell. When results were counted on 8 December, Joe Brown had received 43,395 votes while a third candidate, Pope Brown, had received 38,024. Richard Russell received only 28,362, no appreciable gain since 1906.

Richard Russell, Sr., could find no explanation for this defeat outside the stand taken against him regarding the local option issue. Grieving, humiliated, and disappointed, he wrote to his children who were away at school. To his girls he wrote of his pride in and love for them and of the importance of love when all else fails. To R. B. he reiterated his 1906 theme but added a caveat regarding unprincipled clergy who used the pulpit of the Holy Savior for dirty politics. Although he had lost, he had not lost his manly honor. His greatest regret was that he would not be able to give his son and namesake a better chance, but now, "[Y]ou must fight for yourself. Be a man and you can be a Governor, but if you never are a Governor be a man dear boy.... I know you will not let my loss dishearten you, for you can think about the fact that no boy has a father who loves him better than yours loves you. Be cheerful and work hard to the sake of Your loving father Richard B. Russell."

To R. B.'s great credit, he answered his father's letter immediately. The same day, the boy wrote saying he had studied the returns and was glad to see that his father had had strong support in most counties. He did not seem at all disheartened. With a fourteen-year-old's confidence, he noted that it was too bad to get beat, but they could always run again. He added some advice about when his father could sell his cotton crop.

Getting a profitable price for the cotton was important because Richard senior was now deeper in debt, having borrowed heavily for the 1911 campaign while also paying room, board, tuition and books for four scholars. He also had to calculate the additional responsibility of four children born since 1906. Richard Russell, Sr., was now so famous for his large family that a familiar story in the state told that Judge Russell took his family to the fair, and the children wanted to see the two-headed calf. Stepping up to the ticket booth, the judge asked for fourteen tickets. Seeing the line of stair-step children, the hawker asked, "All them children yours?"

"Yes, indeed," the proud father answered.

"Wait a minute, then," the man said. "I want to go git the calf and show you to it."

Although this story is apocryphal, it was true that one of the judge's colleagues, Judge Bell, on the Court of Appeals, took his Sunday school class to the state fair in Atlanta, and when he was buying their tickets, he was asked if he was Judge Russell. R. B. heard these stories many times and enjoyed retelling them. He was proud of the loving and functional family he belonged to and was early aware of his privileges and responsibilities within it.

Christmas 1911 was a time for family reunion and rejoicing. They did not go to church any longer at the Methodist church, and although Uncle Lewis begged them to attend the little Presbyterian congregation he was helping to build up in Winder, Richard was too sore to go to any church. Ina insisted, nevertheless, on at-home services with hymns and scriptures. Richard senior licked his wounds and made plans for the future. R. B. heard his father dreaming about making Russell a prosperous little village with increased businesses. He would get the textile plant going again, and he had also started a bottling works, a venture with which he planned to rival Coca-Cola.

Papa also planned to build a hotel near the railroad tracks and have a whistle-stop station installed. In 1910 the family had moved into a slightly larger house, called "the Jackson house" after its former owners, but, though larger, it was more dilapidated than the "Gresham house" bungalow. Ina took one look at the plans for the hotel and said that if Richard was going to build anything that large, she was going to live in it. Being a fair judge, he had to admit her case had merit, and by the end of the spring, they had sold the Jackson house and their new home was under construction. They would move in late summer.

Thanks to the move into a new house, Ina told all her children away at school that there would be no summer house parties. She told the older girls that she was expecting her fifteenth child, an unforeseen blessed event which was testing her resolve to remain cheerful no matter what life brought. She did not tell R. B. this news, and he expressed disappointment at not being able to invite friends to spend long summer days in Russell. The Russells had enjoyed summer house parties since about 1907. Sometimes as many as a dozen children and parents, most of them relatives, would visit for several days or a week. In this way, Ina hoped to make up for the isolation from Winder. Now she had to tell R.B. that he and Rob were going to have to be the chief keepers of the farm store for the tenant farmers. The boys would have to record amounts of guana bought and groceries and farm supplies. Ina kept a careful account book of the farming operation, a book wherein she also recorded the numerous garments she made for her family, including underwear, dresses, and shirts. There also would be a large garden to tend as usual. Summer 1912 would not be a lazy one.

Carolyn Lewis put in her appearance on 19 August, which was also Rob's birthday. The family was half-moved into the new house, where Carolyn was born. This work went on until it was time for the scholars to go away again in September.

Although R. B. had succeeded at his studies at Gordon the first year, he found the second year more difficult. He was almost fifteen, an age when many young people left school for good. Struggling to get passing grades in algebra and Latin, he thought of his father's desire to build up the little village of Russell and decided he could quit school and open a store. This would help Papa out in two ways. He would not have to pay school expenses, and he could share in the store's profits.

His mother's response to his letter expressing these plans did not equivocate:

"Quit school! Never by *my* consent. You are preparing yourself now to make a living & to make a mark in the world & a high mark it must be.... Keep a store in Huffs store! Think of it! I can see you with your case of soda water & jar of red candy & box of chewing gun & you, *R. B. Russell Jr.*, sitting on the 'small of your back' waiting for a customer to come along with his *pennies* to trade with you." Ina was not given to sarcasm, but here she could not resist comparing a store-keeping R. B. with his respected and illustrious father. In closing, she softened and advised her son to grit his teeth and resolve that his dreams would come true through better education.[2]

During the winter term, R. B.'s grades did not improve, and his lack of success haunted him, though not enough to frighten him into studying harder. When he again expressed the desire to quite school, his parents wrote a joint letter outlining the circumstances under which they would allow him to leave Gordon. Ina wrote, lovingly but firmly, that he could come home and work on specific projects which she outlined for him. He would, with an axe, clear a gully on the farm of trees and, with their mule, the long-eared Rabbit, haul the wood to the train station to be shipped to Atlanta for sale. The proceeds of this work would be his. In addition, he would plow Rabbit at planting time, then chop and hoe the cotton, learning about nature as he did so. If he should decide to accept this, his mother reminded him that he would have to do better than he did last summer chopping cotton. "You must work & not stop to read the papers until you rest for dinner. Follow the old-time maxim to 'work while you work and play while you play.'"

Ina added that this physical labor would help him grow strong in body. Of course, he would be expected to continue his studies at home with his father helping him with Latin and mathematics, while his mother could teach him to write. He could turn himself into a Ben Franklin, Daniel Webster, Horace Greely, or Abraham Lincoln and work in the day and study at night. If he did this, "[W]e might have a president in the family some day, or to say the least of it, a very smart, strong, healthy boy." The litany of heroes she chose to hold up as models of virtue and achievement might have gone unnoticed at the time, but the power of the word works subconsciously.

---

[2] Ina's italics. Ina Russell wrote regular letters to all her children away at school. She kept them in touch with the family news and exhorted them to work hard, to achieve, and to make the most of their opportunities. She did not mince words about how much their schooling cost, although she made it clear that she and Papa felt that educating their children was the best investment they would ever make. Her letters were remarkable for their warmth, their energy, and their child psychology. When the scholars struggled, she never made excuses for them nor blamed the school and teachers. Instead, she encouraged them to see what they could do to improve their situation.

To these instructions, his father added that he agreed with Ina's plan and concluded: "You are my oldest son and you carry my full name. You can have—and you must have—a future of *usefulness and distinction*[3] in Georgia or it will break my heart. You know now what is my mind about your coming home and of course I often miss you and wish you were at home. So make up your mind as to what you think is best and act accordingly. God bless my boy."

Given this choice between physical and mental labor, R. B. decided to stay in school, but he failed Latin and was therefore ineligible to return to Gordon. This "choice by default," if such it was, did not work with his parents. They arranged for him to attend the Powder Springs Agricultural and Mechanical College in the fall so that he would have instruction in physical skills as well as mental.

At nearly sixteen years old and still in school, R. B. could enjoy the summer house parties of 1913 as much as ever, without worrying about finding a full-time job. As promised, his mother allowed the away-from-home scholars to invite friends to come to visit. R. B. had Tom Thrash as his guest, and pretty girls came to stay with his older sisters. Young men came to call, too, from Winder, walking out or catching the train and getting off at the whistle-stop station that now graced the line about 100 yards from the house. Other young men arrived on the newfangled contraption called a motorcycle, and R. B. was amazed to see his sister Ina hop on the back to ride. The older Russell children loved to dance and to learn the latest hit songs. In her youth, R. B.'s mother had been against dancing, but now Ina bought popular music, even ragtime, and tried to learn the songs herself so that she could play while they danced, sharing the interests of her young, and offering wise comments on lovesick lyrics.

Baseball remained a devoted activity of the summer as the boys eagerly played Winder teams and anyone else who could get up a team to challenge them. R. B. kept collecting his baseball cards.

One night after everyone had gone to bed, a frantic knock came on the kitchen door. Ina went to answer it, and since Papa was not at home, R. B. got up to be on hand in case she needed help. On the dark porch

---

[3] Italics mine. These were two constant tenets of the work ethic of Richard Russell, Sr.

stood Arch Barnes, son of one of their black tenant farmers, a young man only a year or two older than R. B.

Sweating and trembling, Arch said there was a lynch mob after him, and he could think of nowhere safe except in Judge Russell's house. Ina told him to come in and shut the door behind him. Whatever it was that Arch might have done, if he had, in fact, done anything, there was no question of letting a lynch mob have the upper hand.

R. B. leapt to his friend's defense. "Mama, Arch can stay right here in the kitchen all night, and I will stay with him with my shotgun. If anyone tries to get in, I'll shoot them."

Ina did not think anyone would suspect that Arch Barnes was sleeping on the floor in the Russell kitchen, but if they did, she did not believe they would attack the judge's house. She agreed to R. B.'s plan, and the two boys slept on the floor that night, shotgun at the ready. This event might have been R. B.'s first and was most certainly his most notable experience in fulfilling his patriarchal and paternalistic duty. It would remain as proof to him that extraordinary loyalty and friendship existed between those who were black and those who were white in the American South.

As the summer drew to a close, Ina junior fell ill with typhoid fever, and as her case worsened, her siblings saw their mother become more worried than they could ever remember. Dr. Almond came and went frequently but could not give much reassurance. The disease ran its course, however, and Ina senior somehow managed to get the other children ready to go away to school while nursing the sick girl.

Rob would be going off this year to Monroe Agricultural and Mechanical, in nearby Walton County. Mary Willie and Margo were still at Georgia Normal and Industrial College, but Lucy Cobb Institute had been notified that Ina junior would not be able to attend the fall term. She was wild to be back at school, but she could barely walk into the kitchen without collapsing, so her mother said she must not think about school yet. Sister Harriette, now fourteen, would live with Aunt Hattie in Washington to take advantage of the public school there.

R. B. was glad he would not have to wear a uniform at Powder Springs, and the school boasted yet another advantage: girls. Nevertheless, he and Rob both wondered how much physical labor they would be required to do. The tuition at such schools was less than at an academy or institute such as Gordon, but it was understood that expenses were offset by the students' own work. These chores were not so different from the ones R. B. had done at home: chop wood, hoe or pick cotton, feed animals.

Ina worried that because the students lived in dormitories, their manners would deteriorate without the supervision of the maternal authority present in a boarding house. She cautioned both boys against this occurrence, because she wanted them "to be gentlemen and to be good and to have a good influence on those around you." R. B. did not have as much free time as he had at Gordon, but he was still drinking Coca-Colas and eating candy at stores in Powder Springs, although his mother advised against this again and again.

When R. B. received letters from his brother Rob telling about the variety of meals served at Monroe A & M and the indoor bathrooms and electricity, none of which were found at Powder Springs, the older brother wrote home whining about his inferior conditions. His mother would have none of it. She instructed him to make the most of his opportunities and not spend time complaining and making useless comparisons. If his meals weren't as varied as Rob's, he could still give thanks that he had plenty to eat. Both boys were homesick and begged to come home for a weekend, but these visits were discouraged by the schools. R. B., however, managed to get his father's permission and came home one weekend in October. Ina thought he had grown several inches and allowed that his syrup and bread must be good for him.

Neither boy made good marks. Ina was encouraging to Rob, because this was his first time away at school, but to R. B., she scolded: "Look here, son! Why can't you get up a good report to send us once in a while? Your marks are dreadful & I can't understand. Surely you have the sense of intellect to do better. I want you to tell me sometimes why you don't make good marks. I'm worried...." Another time she told him, "I can't have one of you a failure, not one!" The great expectations did not abate, no matter how indifferent R. B. appeared toward his studies.

Ina's letters contained news about all the children still at home, about friends and family in Winder, and about the black families that lived in the little community. White and black people, though segregated officially, lived within that segregation an intense integration. They were in and out of each other's houses on a regular basis, and their lives were intricately entwined with the work of survival. Women like Ina understood this human condition deeply, beyond the law, beyond even custom. Ina often went to the homes of the tenant farmers, white and black, to visit the sick. She kept a small bag of medicines ready for these occasions, and it was she who sent one of the children into town for the doctor when she could not manage. It was customary for the landowner to pay medical bills, but doctors were sensitive to each situation and often rendered their services pro bono.

Laura Glenn continued to be a faithful and competent assistant, and she and Ina rejoiced in each other's children. Laura made special cakes and cookies to send to the Russell scholars. When the cook's prodigal son, missing for fourteen years, returned home, Ina wrote of it to her children with the same joy she would have expressed for any of her own family who had regained a loved one. When Ina junior was well enough to take the twins and Dickson into Atlanta for a day, Laura went with them and laughed when people mistook the twins for Ina junior's children.

Walter, the oldest boy left at home, eleven now, was ecstatic to pick cotton with the black children from the neighborhood—and everyone was pleased that he could pick as much cotton as any of them. For Walter, the chance to hunt rabbits with Arch Barnes and younger black playmates was not to be missed.

Ina Dillard Russell taught a comprehensive and deeply charitable view of how to treat one's fellowman, by precept and example. She did not believe that telling something without showing it in your own life would constitute effective training. Both boys wrote home to tell about a student who came to their school, a "Wandering Jew" named Isador, who was a twenty-six-year-old Russian emigrant who had been a tailor in Russia. R. B. did not write sympathetically. His tone was almost scornful, telling of how Isador did not like Powder Springs because of its primitive facilities. Isador had already been at Monroe A & M and was pleased when he learned that Robert Russell was R. B.'s brother. He told R. B. that Rob had been kind to him at Monroe A & M, sympathizing with his frustration at being forced to attend Christian prayer meetings,

and that Rob did not participate when others called him "Leo Frank."[4]
R.B. knew his mother deserved to hear that news, and he told it.

Ina's responses to both her sons emphasized her life view. To Rob
she wrote that she was supremely happy to learn that she was the
mother of a son who possessed a heart, who knew what kindness was.
"O, Rob, tears are in my eyes now, as I write, and my heart is so glad that
you were kind. Cultivate your heart to be kind. Why shouldn't we be
kind to a Jew? We are told that man was made in the image of God. A
Jew as well as a Gentile—a *black* man as well as a white man."[5] To R. B.
she wrote firmly that he should not criticize others until he had fully
considered their circumstances and how he might behave with the same
background. Clearly, intolerance, narrow-mindedness, and self-
importance were not worthy qualities. She constantly advised all her
children to cultivate kindness, courtesy, tolerance, and love. More
importantly, she lived these teachings in a way that marked them with
the imprint of a truly great soul.

Ina did not fail to praise R. B. when he did well. Both parents were
highly pleased when he was elected president of his literary society in
winter 1914, because this would give him a chance to speak publicly and
often. Ina sent him a speech of Patrick Henry's and urged him to learn it
and be able to recite it. In general, R. B. ignored both admonitions and
encouragements. Although his parents continued to expect great things
from him and to tell him so, he did not seem to worry about his poor
performance in school. At Powder Springs he continued as he had at
Gordon, apparently without any ambitions except to dance with a pretty
girl at a school party, figure out a way to get into Marietta (walk) so that
he and a friend could catch a train into Atlanta, and to graduate with as
little distinction as possible.

Graduate the eldest son did, in spring 1914, but Richard senior was
not satisfied with this diploma. He declared that R. B. must go back to
Gordon for a year and receive a diploma from this more academically

---

[4] Italics Ina's. Leo Frank was a Jewish man from Atlanta who in 1913 was accused
and convicted of a murder based on questionable evidence. While his case was being
appealed, he was taken from prison and lynched. The case was sensational news for
months.

[5] Italics Ina's.

prestigious school, then enroll in law school at the University of Georgia. It was usual for aspiring lawyers simply to study with other lawyers, then take the bar exam, but Richard senior had taken a law degree at the University of Georgia, and he expected his son to do the same.[6]

Gordon Military Institute refused to accept R. B. Russell, Jr. again until he had passed Latin, so he was sent to the university to take Latin in summer school. Being in Athens and living with his cousin, William Henry Quarterman, under William's mother Mamie's supervision was not a hardship because the boys were old enough now to stay out late. Horrified when Mamie reported that the boys stayed out most nights until after midnight, Ina wrote R. B. that she was sure he could get in a little fun but study more as well. She continued, detailing the farm work she, Rob, and even the small fry were doing: "We have had some good rains now. Rob, Luther [a farm hand] and I planted the two upper oat terraces in peas. I sowed them & then the twins & I piled rocks. You know there are a *few* over there...." The unspoken message was clear: *You are fortunate to be in school. Make the most of your opportunity.*

Other times she made the message as overt as possible:

"Son, mother loves you so, & I'm always hoping & wanting you to do the right thing. Be gentle, be kind, be polite, be thoughtful of others, practice patience & unselfishness. Remember that all these begin at home. Be nice to your sisters. Be thoughtful of Mamie. Just be an all round good boy, such as you know your mother wants you to be...."

Ina junior had not been able to return to Lucy Cobb Institute, but she had studied to take a teaching exam, and that year there was a rural school a few miles from Russell that would hire her after the cotton was picked in late autumn. Twenty years old, restless, bored, and feeling confined, Ina junior needed a job. Richard senior had succeeded in securing state funds for a teacher at Russell, but hiring his own daughter for this post was not an option for Papa. The school was open to all white Russell residents, and "Miss Pearl" McBrayer, wife of a retired Methodist minister living in Russell, became the teacher. Almost forty children showed up for school during the first term.

---

[6] Aspiring legal or medical students were not required to take a four-year university degree before entering their specialized study at the time.

The feud with Winder over the creation of Barrow County heated to the boiling point in summer 1914. Winderites were determined to get the county through the legislature during the summer term. Richard senior went off on one of his Royal Arcanum trips to New York City with Ina and Ina junior, where they hoped to visit Mary Willie, who was in summer school there. While Richard was away, Barrow County was voted into existence by the Georgia legislature. The county was named for Dave Barrow, chancellor of the University of Georgia and longtime friend of both Ina and Richard.

People in Winder were in a celebratory—and vindictive— mood. They filled up several cars with Barrow County supporters, both men and women, and rolled out to Russell. Driving around and around the circular drive, ringing cow bells, they sang, "Let's hang Dick Russell from a sour apple tree," and shouted, "Glory to Barrow County! Glory to Barrow!" Some men got out of the cars long enough to paint "Barrow County" in bright letters on the whistle-stop station. Rotten tomatoes and eggs crashed onto the porches, front and back.

In his parents' absence, R. B., as the eldest son, felt keenly the responsibility to protect the homeplace. The younger children—the twins, Jeb, Dickson, and Carolyn—were frightened by the hullabaloo. As caretaker, Pipey tried to soothe them, with help from Patience and Harriette. Margo, always feisty, was surely urging her brothers "to do something." R. B. reached for his shotgun and raced upstairs to a corner window on the front of the house, followed by Rob and Walter.

It was dusk, and as the cars circled and jubilant passengers sang and shouted, R. B. ground his teeth and vowed to his brothers that he would fire on somebody if they did not get off the property. This attitude was the most frightening thing about the whole scene, and Rob thought better of that plan. R. B. raised his gun to his shoulder, but Rob put a quieting hand on his arm. "That ain't going to do any good, R. B. You know that." He might have whispered something about setting a good example for the four little boys who had followed the big boys up the stairs and were huddled terrified at the bedroom door. R. B. lowered his gun. No one was going to be hurt over something as silly as a new county, but no one who was there that night would ever forget what happened or what could have happened.

The next morning Patience, Walter, and the four little boys scrubbed *Barrow County* off the station wall.

R. B. passed his Latin course at the university, but he did not go back to Gordon until January 1915 because of Papa's financial struggles and the fact that he needed only half a year to receive his diploma. Thus, R. B. and Ina junior were at home all autumn, commiserating about their desire to leave Russell. Ina senior, hoping to cheer up her daughter, agreed to a house party in October, before the girl was to start her teaching job. R. B. entertained the four girls who spent the week at Russell, making them laugh at his ability to turn a handkerchief into an apron for candy-making sessions and at his recounting of exciting moments in football games in Atlanta. Younger than the girls, he chafed when older "men" from Winder came to call and whisked the guests away.

With three daughters soon to be of marriageable age (Russells and Dillards tended to marry late, well into their twenties) and R. B. now nearly seventeen, Ina made every effort to give her children a pleasant social life. She was exceptionally good company herself, and sometimes her daughters' friends begged to stay with her, even when her own children had to return to school or work. Young men wrote glowing letters of thanks for their time spent at Russell, and R. B. realized as he grew older that he had seen the best a woman could offer in the role of hostess in his mother's home.

When R. B. left for Gordon in January, he tried to comfort Ina junior that she would be all right in Russell, even if she was "at home with her mother." This remark hit a sore spot with their mother, for all her composure and willingness to let her children go and grow.

In March Ina had a sad letter to write to her children away at school. Her friend and right-hand helper, Laura Glenn, died suddenly of what was likely a brain hemorrhage. Ina helped to dress Laura for burial, including underclothes that Ina herself had made, and Ina junior quickly made a white lace cap for her. As was the custom, friends, black and white, united to give the respected and beloved woman a decent burial. Richard senior bought the coffin, while black friends paid for the grave and two buggies from the livery stable. Ina junior made an elegant cross of evergreen and jonquils, and black friends sent other floral creations. Ina took all the children except the baby, Carolyn, to the funeral, for the little children were all brokenhearted. Ina wept throughout the service. When Papa insisted she go with him on a trip to Knoxville, Tennessee, soon after, she refused, saying she was grieving Laura and could not be expected to go.

The final term at Gordon Military ended with a diploma for Richard Brevard Russell, Jr., and he was accepted at the University of Georgia law school for the autumn term of 1915. Although R. B. disappointed his parents with a lackluster academic career up to this point, they never lost faith in him, and neither did they fail to let him know that their expectations were not lowered. One instruction that they both gave him was to make friends while in school, and this, at least, he followed. Ina and Richard each had a gift for friendship, and R. B. inherited the double gene. Richard senior had, by this time, waged four statewide political campaigns and knew the practical value of having real friends in these battles, but this charismatic couple proved sincere in all friendships. Ina was particularly forgiving when political "friends" proved false on Election Day. Having been to two schools with rather different types of students, R. B. had made friends all over the state, in all classes.

Rob finished at Monroe A & M, and he, too, would take a final year at Gordon to earn an academic diploma. Richard senior was struggling financially, trying to repay old campaign debts and keep his children in school on the $4,000-a-year salary of a Court of Appeals judge. Mary Willie, continuing in her special bond with Rob, volunteered to pay his tuition and books from her teacher's salary, and although Papa chafed to have to accept, accept he did. Once, he also accepted Mary Willie's purchase of a train ticket so that he could go to Savannah to a meeting there. No one in the family took this behavior as exceptionally virtuous, although it was commended. As the eldest child and now employed, thanks to a good education, Mary Willie felt a sense of duty toward her home and family, but in this family, duty was performed with a loving and grateful spirit. As R. B. absorbed these lessons of family loyalty and love, he, too, began to develop, unawares, a strong idea of his duty. He was the favored eldest son, but nothing obscured the tenet that position brought not only privilege but also responsibility.

Richard Russell, Jr., almost eighteen years old, began his studies at the Lumpkin School of Law at the University of Georgia in fall 1915. He joined the Sigma Alpha Epsilon fraternity and continued his habit of enjoying an active social life, while studying just enough to ensure passing grades but not much more. At this juncture, he experienced a typical teenage dissatisfaction with life in general. He complained to his mother about everything, and this first experience with a restless young male was painful for her. Ina was constantly advising Ina junior and Margo, both of whom were out of school now and hoping to teach in rural schools near home when the cotton was picked. She instructed the girls to cheer up, find something to be happy about, think of others, not themselves, and give thanks for their many blessings. She did not appear too surprised nor too worried about the girls' laments, but she took R.B.'s remarks more personally. Remembering what a sweet little boy he'd been, how he'd adored her, and how proud he had been to be her escort, she could not bear to think that now he did not love her.

Ina, with several of the younger children in tow, made a special trip to Athens in November to visit R. B. for his birthday, taking a box of sandwiches and a cake, traveling via a rented car and driver. R. B. was not openly grateful for the visit or the food, saying, instead, that he regretted that the hog had not been slaughtered, so that he could have some good country sausage. His mother, although hurt by his indifference and careless remarks, wrote the next day and advised him to stop thinking about himself so much, to be more thankful, and to make a joke out of some of his distresses to see how quickly they would disappear. She closed with staccato advice: "Be happy, be *kind*, be *considerate* to those around you. Follow the Golden Rule,"[7] and, as usual, she sent "hearts of love." R. B. continued to request clothing, such as shirts and pajamas, and when he paid a quick visit home, Ina worried that he was not wearing a sweater. She hoped to be able to afford to buy him an overcoat soon. In December she wrote that they had killed the hog and had good and beautiful meat for Christmas.

The Christmas holidays of 1915, however, proved to be the worst the family had ever spent. Usually Christmas was a time of increased gaiety as they celebrated the deep joy of being together again, but R. B. returned home with a severe cough, which he had had for several weeks. By Christmas Day, he was fighting for his life against a virulent pneumonia. Everyone tiptoed through the house, from the youngest to

---

[7] Italics Ina's.

the oldest, as Dr. Charles Almond came and went. Running a high fever, coughing, aching, completely weakened, and frightened, the young man begged his mother not to leave his side, and she did not. Doctor Almond told a visibly shaking Richard senior and Ina that the next twenty-four hours would be critical. If the boy survived those, he would likely survive the illness. There was no Christmas revelry as the family prayed through the night.

There was slight improvement the next day, so Doctor Almond recommended that they hire a full-time nurse from Atlanta to come and care for R. B. until he fully recovered. Miss Dovie came the next day, 27 December, and remained with the family about nine weeks. R. B. suffered horribly through his recuperation, coughing blood, feeling feverish, and seemingly wasting away in the early period. Often he could not eat, and he developed painful groin abscesses, which had to be treated with constant hot compresses. At first he refused to try exercises to restore his withered limbs. His mother feared he would never be able to straighten his stiffened and bent left leg and would be permanently crippled.

Miss Dovie and Ina persevered, however, managing to get him out of bed and urging him to exercise. Ina used a small kerosene stove in the room for heating the water for the hot compresses she applied constantly. Miss Dovie scribbled notes of his progress daily.

Gradually R. B. began to improve, but he still did not like for his mother to leave his side, and she spent as much time as she could with him, using the time he slept to write letters to her children away at school. Mary Willie was teaching in Virginia, and it was to this eldest child that Ina confided some of her fears for R. B. Harriette was at Georgia Normal and Industrial College, alone now that Margo had graduated, and she fell ill with the chicken pox and had to be quarantined for several weeks in the infirmary. Ina wrote long letters to her as well, keeping her "chicks," as she called the children, particularly those far away or in trouble, in touch with home.

By late March 1916, R. B. was well enough to go to Sea Breeze, Florida, to spend a few weeks with his father's aunt, Aunt 'Pheme (Euphemia Russell), who ran a boarding house there. His mother's faith was tested as she sent him off to be under the care of another woman, but she knew Aunt 'Pheme was a loving and capable caretaker.

Euphemia Russell's fiancé had been killed in the Civil War, and she had remained faithful to his memory. She and a bachelor brother managed to support themselves with a boarding house in Mount Eagle, Tennessee, and another in Sea Breeze, Florida, living the summer months in Tennessee and the winter in Florida. Uncle Henry had fought for the Confederacy in Virginia, and in their company, R. B. heard tales of the war that stayed with him all his life.

Meanwhile, Papa was having a "hard go of it," unable to meet his debts, recurring school fees, and normal living expenses for a household of fifteen people. He had sold almost all the real estate he'd bought as a young man except his farm in order to keep afloat, and now, even with three daughters working and contributing to the budget, he felt that he should resign from the Court of Appeals and open a law practice. There ought to be sufficient clients happy to pay a former Court of Appeals justice for his legal expertise. Although he dreaded the months of building a practice, going private again seemed the only way to get out of debt and educate the nine younger children.

Ina was pleased with this decision because to her, the education of the children always came first. She did not, however, know that there was another political campaign embedded within the change. Once Richard senior knew that R. B.'s health was on the mend—reports from Florida told of his riding a bicycle and getting stronger daily—he decided to announce his candidacy for the US House seat of the Ninth District. Friends in counties north of Barrow, Walton, and Gwinnett encouraged him to challenge Tom Bell, the longtime congressman from the district. Bitten again by the campaign bug, Richard senior wanted, he said, to write part of his history into national history.

It was no secret that Ina had hoped and prayed that their campaigning days were over. Only one thing made the new foray a little less onerous than previous tries: Richard senior bought an automobile. With the acquisition of an automobile came the critical need for drivers. Neither Richard senior nor Ina showed the least interest in learning to drive, and why should they? They had, by 1916, at least five children old enough to drive and wildly eager to do so. Richard senior would need Rob and R. B. during the summer campaign, and they were offered driving experience first. Driver education in the formal sense did not exist, but the five older children learned, from practical application, to drive within weeks, vying for the privilege of taking Papa and Mama anywhere and everywhere. It is likely that R. B., Billie, and Margo had all had some experience driving Uncle Lewis's and Uncle John's cars. Rob and Ina junior were eager to get behind the wheel too. Both girls and boys were encouraged to drive, though only the boys would participate in campaign driving.

One of Ina's most thrilling early rides was to Rob's graduation from Gordon Institute in May 1916. She was amazed at the speed with which they could travel, and she embraced the new mode of transportation with great enthusiasm. Before buying his own "flivver," Richard senior rented a car and had his stenographer on the court, Mr. Crooks, drive him and Ina through north Georgia, since R. B. wasn't home from Florida yet. He needed to learn if the transport would be effective for his campaign. Ina was enchanted by this journey. They spent nights in Blairsville, Blue Ridge, and Jasper, and one evening their ambition got them stuck on the mountain, unable to continue safely on the rough mountain road with primitive headlights. Ina thought it a grand adventure that they had to sleep in the car until daybreak.

R. B. was the offspring who spent the most time behind the wheel chauffeuring his father over the rough dirt roads of north Georgia's Ninth Congressional District during summer 1916. At Chautauquas, Sunday school associations, fiddlers' conventions, court sessions, commencement exercises, Oddfellows meetings, and reunions of Confederate veterans, the young man saw his father receive warm applause and provoke laughter—Richard senior always found a joke or a witty remark for any situation, a talent which made his family proud. When not making formal speeches, Richard senior was on the streets, shaking hands, mixing, and telling voters how eager he was to serve in Congress. The Great War had piqued his interest to serve on the national level, he said, and he believed his long service had uniquely prepared him to make a lasting contribution in a changing and troubled world. His audiences listened and applauded, but Tom Bell had brought considerable federal money to the district, and the majority of voters saw no reason to change horses in the middle of the stream. On 12 September 1916, the voters of the Ninth District went to the polls and confirmed that they preferred to keep riding the Bell horse.

Thanks to his experience driving his father all over the Ninth District, the judge's son accepted a job delivering an automobile from Gainesville to a Blairsville automobile dealer, along with five or six other young drivers in new cars. For the next fifty years, R. B. felt the accomplishment of bringing one of a half dozen cars into a mountain town, in spite of rough and dangerous roads, was an adventure worth recounting.

Working with his father campaigning in summer 1916 convinced R.B. that he wanted to go into politics himself. He noted the respect his father had with people in all levels of society, and the boy decided that he would change his name. He wanted to be called Dick Russell, Jr., not R. B. People knew the name of Dick Russell and liked it. When he told his father this, Dick Russell, Sr., was altogether behind the change. Happy to hear of his son's political ambitions and his conviction that his father's name would help him, Dick senior announced to everyone that "Dick" was R. B.'s new name.

Dick junior did not see how there could be two Russell sons with the same name and suggested that Dickson's name be changed. Richard senior agreed and changed the six-year-old's name to Alexander Brevard, a revered name in family history on his mother's side. Alexander Brevard, from Brevard, North Carolina, had the status of hero in family tales, having practically single-handedly helped George Washington win the American Revolution during more than one battle. Mother Ina must have felt the pain that such a change would cause the little boy. He'd been "Dick's son" and now he wasn't? Yet she believed this little boy one of her most intelligent and sensible children, and she invariably went along with the patriarch after she had her say. Fourteen-year-old Patience, Dickson's special sister and caretaker, was horrified and said so, an unusual occurrence in this patriarchal home. Richard senior felt that by giving the little boy another part of his own name— Brevard—he was doing the best he could do for both sons, and thus all other parties must be satisfied.

Because he had finished one term in law school in fall 1915, Dick junior did not go back to the university until January 1917, when he resumed his studies and his casual lifestyle. Living at the SAE fraternity house, he had numerous opportunities to attend dances and to go on dates with pretty and popular female companions. He wrote his mother that he was confident doing the one-step but was in mortal dread when the band struck up a waltz or fox trot. Nevertheless, having seen his father dance with alacrity and joy from before he could remember, Dick Russell, Jr., felt right at home on the dance floor. His brief estrangement from his mother evaporated. He wrote to her and she to him with affection and respect.

Ina was not shy about admonishing her son regarding the repugnance of a habit many young men turned to as they grew up: chewing tobacco. Having spent her marriage trying to get Richard senior to give up chewing tobacco, his mother was sure that the habit had "hurt papa." Although smoking tobacco was more acceptable, any use of tobacco was unwise, according to Ina. It hurt her to see those she loved put themselves "under the dominion" of such a thing. As a final note of persuasion, she hinted that Dick might be less attractive to those pretty girls, and perhaps a very special girl some day, if he kept up the use of tobacco.

At the moment, however, R. B. was popular both with girls and boys, making friends all around, as his parents had advised and shown him how to do. With Russells and Dillards, making friends was a natural part of life.

War Is Not a Game

A shadow over Dick Russell's young world lengthened and darkened during this period. Until America's entry into the conflict, war news had been inconstant, appearing only in newspapers, and in the Athens and Atlanta papers, it was not likely to be prominently displayed. It had been easy for Americans to remain insulated from the conflict, but many, including Ina Russell, worried over the looming horror. When President Woodrow Wilson asked Congress to declare war against Germany on 3 April 1917, America felt its membership in a harsher, wider world. Dick feared he would be among the first to be called up, but he was naively sure that no American troops would be sent to Europe.

For one who had gloried in childhood warfare, Dick viewed the possibility of fighting for his country with alarm. He wrote to his father that he admitted to being a coward and if he had to serve, he would join the Navy rather than the Army. The war news, he said, had demoralized the entire campus, and none of his friends were eager to serve. It was too bad that his generation was not as brave as that of 1861. He was overjoyed when he learned that as a student he would be permitted to finish his first year of law school. A later extension of student deferment allowing him to complete his law studies meant he could spend summer 1917 at home going out with the local girls or visiting girls in Athens and other towns. He had made grades above seventy-five in every course in 1917, so he was not under academic stress. The possibility of soon being part of a bloody war scene retreated.

In the early days of America's involvement in the Great War, it was the Russell girls who experienced the most dramatic life changes. Billie, Ina junior, and Margo were all teaching, and Harriette was at Georgia Normal and Industrial College. Only Ina junior was still living at home. Billie, teaching near Columbus, Georgia, had frequent dates with young officers at Fort Benning, which sometimes included rides in automobiles with other couples. She wrote home about a special young man, Gordon Green, from Gray, Georgia, a Georgia Tech graduate. Harriette reported the astonishing news that the town of Milledgeville was full of soldiers, and that they were invited on campus so the girls could make them feel welcome. Girls were actually assigned soldiers, and although Harriette enjoyed showing her "soldier boy" around the campus, she lamented the bad luck that he was married.

Dick's mother and sisters wrote to him of these dramatic changes while he was at law school in autumn 1917, but he was well aware that the tense and uncertain times were loosening Southern society's tight hold over the lives of women. The university was not coeducational, but he had no trouble finding dates for any social activity on campus. During this time, Ina senior watched Ina junior closely as she entertained at least two young men seriously. The young woman, still dissatisfied at home, knitted a warm sweater for Charlie and told her mother that Van had asked her to marry him. Billie and Gordon's romance heated up, and by Christmas 1917, Dick, who once recorded in his journal that he was thankfully not in love at that time, had formed a close relationship with Laurie. Margo was dating a Winder boy named Ralph Sharpton, her beau for a couple of years, who was going into the Army. Conversations during the holidays were filled with exciting and humorous stories of couple adventures.

Richard senior and Ina listened to these tales with attention. Early marriage was frowned upon in the Russell and Dillard clans, and even though Ina junior and Billie were now in their twenties, their parents viewed any prospective mate with caution. Gordon Green, who was from a good middle Georgia farm family and was extremely bright, college-educated, and an officer in the Army, was not marked off the list. Ina senior advised Ina junior not to consider marrying someone she wasn't wholeheartedly enthusiastic about just to get away from home. Marriage was too long a proposition for doubts. Ina junior refused Van's proposal but continued seeing Charlie. Ralph Sharpton could not afford to get married, so there did not seem to be an immediate concern over Margo's situation.

Richard senior advised Richard junior that if he wanted a successful political career, he should consider staying single. "He travels fastest who travels alone," he said. This advice, coming from a father of thirteen children who cherished his family and who could, perhaps, be considered the most famous father in Georgia, might have amused his eldest son, and it did not deter him from falling in love. During his final year at law school, Dick Russell, Jr., fell enthusiastically in love with a young woman whose name he would never disclose. Sure that they were destined to be together, he dreamed of starting a home and family. He said nothing to anyone about these dreams. How could he propose even a long engagement? He was still a student, with no means of support and a military obligation to fulfill. Yet he gave himself over to the hope and the joy of being in love.

Then tragedy struck. His sweetheart fell ill, perhaps with the influenza that took the lives of so many in 1918, and she died, leaving him bereft. Because they had told no one of their deep attachment, the young man could not share his grief with her family or with anyone. It would be years before he would even talk about this love, and then only to one or two trusted friends.

In February 1918, word came from Billie that Gordon had received orders for France, and the couple wanted to be married immediately. Richard senior, Ina, and Ina junior travelled to Washington with Billie to meet Gordon, who was stationed in New Jersey. The couple married on 1 March, in the home of Uncle Ed (Richard's brother) and Aunt Susie. Richard senior was in such shock at giving up his eldest daughter that she had to help him put his shoes on as he sat weeping on his bed the morning of the wedding. Dick, unable to leave school, heard through letters about the simple but elegant ceremony, the capital city thronged with soldiers and sailors, and the joyous couple who boarded the train on their way to New Jersey. What he did not hear about was an idea that had come to Ina junior during this visit. No one heard about it, for Ina junior kept it to herself until she could execute it.

While in Washington, Ina junior learned that many civil service positions were open to women so that men could be released to serve in the armed forces. She heard about women being allowed to join the Navy to serve in clerical positions, but she had no interest in joining the Navy. A job in Washington, however, was tempting. She arranged to take the civil service exam in Atlanta and took it, not saying a word to anyone. Perhaps she would not pass.

Spring, never slow in Georgia, seemed to fly faster than ever that year. Harriette completed her studies at Georgia Normal and Industrial College, and Dick graduated from law school. His grades had improved slightly, but, in truth, there was nothing in his school record to indicate his superior intelligence and keen political mind. As the school year ended, he wrote his mother that he knew he ought to join the Navy, but he ought also to help his longsuffering father in his law practice. Watching his friends go off to war, some of whom he had been in school with for six or seven years, made him blue. He also was afraid that his easy student life would make work in the real world hard to face. Apologizing if he had bored her, he closed with a line that Ina senior was sure to cherish. "I felt just like a child again and just wanted to confide in you."

The new graduate came home, knowing that he would have to go into the armed services soon. He wanted to join the Navy because of his admiration for Uncle Rob, but he found it hard to put his name on the line. He dawdled through the summer until his younger brother Rob, barely eighteen, decided to join the Army. On 12 September, not knowing that the war was, in fact, almost over, R. B. Russell, Jr., joined the Navy and was stationed in Athens. Rob was stationed there in an Army unit, since both the Army and Navy had training camps on the University of Georgia campus.

About this same time Ina junior received word that she had passed the civil service examination and a job in Washington with the Bureau of War Risk Insurance[1] was waiting. She revealed her plans to her parents, who were shocked, but her mother was not disapproving. Ina junior had never liked teaching, and this was a chance at different work. She could live with Uncle Ed and Aunt Susie, and her longtime dream of leaving Russell would be fulfilled. Richard senior, unhappy with the idea of losing another daughter, said she could give it a try. He would come to Washington after a few weeks and check out the situation. If dissatisfied, he would bring her home.

Dick found the apprentice seaman's life even more difficult than he had expected. Not only must he stand guard duty and take part in drills, activities no less tedious than they had been at Gordon, but he must also scrub barrack floors. Further oppression came in the form of science subjects, which had never been his strong point. Hours in study hall with books on physics, mathematics, and navigation left him weary and depressed. There was scant time for meeting girls, going to dances, not

---

[1] Later, the Veterans Administration.

even time for a weekend at home. When the flu epidemic put all military personnel under quarantine, he felt so low that he wrote his mother he had made a terrible mistake by joining the Navy. Underscoring his earlier worries about adjusting to real life, a remark made by his youngest sister, Carolyn, might have said it all. Upon hearing her mother read aloud from a letter about how hard her sailor brother was forced to work, the six-year-old said, "Mama, Dick can't be lazy now, can he?"

Reports from sister Billie (Mary Willie) about the advantages officers enjoyed could have made military life look more attractive, but when Dick thought of the work and effort needed to become an ensign, he elected to remain a seaman. Because he never saw more water than the Oconee River, he at least could display characteristic Russell humor by referring to himself as the "admiral of the Oconee."

Like so many other American servicemen of the period, Dick Russell also began to smoke tobacco. Few were concerned with the health hazards that cigarettes posed. For the first time, tobacco was rolled ready-made into cigarettes sold in packs, and this convenience, coupled with the cheap prices charged to servicemen, made addiction inevitable.

When Richard senior was in Athens working on a law case, he visited his sons but was allowed only to speak to them through a fence because of the quarantine. He found both boys well but Rob more cheerful than Dick junior. Naturally the entire family rejoiced when the Armistice was signed on 11 November, and their sailor and soldier were discharged before Christmas. Dick Russell, Jr. had spent seventy-nine days in armed service to his country.

Richard senior made good on his promise to check up on his daughter in Washington, but by the time he arrived, Ina junior knew beyond any doubt that she would stay there. She had just received her first paycheck.

After the war ended and Billie and Gordon were stationed near Washington, they rented an apartment with Ina junior and shared expenses. It would be another fifteen years before Dick would arrive in the nation's capital, and it would be a great boon to him to find two beloved sisters there to welcome him.

In January 1919 Dick Russell, Jr. began working with his father in the law office in Winder. His brother Rob went to Atlanta to work as a tombstone salesman, where sister Margo was working for the Federal Reserve bank, living with Miss Hettie and her husband Jim Langley. Dick moved back into his parents' home, apparently never giving a thought to leaving home. In spite of political disappointments, Richard senior saw one lifetime dream come true as he and his son began to work together. With the sudden death of Richard senior's sister, Mary, from pneumonia in late 1919, his brother Lewis also moved into the Russell home, and soon son Rob gave up tombstone selling and came home to study law. He passed the bar before he was twenty years old, and the practice now had four Russell lawyers.

A fifth lawyer was added when Joe Quillian, who had been practicing in Winder, suffered a debilitating loss. Joe's wife, critically ill with influenza, died at the birth of their third child, who lived only a day. Joe, a distant cousin of Ina's, was so undone that his other two children were sent to live with relatives, and he moved in with the Russells until he could recover. Lewis and Joe roomed together, as did Rob and Dick junior. Helping family members in trouble was neither unusual nor heroic, but simply the order of the day.

Thus, by 1920, Ina Russell had five lawyers living under her roof. Only Billie, Ina junior, and Margo had left home. Patience and Walter were away at school most of the time, but William, Fielding, Jeb (Edward), Alex, and Carolyn were at home. By this time the family had a "flivver," and getting to school in Winder was not a problem for the youngsters. Joe and Lewis also had cars, as did Dick. Someone was always available to take five children to school. Ina rose before everyone else each morning and prepared breakfast and lunches for twelve people, then watched them depart in a hullabaloo, leaving her alone in a strangely quiet house.

Winder had been a dozing village crossroads of about 1,000 souls, still dreaming of future prosperity, when Dick was born. By 1920 its population had tripled, and it had several manufacturing plants in operation. The fact that Winder had become the county seat of Barrow County was undoubtedly one of the keys to its growth. The old quarrel with Richard senior still rankled with some of Barrow's barons, and Papa was seldom seen in the Winder office. He worked out of an Atlanta office and had plenty of clients to keep him busy. Dick and Lewis had no quarrel with Winderites, Lewis having supported the county and Dick having held his fire the night the county was celebrated in Russell. Their law practice in a court town began well.

The City of Russell, which came into existence five years after the birth of Richard B. Russell, Jr., boasted seventy-six inhabitants in 1920. Thirteen-year-old Fielding, one of the Russell twins, was paid $5 to take its census. It was not thriving as a developing community, but to the Russell family, especially its eldest son, it was the finest place on earth. From this old-fashioned setting, Dick Russell, Jr. would slip easily into the Roaring Twenties and the era's headlong flight into modernity.

PART II

1921–1932

Boy Wonder of Georgia Politics

The family had not yet settled down from the giddy excitement of Margo's wedding to Jim Bowden on 24 June 1920, a celebration that filled the house with kin and daisies, when Dick caused another stir. A surprising announcement appeared in the local paper in early July: Dick Russell, Jr. was a candidate for the Barrow County seat in the Georgia General Assembly and was asking for the support of all the white voters of the county.[1]

A twenty-two-year-old unknown, Dick Russell did not expect to win against the opposition, an elderly and popular newspaper editor named Albert Lamar. His main goal was to use the race to become better known and thus bring in more clients. Although Dick had enjoyed law work from the beginning, especially meeting people and trying to help them with problems, the Russell firm was not the only one in town, and competition was stiff. In rural Georgia in 1920, people often could not pay lawyers, doctors, or dentists, and, consequently, many of Dick's bills went unpaid. Locally, people understood and duns were rare—everyone was struggling to make ends meet—but the Chicago firm that had sold R. B. Russell, Jr., a set of law books wrote repeatedly demanding payment. Dick had watched his father increase his income since 1916 in private practice by increasing his efforts. If the son campaigned as his father had done, going door to door, he would get to know most of Barrow County, he figured, and they would get to know him. He was confident this plan would result in more clients.

The day after he announced, Dick Russell closed his office early and set off for Bethlehem, a hamlet about five miles from Russell, excited about starting his campaign. Although Bethlehem boasted few stores, these would still be open, and people would be on the streets, moving slow in the July heat. He could shake a few hands and practice the brief speech he'd been going over in his mind about what he had to offer.

---

[1] A common statement of the time, "white" and "voter" went together almost as one word.

In spite of unpaid bills, Dick managed to have his own car and to keep gas in it. He drove down the dirt road that ran from his house in Russell to Bethlehem and pulled into a parking place on the main street, next to the hitching rail. He could see a group of eight or ten men gathered at the end of the street, near the train station, so he walked down there. As he approached, he saw that they formed a rough semicircle, watching something intently. When he reached the spot, he saw that across the street a hound was crouched against a building within a thin line of shade. It stood slightly hunched, drooling and panting.

"Well, if it ain't Dick Russell, Jr.," someone said, extending his hand, and Russell shook it.

The man looked at the others and said, "I hear Dick's a good shot, and I'll bet he's the man to take care of this here mad dog for us without no one gittin' too close."

There was a murmur of approval. The fear of rabies was acute in rural America during the nineteenth century and well into the twentieth. Summer was an especially dangerous time for the disease, when the hottest periods were sometimes referred to as "dog days" because of the fear of mad dogs. Someone handed Dick Russell a pistol.

The eldest son in a numerous clan, Dick Russell, Jr. was not afraid to take responsibility where he perceived a leader was necessary. He took the gun, checked the chamber for shells, then cocked the hammer. As Dick aimed, he noted that the dog panting and drooling against the weathered building was a healthy-looking one, its darkly amber coat sleek. He lowered the gun and asked, "Whose dog is that anyway?" No one knew. "What makes you think it's rabid?"

Answers varied. "He's actin' funny." "No need to take a chance." "Better safe than sorry."

The candidate uncocked the gun and returned it to the man who had given it. "You know, boys, I'm running for the legislature this summer, and I think this would be a bad time for me to shoot somebody's dog."

The men present would recall this event many times in the community as a sign that here was a thoughtful and honest young man, one who would not go off half-cocked.

As the summer progressed, Dick found his campaigning going more smoothly than it had on that first day. Endowed with a wealth of his father's and his mother's charisma, along with their examples of hard work on the road to success, he went from store to store in Bethlehem, Statham, Auburn, and Carl, Barrow's small towns, as well as in Winder, and from door to door at every neighborhood house and farm. As he talked with the voters, he perceived that they were listening and that they warmed to his forthright approach. He began to believe that he could win the Barrow County seat in the Georgia General Assembly. Rob, watching his brother's good manners, his sincerity, and his genuine friendliness strike answering chords in the voters, encouraged him to keep working. Richard senior did not spend much time in Winder, preferring to work out of his office in Atlanta, where he found many clients—ones who could pay—but the father was proud to see his eldest son embarking on his political career and said so.

On 9 September 1920, the white male voters of Barrow County went to the polls, and both Dick and Rob felt assured that Dick would be a new representative to the 1921 Georgia General Assembly by nightfall. Their excitement at the breakfast table that morning infected Ina. Although she had never dreamed of going to the courthouse on election night to await the count for one of Richard senior's contests, women were now on the verge of getting the vote, and Ina thought she would like to hear the first announcement of her son's success. Billie was visiting during this time, and having lived in Washington and held down a part-time job in the big city, she felt going to the Barrow courthouse a simple assignment. Neither woman suspected how rough election nights could be. Nineteen-year-old Patience wanted to go too.

Driving a Chalmers, which Ina had purchased with money inherited from her sister, Hattie, Billie took her mother and sister into Winder to hear the voting results. All three women were disquieted to see men staggering drunk on the sidewalks and in the streets, shouting and cursing. Billie parked the car near the Opera House across from the courthouse and the women got out. Before they could move away from the automobile, a man stopped near it, pulled a pistol from his pocket, and pointed it at another man coming down the street. The shouts of the pistol-packing drunk that he was going to kill the other man sent the ladies scurrying back into their car and home without hearing any election results.

Later in the evening the men came home—a little drunk themselves—to announce that Russell had been chosen over Lamar by a vote of nearly two to one. At the age of twenty-three, Dick Russell, Jr., would have the best of both worlds. Most of the time he would enjoy the intimacy of small-town lawyering, but he also would have the experience of living in a city for a few weeks every other year, making laws and friends.

Family life at Russell was hectic. Seven-year-old Carolyn and her four older brothers, so close in age, were talented at producing school problems. Dick was not only expected to take them to and from school, but he might also have to pay for school supplies or a yearbook. As for his aging Dillard aunts, Pipey and Aunt Annie, who lived next door, the young man was called on to take them to town for shopping or to Atlanta to the doctor. Sometime during the 1920s, the Dillard sisters were joined by their brother Ben. Ben Dillard, now in his seventies and in ill health, had finally quit working, but he had nowhere to go and no money upon which to live. His sisters took him in as they had taken in his children more than a decade earlier. Family loyalty remained a workable ideal.

Ina Russell was talented at making people feel at home, and Dick's mother's easygoing and competent way of running her home drew her eldest son back into this comfortable fold. After his unhappy experiences in the Navy, Dick wanted to be nowhere else but at home, and he accepted that he had family duties to fulfill. Unlike his father, he participated in Winder community activities, playing right end on a city football team and teaching the men's Sunday school class at the Methodist Church.[2]

The newest Russell lawyer, Robert Lee, shared many of the home duties with his older brother, but Rob was considering starting a home of

---

[2] After Richard Russell, Sr., left the Methodist Church because of politics in 1911, Ina wrote to her four eldest children, who had joined the church by that time, that they must continue going to church, but that each must make his or her own decision about which church to attend. Dick Russell, Jr., would remain a Methodist all his life.

his own. While Patience was at Georgia Normal and Industrial College, her roommate there turned out to be a Winder girl, Sybil Millsaps. When Richard senior met Sybil, he said to Dick and Rob: "One of you has to marry that girl. We've got to have her in the family." Dick, keeping his eye on his first political duties and his monthly budget overruns, elected to follow his father's advice about traveling alone. Rob, though, agreed with his father's assessment of Sybil as an extraordinary woman. He started saving and courting.

When Dick Russell, Jr. arrived in Atlanta in June 1921 to take up his legislative duties, he was, at twenty-three, one of the youngest members of the 198-man General Assembly.[3] Possessing confidence born perhaps of youth and ignorance but also from hearing Georgia politics discussed firsthand since before he could remember, he was ready for the scene. With other young men in the assembly, and mindful of Georgia's "redneck" image, Dick Russell wanted Georgia politics and governmental administration to reflect a more progressive state. Yet he also knew and respected many of the older representatives who were his father's contemporaries, and he was thus disposed and able to avoid unproductive confrontations. Growing up in a large family under the guidance of a woman who was a master at compromise had not been wasted on Dick Russell, Jr. He had absorbed his mother's wisdom, strength, and modest manners. A natural leader and a clear thinker, Dick early showed a willingness to work behind the scenes, without fanfare and without concern over who received the credit, but with deep concern over getting a creditable job done.

In his first session, Russell from Barrow supported education and highway legislation but avoided inflammatory issues such as the Ku Klux Klan and lynching. The Ku Klux Klan was making a comeback in Georgia with such strength that within a year or two, politicians hoping for election would feel forced to espouse the Klan or, at best, avoid criticizing it. Although retiring governor Hugh Dorsey castigated Georgia's lynching record and spoke at length that first day of Dick's

---

[3] Richard Russell, Sr., at twenty-two, was the youngest member of the Georgia General Assembly when he served his first term in 1882.

legislative career about the horrors and injustices of lynching, the General Assembly refused to confront the issue.

The approach Dick Russell, Jr., employed of working on obviously needed projects, while making friends instead of fanfare, proved effective. He was unopposed in the 1922 election.

Preceding those summer elections, the family had a crisis in which Dick showed strong leadership. Richard senior, struggling to cope with an ailing digestive tract, was unable to dispel his lethargy and depression. He became harder and harder to live with, so weak and discouraged that both Dick and Ina feared for his survival. Then Henry Braselton, an old friend living in nearby Braselton, Georgia, told Richard senior that he wanted to go to Hot Springs, Arkansas, for a cure, but was afraid to go alone. Ina and Dick urged Richard to go with him. Braselton, a wealthy man whose town had done much better than Russell, offered to pay Richard's expenses if he'd go. Dick urged his father not to worry about money. He had two sons who wanted to and were able to help.

Richard senior had succeeded in paying off his campaign debts by this time, and he had educated eight children too.[4] That would have been a decent life's work by any standard, and his money situation was easing at least a little. There were still five children to send to school, however, and he was pleased to be solvent enough to be able to lend Billie and Gordon $500 when they needed it after the birth of his first grandson, Richard Russell Green. He was not about to accept Braselton's offer, but he did decide to go to Hot Springs in search of a cure, and the two men travelled together. Richard chose the Lamar Hotel, which cost $10 a week, room and board, thinking a man as wealthy as Braselton would go to a more luxurious lodging. Henry Braselton, however, preferred the company of Richard Russell, Sr. to luxury, and stayed right by his friend's side, much to Richard's surprise and perhaps dismay.

Papa received letters from his five oldest children all on one day when he arrived, as the family rallied to support their ailing patriarch. Dick and Rob wrote different types of letters. Rob wrote with warm affection, while Dick wrote of practical matters, much as his mother

---

[4] Patience and Walter had finished their schooling in 1921. Patience was teaching in Cochran, Georgia, and Walter, trying to decide whether to go on to school, was doing farm work. He could pick cotton as well as any hand, black or white.

wrote to her children. Dick told of the death of a local and prosperous farmer, Leet Smith, whom Dick was sure had simply given up the fight for life. His unspoken and worried message to father was obvious. Richard senior took heart as he considered the double blessing of being able to work with two such fine sons. He had longed for the chance to work with his R. B. junior, but he had not dreamed of the unexpected delight of a second son with whom to share the love of the law. That Dick and Rob were best friends made the situation even sweeter.

Richard Russell, Sr. returned home from Hot Springs revived, determined to live and to live well. Dick and Ina breathed sighs of relief, expecting Richard to continue his lucrative law practice.

On the last day of June 1922, late in the evening, Richard senior was in his law office in Atlanta with several friends, including his ardent supporter Walter Brown, also an Atlanta lawyer.[5] Politics was the subject of conversation, for it was the last day to qualify for the Democratic Primary on 9 September. Everyone wondered what would happen in the governor's race. The current governor, Thomas Hardwick, had been elected in 1920 over Clifford Walker, largely because Hardwick had supported the Ku Klux Klan and Walker had not. As governor, however, Hardwick denounced the escalated activities of the Klan, and Walker, on the other hand, had become an avowed Klan fan. What would be the outcome of such a fight?

Walter Brown, recalling Richard's courage in 1906 when he stepped into an equally bitter gubernatorial campaign, regretted that there was no office open to his friend, whom he considered a consummate public servant whose talents were being wasted. But wait. There was an office for which Richard Russell, Sr. was eminently qualified, one which should, by rights, be his some day. It seemed to Brown unfair that the current holder would live long enough to be reelected, and then die in office, giving the governor the right to appoint the next chief justice of the Georgia Supreme Court. This very scenario had played out in 1904 when Richard Russell had run against a failing T. J. Simmons, and lost. Simmons did indeed die in office, and the governor appointed William

---

[5] Son Walter Dillard's name had been changed in about 1912 to Walter Brown because Richard senior had been so hurt by the Methodists' stand against him in the 1911 election.

Fish, who was now the ailing and elderly chief judge. The men in Richard's office that night mused over how the electorate was effectively excluded, in these circumstances, from having a choice in choosing their judges. Yet it was almost unheard of to run against a sitting justice who was doing his job.

As Richard and Walter talked, the old passion stirred. If Richard could convince the voters of Georgia that electing him as chief justice was in the interest of democracy, if he could emphasize that Judge Fish deserved and needed a rest.... It would all be a challenge in persuasion, but Richard Russell, Sr., had rarely doubted his ability to persuade. A campaign would cost money, but for once he had some savings so that with a few contributions, he could finance without borrowing. If elected, he would finally achieve at least one of the dreams he had dreamed as a young man who wanted to serve his state in the top posts of all branches of government.

The idea and the discussion produced instant intoxication more serious than that of the whiskey they sipped as they talked. With Walter Brown urging him on, Richard paid the qualifying fee of $150 shortly before midnight, and his political hat was once more in the ring.

The sudden decision took everyone by surprise, especially his family. Ina could not help fearing another defeat, but Dick, Rob, and Lewis did not question Richard's decision. They went to work immediately, setting up campaign headquarters in Atlanta. Lewis would manage, with Dick and Rob as first assistants. Dick's contacts in the legislature were bound to be helpful. If they worked hard enough, they just might win this thing.

Richard Russell, Sr. formally announced his candidacy for the post of chief justice of the Georgia Supreme Court on the Fourth of July, and from that date until the election on 9 September, Dick and Rob spent every spare moment working on their father's campaign. Chauffeuring, they drove all over the state to various speaking engagements, and they did office work, such as typing, answering phones, stuffing envelopes, and greeting visitors. Lewis remained the indispensable, faithful, multitalented, and competent staff he had been for his brother on so many other occasions. The boys were amazed at Uncle Lewis's stamina and learned from him how to keep working until the last job was done, no matter how bone-tired they were. Although Lewis was given to witty sarcasm which could have been devastating, neither Dick nor Rob was perturbed by his remarks. Russell wit was often sarcastic, while Dillard wit, equally quick to see humor and comment on it, was gentler, never intending to hurt anyone. Dick and Rob had lived with both kinds. On the political battlefield, it was the rapier-like wit that would naturally become the weapon of choice.

Dick was given the job of chauffeur more often than Rob or Lewis, because all the men understood that it was important to Dick's own aspirations for him to meet people all over the state. The apprentice learned invaluable lessons from his father's approach. Richard senior was past master at reasoned arguments, and he kept the subject most important and likely to win support in the forefront. He refrained from criticism of Judge Fish, but pointed out again and again that if the public wanted younger and more vibrant judges, someone had to run against incumbents. Let Judge Fish retire to a well-deserved rest. Judge Russell was willing and able to serve and would not be an old man even by the end of the six-year term.

Wherever they went, Dick urged his friends to support his father's candidacy. The son sometimes made speeches for the father as well. Dick Russell, Jr. was right at home in the simmering political pot.

The issue of Prohibition seemed to be rearing its head again when the Women's Christian Temperance Union (WCTU), harking back to the election of 1911, endorsed Justice Fish. Although Dick had written to scores of friends asking for support for his father, he felt unable to write Aunt Lella. Instead, he wrote to his mother asking her to ask Lella to use her influence in the statewide organization to dismiss such ridiculous publicity. The chief justice would have no legal jurisdiction on liquor cases, he pointed out, and besides, with Prohibition the law of the land, local option was "as dead as slavery."[6]

Ina, wanting to do her best to support her husband, wrote to her sister-in-law, but she also wrote to her eldest son to remind him of the personal nature of campaigns. "Now I want to tell you and you can tell Rob," she wrote, "You and Rob and dad...have made it very hard for me to go to aunt Lella this time.... When Sister Lella came to Winder and conducted her meeting and made her beautiful speech, I couldn't get one

---

[6] To his credit, Richard senior also wrote to Lella, asking for her support.

of you to go near. You all are not even nice to her children, my own blood kin, and those children are dear to me, for their father was my greatest help in many ways when I was young and wanted to go off to school....

"I have grieved over Rob's hostility and haughty spirit and fierce criticism—just because somebody didn't think as he did. Papa has been harsh and hurt me so, in things he would say about aunt Lella. Aunt Lella gave papa the opportunity of running on her ticket. He didn't believe that way. I don't see that she could well be for him. But I don't believe she ever said one ugly thing about him, and many men did, that you *all* are friendly with now...."

That politics could be painful in family relationships was clear, for it was uncharacteristic of Ina to protest during a campaign. Yet this time she wanted them all to know how she felt, and her sons could not be unaware of the just nature of her complaint.

The WCTU issue was important in a way beyond the liquor question, however. Georgia women had the vote in 1921 for the first time, and Richard senior went after this vote. Although no one knew how many women would come out to exercise this right, the judge promoted his wife and his mother as exemplary women of intellect who deeply influenced his life in his campaign speeches. No less a personage than Rebecca Felton, Georgia's distinguished and longtime woman in politics, came out for Richard senior. At eighty-seven years of age, Felton wrote a popular column for the Atlanta papers, and she quoted with approval Richard senior's statement that "I ask nothing better for my own children than for them to be such characters as my honored wife and my blessed Mother."

Richard senior's recognition of a significant change in society was not lost on Dick Russell, Jr. He had grown up on stirring stories of his paternal grandmother's intellectual abilities, how Harriette Brumby had insisted on taking chemistry with her father, and Dick never tired of hearing of her heroic deeds during the War Between the States. Dick also knew that Harriette had homeschooled all her children and that his father, as her eldest, never ceased to give her credit for his achievements, in public and private. Dick saw firsthand how his own mother's keen intellect, coupled with a great heart, kept track of her large brood and her extended families, Russell and Dillard, through countless letters written each week. She kept a Bible and a dictionary by her bedside, and encouraged reading and education tirelessly. That women were now to vote was not cause for alarm.

The campaign again showed Dick that others realized he had parents of sterling character whose life path he would do well to follow. As he travelled over the state with his father, the young man's appealing personality made him a quick favorite with the old guard, who recognized a young and talented politician. They congratulated the father on his progeny's prospects. All his life Richard senior had said that he wanted his own career to promote his son's, and Dick sensed early what the respect given to his father would mean for him. Richard senior sometimes apologized to his family that he had not made enough money to indulge them. Dick knew from the earliest days of his own political career that he had capital far above the price of rubies and that it was up to him to utilize it wisely.

As the summer wore on, more and more family began to serve in the campaign. Billie and Gordon, stationed for a short tour at Fort Benning, Georgia, worked hard in Muskogee County, strong Fish territory. Pat, Margo, and Harriette worked in Atlanta in the campaign headquarters, typing and posting general campaign mailings and writing to former classmates at Georgia Normal and Industrial College. Uncle Lewis continued his indefatigable letter writing and typing. In addition, several part-time stenographers were hired in spite of the expense, proving that Richard senior had done well in his law practice. The law work of everyone concerned was suffering, but they counted this an expense of the campaign.

On 9 September 1922, Richard B. Russell, Sr. was elected chief justice of the Georgia Supreme Court by a comfortable margin, at last fulfilling one of his lifelong ambitions. Two days later the proud people of Barrow County honored their judge with an ovation.

Friends from all over north Georgia began to appear at the Russell home late in the afternoon, and soon the road was lined with cars, and the yard filled with them, as more and more friends came to share in the judge's triumph. Ina, amazed and gratified, watched as other women took over her kitchen to prepare punch and other refreshments to welcome the crowds.

About a hundred women, by Ina's count, congregated in the house, while the men, over 400 in number, stood outside on the porch and in the yard, shaking hands, laughing, and talking. Richard was in his element, and his main campaign staff of his sons and his brother shared the joy. Dick was particularly energized by the crowd, and he had many thanks to give, having received every one of the 1,247 votes cast for his legislative seat.[7] About seven o'clock, Governor-elect Walker and his wife arrived from nearby Monroe. They had thoughtfully gone by Monroe A & M School to pick up William, one of the Russell twins in school there, so that the fifteen-year-old could celebrate his father's accomplishment. Other family members had come from Atlanta: Margo, Jim, and Harriette.

G. A. and Sunie Johns, close friends from Winder, had organized the ovation, and after the governor-elect arrived, Mr. Johns mastered the ceremonies by introducing speakers on the porch of the Russell home while the crowd stood in the yard. On this occasion three distinct branches of state government were eminently represented, Johns said: the judiciary, the executive, and the representative. Sitting inside the door of her home beside Mrs. Walker, Ina marveled that two of those branches were represented by her family.

Then the judge began to speak. Richard had been an accomplished orator since his college days on the debate team, seasoned through many campaigns, and he spoke now with the sauce of success to sweeten his words. He made the crowd laugh—he was famed for his ability to make crowds laugh—clap and cheer. They threw hats into the air and shouted for joy. Inside the house, Ina smiled and let happiness fill her frame, because "dear dad was getting just what he had deserved for so long."

Following this speech, Johns introduced Governor-elect Walker, but the executive branch said this was Judge Russell's ovation and he was there only to pay him tribute. Then it was Dick's turn to speak for the legislative branch, and his mother felt he made a fine speech. Even allowing for a mother's prejudice, Dick was gaining a reputation as an accomplished orator, and the young man also made people laugh, cheer, and exult in their representative. The son had known from an early age

---

[7] Richard senior received 1,100 of the 1,247 votes cast, showing there were still some Barrow Countians who had not forgiven him for opposing the county.

how his father had worked and struggled. He had seen the bitter tears of defeat. Working for months on this campaign, traveling the state, and getting to know its people, he began to love Georgia in a way he could not have suspected was possible. There in the deepening September twilight, gazing out at hundreds of friends who had come after so many losses to share the sweet wine of victory, sensing his mother behind the screen door, her face shining, her heart happy for her husband, Dick's pride in his father and his conviction of the worthiness of the course filled his heart to overflowing.

Changes resulted for several family members from the election. Richard would still be living in Atlanta, but he could come home regularly on Saturday afternoons now. Lewis was employed as executive secretary by the newly elected Georgia senator Walter George in the late autumn and moved to Washington in time to see the first woman senator, Georgia's Rebecca Felton, be sworn in and take her seat for two days. Walter George's election had been the result of the death of Senator Tom Watson, and Governor Hardwick appointed Felton as a gesture to the emerging status of women. The Russell men were well aware of the historic nature of the occasion, and Lewis, pleased to be invited to dinner with Senators George and Harris, wrote home for all the family to share in his success. All the Russell men were thinking of Harriette Brumby Russell's ambitions, for herself and for her sons. When Lewis needed to attend dances, he invited his niece Ina, proud that she was a good-looking, diminutive young woman of wit and fine spirits, a career woman in the nation's capital.

Dick remained at home and took seriously his duty to help his mother handle the crises that inevitably emerged among the many younger members of the family. Dick had recommended that Walter try Oglethorpe University, a small school, for his first year, but Walter chose the University of Georgia instead, where in the first week he was part of a group of students who climbed the Athens water tower to paint "[Class of] 26" on it, nearly scaring the wits out of his mother and father when they heard about it. A day or so later, Patience, now teaching in Cochran, Georgia, was injured in an automobile accident on her way to a concert in Macon. When the news made the front page of the Atlanta papers, Dick and Rob tried to hide the papers from Ina so they could break the news to her gently.

Rob, deeply in love with Sybil Millsaps, who was now a grade school teacher, decided that marriage to the right woman was clearly preferable to bachelorhood, and their wedding was set for June 1923. The young couple was delighted when Rob was hired as his father's stenographer on the Supreme Court. Rob would learn the law thoroughly, and they could live in Atlanta in a cottage across the street from Margo and Jim, with electric lights and indoor plumbing. Dick rejoiced with his brother, but must have felt a pang of regret at seeing his best friend initiate a family that would inevitably take precedence over his original group.

In spite of his bachelor state, Dick continued to have a demanding family life. In the case of an exciting murder trial in which he was the lawyer for the defense and Joe Quillian one of the prosecuting lawyers, people flocked from all over the county to witness the three-day trial. Dick was so thrilled when his client was acquitted that he forgot to pick up the children from the Glee Club Concert, as he had promised. Instead, he dashed off to the jail to consult with new prospective clients, two men accused of robbery. Someone finally brought the Glee Club singers home close to midnight, about the same time Dick showed up. Fielding, Carolyn, Jeb, and Alex teased their brother unmercifully about his neglect. They added the face-reddening news that it was all over town that when the robbers were brought to the jail, Dick had almost accepted their case in exchange for a Buick automobile they were driving. When the car turned out to be stolen, he had decided to give up their defense. His mother wrote long letters describing these escapades to his sisters, Ina junior and Billie, in Washington, DC, and Pat and Harriette, rooming together in Atlanta, where Harriette worked in a bookstore and Pat taught third grade.

Dick took all manner of cases during these years, and this experience made him believe strongly in American law and the American system as he saw it. He had great faith that the system achieved justice most of the time, and his interest in creating laws increased. His contemporaries in the legislature, aware of his sincerity and his ability to make idealism a practical reality, and in keeping with their wish to change Georgia politics, banded together and elected Dick Russell, Jr., Speaker Pro Tem of the Georgia House of Representatives in June 1923. This office was a pivotal post from which Dick could work with both the younger and older elements of the legislature, putting his skills at compromise and political maneuvering to good use. He would have the chance, from time to time, to preside over the House, and, with increased popularity, would be in line to become Speaker of the House, the most powerful legislative post in state government. Even as early as 1923, he was considered a leading member of the Georgia House of Representatives.

It was a good thing that Dick could continue to live at home and reduce expenses when he was not in Atlanta, because his law practice did not thrive. Winder was a depressed farming community, as was Barrow County, in the 1920s, and many fees went unpaid. He did not seek clients elsewhere. His bills, whether for dental work, office supplies, or on a bank car loan, often were past due. Dick still stepped in to help pay bills for the younger children from time to time, and seems not to have worried about unpaid bills, simply continuing to pay as money came in. He knew the poverty of the South and accepted that all were caught up in it and all would have to be patient.

In the meantime, in 1923 Dick saw his uncle Lewis give up his Washington job in order to accept an appointment as superior court judge to the newly formed Piedmont Superior Court Circuit, part of the old Western Circuit, where Richard senior had presided as judge. Unfortunately, Lewis was not elected to the post when he ran in 1924. Dick, Rob, and Joe Quillian worked hard on his campaign, but to no avail. The defeat so embittered Lewis that he left Georgia late in the year to try his hand at selling real estate in Florida. The fact that political endeavors tiptoed on the razor's edge of defeat was never far from Dick junior's consciousness.

In typical Russell support mode, it was decided that William, indifferent to academics, being the only one of the Russell children not to have an intellectual bent, would go to Florida with Lewis to try his hand at running a café. Dick and Rob accompanied the two to Florida to help them get set up, and the group stopped to visit the Florida legislature and supreme court in Tallahassee on the way to St. Petersburg.

Walter quit school and moved to Washington, DC, in 1923, and he lived with his sister Ina while he looked for a job. He eventually went to work for the A&P grocery store chain while taking college night courses. Everyone at home missed William and worried that he was so young to have gone away. Ina read his letters aloud at the supper table, where Dick sat in his father's place to the right of his mother, who was always at the head of the table. When the judge was at home, Dick sat next to him. His place as patriarch-in-training was obvious.

Dick Russell, Jr., however happy he was in Ina's home, did not abandon his interest in women. He escorted Winder girls Runette, Dot, and Mary Louise to picnics, dances, and tennis matches. When friends from the legislature were in north Georgia, they came by to solicit his company for a foray into Athens to spend time with girls they'd known in college. His younger brothers watched with admiration.

Dick's life in Atlanta, however, was another scene altogether. Whether in the city for legislative duties or simply to meet friends to socialize, the charismatic young lawyer was in demand everywhere, and he had many dates with women who were enjoying the freedom of the Roaring Twenties. As the decade wore on, letters he received from these women friends reveal that they were willing to play the dating/mating game on new terms, and perhaps with his father's advice in his ear, Dick Russell took them up on the offers. He had a strong example of a bachelor with many of the benefits of matrimony in his uncle Lewis. Although never married, Lewis had women friends of long and affectionate standing. Dick, likely without realizing that it was a decision at all, made the choice to have women on the side, not at the center of his life. He was attractive enough to make this approach work to his satisfaction.

By 1926, the climate in the General Assembly was encouraging Dick Russell, Jr., to think of running for the most powerful legislative post in the state, Speaker of the House. Speaker W. Cecil Neill indicated that he would not seek reelection in 1927. Although Governor Walker called a special session of the legislature in February 1926, which turned out to be a battle between the governor and the legislature, Dick managed to let his friends defeat the governor's program while keeping a low profile. Because he had not made up his mind entirely about the Speaker's race, Dick did not want to be divisive and sabotage his chance, should he decide to take it.

In June, Richard senior made a bewildering move. The chief judge announced that he would run for the Senate seat held by Walter George, whom his brother Lewis had served as executive secretary. George, popular and well-liked, had not expected opposition. In the judge's family, the announcement was met with dark despair. Dick and Rob, who would be expected to run the campaign, were embarrassed to be going against such a popular figure, whose record they did not criticize. Ina was weary to the bone of her husband's politics and had thought he had settled in as chief justice for the duration. Nevertheless, the word of the patriarch was law, and everyone rallied to support him in this race. Lewis was thankfully in Florida and would not have to campaign against his former employer. For the first time in more than twenty-five years, Richard senior would not have his youngest brother by his side in a campaign.

Dick worked hard for his father, as did all the other children. Living on a judge's salary of $7,000 per annum, with Fielding in college and three others on the way to college in the next four years, Richard senior did not have the money he'd had to finance the chief justice race. Six of his sons were called into service, without pay, to man the office, drive, or, in the case of Dick, make speeches. Walter, Alex, and Rob worked in the office, while Fielding and Edward served as chauffeurs. Only William was not drafted because, in debt with his café in St. Petersburg, he could not leave Florida. He wrote home and offered to come, but his father told him to stay at his post. Billie's husband, Gordon Green, was stationed near Washington and went to the Senate to hear George speak, reporting anything he thought might be helpful. Harriette, Pat, Margo, and Billie wrote to Georgia Normal and Industrial College and Georgia State College for Women classmates on their father's behalf.

Dick and Rob were soon caught up in the kind of fight they relished. They had never taken intimate part in a campaign in which their father or Dick had been defeated, and the remembered euphoria of victory spurred them on. Ina worried that "dad's race might hurt Dick," but, in fact, the young man found time as he accompanied his father over the state to campaign quietly among legislators on his own behalf for the Speaker's job. Dick already had many friends who supported him, and he made new ones among his father's friends.

When they attended the Georgia Bar Association meeting in Savannah, a prime place for the chief justice to politic, Dick took time off to have a few drinks with younger Savannah lawyers, one of whom was

Spence Grayson. Spence and Dick, mellowed by their imbibing, decided after midnight to go swimming in the Tybee tide. Stripping on the dark beach, they dived into the cool ocean and swam and talked. Dick waxed evangelical and persuaded Spence that he ought to run for the legislature. He could do great things for his home state. Spence Grayson listened and was elected to the Georgia legislature at the next election, becoming an able legislator who helped Dick Russell pass legislation as Speaker and governor.

As the Senate campaign wore on, in spite of a determined and positive attitude in the camp, family history and a host of negative newspaper publicity against Richard senior heightened the haunting specter of defeat that accompanies all races. The derisive, often brutal, editorial response to Richard's candidacy had to be discouraging, even painful, to a family who respected and loved their father. Some newspapers, however, defended Richard's work on the bench, and voiced the general attitude that no change was necessary. The judge should stay on the court, and George should stay in the Senate. On 9 September, the electorate agreed and returned Walter George to Washington by a large majority.

Although the race could be judged as a minor tragedy, the last symptom of the judge's lingering malaise of longing for the prestige of high office, this analysis does not give the complete picture. Although his platform in this race had been called reactionary, naive, and backward, the facts are that Richard senior was genuinely alarmed by Walter George's support of the World Court and what Richard viewed as George's lack of support of the farmer. As a judge he was appalled at the risky idea of agreeing to support a court whose laws were not yet known, and although Georgia was promoting industrial development, she was still an agricultural region by a heavy majority. Richard Russell, Sr., longed for achievement and recognition, but he also wanted to help his native state and his nation in this time of great growth and apparent prosperity. He had repeatedly asked others to take up the fight, but when no one responded, he took it up himself. It was an old theme with him that for democracy to work, the minority must have its voice. Although he knew he had no chance to win, he thought it important that he give the minority a candidate. When the race was over, he was satisfied, in the sixty-fifth year of his life, that he had been unafraid to make a stand on issues he believed to be critical. Sixty-one thousand Georgians had made their voices heard because of him. His son, working closely with him, respected his father's innate wisdom and sincerity. Dick detested hypocrites, and he felt there was no reason to apologize for his father's stand.

Dick's race for the Speakership was not harmed by his father's race. On the contrary, his support grew as the summer progressed, and before the next legislature convened in June 1927, he and his friends had plans in place to ensure that he was the first choice for the job. In addition, Dick and Rob had learned much that would help them to conduct their next statewide campaign, Dick's battle for the top executive post in Georgia. Perhaps more importantly, his father's unsuccessful and much-maligned race confirmed Dick in his own conviction that the responsible leader stands by those who elect him and represents them, even when they are the minority. When Richard Russell, Jr. stepped onto the national stage, the concept of the voice of the minority would be a strong component of his ideology.

Each statewide campaign Dick had made with his father increased his affection for the people of Georgia. From Brasstown Bald to Tybee Light, the more he knew of both black and white Georgians, the more he admired their willingness to work hard amidst severe poverty, maintaining their dignity and their hopes. Dick longed to be one who could help; he was yet too young to know to be careful what you wish for.

On 10 June 1927, Dick Russell, Jr. was elected Speaker of the Georgia House of Representatives. His network of friends throughout the state had let it be known that he was the preferred choice and that those who wanted support for their legislation in the next session would be wise to get on the bandwagon now. Dick had asked Hugh Peterson of Ailey, Georgia, Montgomery County, to place his name in nomination, and Peterson made a masterful speech in so doing. Dick and Hugh had become friends when Peterson was elected to the legislature in 1922, and Peterson knew that his speech would give his friend good press coverage. He said that Dick Russell, Jr. would preside with wisdom and decorum, that he was a man of superior abilities, and that he was a judicious, conservative, and fair leader. When the vote was called, all members of the legislature present that day agreed with Peterson. Newspaper articles in Atlanta and in his hometown of Winder declared Dick Russell, Jr. one of the most popular young legislators in Georgia's history.

At the inauguration ceremony on 25 June, it was evident that the Georgia legislature was led by young, vigorous men as the twenty-nine-year-old Dick Russell, Jr., and the thirty-three-year-old E. B. Dykes, president of the Senate, sat on the platform with Governor-elect L. G. Hardman of Commerce, seventy-one years old, and Chief Justice Richard B. Russell, Sr., sixty-six. Dick Russell, Jr. had no trouble taking on the mantle of leadership, in spite of his youth. He had been reared from childhood to think of himself as a leader, and now he recognized that he was working for his state in high office and felt both the honor and the responsibility. Upon taking his post as Speaker, Russell called on his colleagues to consider all legislative proposals, regardless of past political affiliations, and to take care of the state's business as speedily as possible. He would be a consensus leader.

Russell's different view on how politics could operate emerged early in the session. For years, certain special interests had been able to use their influence to have legislators friendly to their projects placed on key committees. When, at the beginning of the session, a prominent citizen approached Russell with a written list of names he wished to see appointed to committees, Russell let him know in no uncertain terms that if he wanted any of the individuals on his list named to a committee, he'd better not let Russell see it. The man was shocked into commenting that this must be a new day in Georgia politics, and Russell replied, "Yes, sir."

Although Russell was clearly asserting his authority, having sipped the heady wine of power, it was soon evident that he was fair and considerate. Indeed, he was judged to be a hardworking and responsible public servant, trying to put the welfare of the people above any special interests. His first session was characterized by acrimonious controversy as the lawmakers tried to find ways to secure state funds needed for roads and education, but Russell's leadership in no way encouraged bitterness. It often had been the practice of legislators to make appropriations without increasing taxes to provide the money, whereas Russell strove toward fiscal responsibility. If the Assembly made an appropriation, it must provide the money to pay for it through taxes. As ever the case, no one wanted to be known as the legislator who increased the gasoline tax or passed a sale tax.

Struggling with these numerous roadblocks, Russell drove the members of the House to finish their work in the sixty days allowed for the session, and the final days were hectic as he called Saturday and night sessions and started an hour earlier in the mornings. In spite of his efforts, which included covering the clocks so they would not have to adjourn at midnight, the hard decisions on taxes for highway and education appropriations were postponed when the House and the Senate failed to agree on the measures. Russell, however, came out of the session with an enhanced reputation as a capable leader who worked hard to get lawmakers to face up to the state's major problems. Nevertheless, the *Atlanta Constitution* pointed out that Georgia was left with looming deficits totaling millions of dollars because the legislators had not provided revenues to meet the appropriations of 1928 or 1929, and the state still owed $8 million for 1927.

Dick Russell, Jr., enjoyed the hectic political pace in Atlanta, and during these times, he found that his social life was as full as he wished it to be. Letters from women friends arrived at his Atlanta address expressing pleasure at the prospect of dates with him. Following a date, Nell wrote that she had had a wonderful time and regretted nothing. Another woman wrote that when they were together, they were going to do everything. Margaret called him "Richard the Great" and "Sir Richard" in various epistles and longed to hear from him often, though she realized that she would always be second to politics.

It appears that at this early stage, Dick Russell, Jr., made an active decision to take women on these terms rather than pursue the traditional course of courtship and marriage. It was obvious that he put his career and the resulting public service that it demanded first. Nevertheless, Dick was a strong family man and likely had the same dreams as most young men of finding the perfect wife and starting his own family. That he could enjoy a happy hearthside in his boyhood home, while having unusual freedom to come and go, must have made it easier to forego establishing his own home.

When the legislature adjourned at 6:00 A.M. on Sunday, 21 August, Dick Russell, Jr. was ready to go back to Winder for a rest. He needed to shore up his law practice which had, due to his father's campaign and his own for the Speakership, suffered sharp decline. Exhausted, the young man decided, however, to go to Ailey, Georgia, for a hunting trip with Hugh Peterson on his plantation in Montgomery County. The camaraderie and the physical activity of hunting would remain one of Dick's preferred recreations throughout his life.

In spite of money worries, the fact that he did not have a home to support meant that on 10 September 1927, Dick Russell, Jr., could set sail on the *Leviathan* for Paris, where he would attend an American Legion meeting. This convention was his first chance to see Europe, and he reveled in all activities. After seeing such French monuments as the Louvre, Versailles, and Napoleon's tomb, he travelled to Italy for a look at Venice, an early model of democratic government. He visited Vienna and Prague before going on to Scotland, Ireland, and England. Dick's admiration for Anglo-Saxon heritage increased during this visit. He was surprised to see how quickly Europe had recovered from the ravages of the War to End All Wars, but observing that many countries were maintaining large armies, he predicted that another war was sure to come. Heeding her old advice to keep in touch through letters, he wrote often to his mother during the trip.

There were young women on the trip, wives and daughters of other Legionnaires, and notes from them indicate that Dick Russell, Jr., was a sought-after companion. He was not a ladies' man in the usual sense of the word because he did not set out to make conquests, but endowed with a powerful and natural charisma, it is perhaps surprising that he did not use this gift more flamboyantly. Yet he was heir to clear codes of honor and honesty, and he had been bent toward those ideals. Perhaps it was the knowledge that he could not be fully committed to a wife and family that kept him breaking off relationships when they threatened to become too serious. Having seen his mother forced to rear her family alone because of his father's campaigning, Dick also told friends that it wouldn't be fair to ask a woman to marry him.

As 1928 unfolded, Dick Russell, Jr. practiced law in earnest, inviting his brother Rob to come in with him. When Rob and Sybil decided to move back to Winder, Dick gained as capable and trusted a partner as his father had had in Lewis. Rob and Sybil now had two children, Bobby

(Robert Russell, Jr.) and Betty, who were favorites with their uncle Dick. Lacking his own young family, Dick enjoyed his brother's children completely, as he did other nieces and nephews, the children of Billie and Margo, who came to visit in the summers. The Robert Russell youngsters were bound to become favorites because they were in and out of Grandmother's house, which was also Uncle Dick's house, as if it were their own.

The Robert Lee Russell, Sr., family lived at the homeplace while renovating a cottage owned by Richard senior next door. Because so many newlyweds or young families had lived there, Ina called it the Weaning Cottage. Exciting the most interest was the arrival of electricity and plumbing for the new home. Dick and Rob took up the arduous task of persuading their father to have lights put in the big house at the same time. Richard senior had lost an important and hard-fought case against Georgia Power nine years before, when in private practice. His vow to never allow a power pole on his property was not forsworn without an epic struggle, but his sons finally dragged him into the twentieth century. Dick's offer to pay for the lights was too good to turn down.

When Ina first asked Richard senior if they, too, could have electric lights, he told her that they could not afford it unless he took one of their three sons out of college. Ina said she would use pine knots before she'd allow that. Fielding was a senior at the University of Georgia, Edward was a sophomore at Davidson College in North Carolina, and Alex had just entered Georgia as a freshman. Carolyn was in her junior year of high school. When school endeavors required extra cash, any of the family might be called on to supply a little for travel or other expenses. Fielding was on the boxing team at Georgia, and Edward wrestled for Davidson, and their eldest brother offered financial aid to them on various occasions.

The old folks in the Dillard house next to Rob and Sybil's home grew more feeble daily. Uncle Ben lost his mind, and Pipey and Annie had days of not knowing where or who they were, though both women remained able to care for themselves. A black man called Uncle Mitchell cared for Ben during the day, helping him into and out of bed and to the outhouse. Incontinence plagued them all. With Carolyn's help, Ina sent meals over to the house, even when she had as many as twenty-two people for Sunday dinner. Ben died in summer 1929. Pipey and Annie carried on.

In a home ceremony, sister Harriette had married Ralph Sharpton in 1927 after a long courtship. Richard senior flagged the train for the first time in many years, harking back to Dick's school days, so that the couple could leave for their new home from the Russell homeplace. They would live in Florida, where Ralph worked for a railroad company. Walter had married Dorothea Bealer, his third cousin on the Brumby side, earlier that year and was still working for the A&P grocery store chain. This couple lived in the southeast, wherever the work carried them, and soon William went to work for A&P, managing a store in Sylva, North Carolina. Dick kept up with all his siblings through their letters to his mother. By 1929 he was especially interested in a romance ripening between his sister Patience, teaching in Atlanta, and his friend Hugh Peterson.

After being unanimously reelected Speaker of the House in 1929, Russell faced the formidable task of uniting the legislature in the determination to move Georgia forward along progressive lines. Reelected governor Hardman wanted to pay off the state's deficit of about $4 million, and both the legislature and the governor knew that highways were going to have to be paved in Georgia. Finding the means to pay for these roads was the most pressing question.

Early in the 1929 session, it became apparent that a group of legislators was pushing the sale of $100 million worth of highway bonds to fund a statewide road-building program. Contractors naturally supported this method, but Russell had always opposed bonds as a way of achieving this end. Although he promised as Speaker to give the bond resolution full hearing, he said that as a representative from Barrow County he was openly opposed to this method.

Russell's solution was, instead, to raise the gasoline tax by two cents a gallon. One half of one cent of the tax would go for schools and the rest for highways. In spite of four full-time lobbyists hired to promote the bonds issue, when rumors became strong that big corporations were trying to influence legislation, thereby threatening the integrity of House members, the anti-bond members and the pro-schools group combined to pass the gas tax measure in both houses. A limited sales-tax bill and an income tax measure also became law, in spite of controversy. Now the state had a responsible way to meet the funding of its vital services.

Hugh Peterson, along with Governor Hardman, was keen to push the reorganization of state departments in order to save the state an estimated $1 million a year, and Russell supported the idea. His sharp political sense, though, told him the time was not right. If he tried to force this issue, he would make enemies with little to gain. It would be wiser to let the 1929 session prepare the way.

Sometime after the 1929 session opened, Dick began escorting Josephine Hardman, one of the governor's three daughters, to various official functions, and in spite of his preoccupation with politics, he felt twinges that warned he was falling in love. Good-looking, cultured, vivacious, and experienced in political life, Josephine was the ideal candidate to become a politician's wife. She was only nineteen, but her mother, Emma Griffin, from a prominent Valdosta family, was twenty-five years younger than her husband, Governor Lamartine Hardman. The twelve years separating Josephine and Dick would not have seemed such a gap. Hardman, a physician, farmer, and textile manufacturer, was one of the wealthiest men in north Georgia and one of the most respected. Perhaps he would have liked to see his daughter marry the rising young Russell, but the Speaker of the House did not get obvious encouragement from the governor's daughter. Although he looked forward to the events at which he was to be her escort, however official they might be, Dick feared that Josephine was simply fulfilling an obligation to her father, a situation he understood full well. At first the pair did not put much emphasis on the fact that they were "dating."

Yet Dick and Josephine enjoyed each other's company, and either would have been considered a "catch" in anyone's book. Russell worked long hours during this time in Atlanta, but he found time to continue seeing Josephine whenever she would accept his invitations. Following his usual pattern, work came first. He worked harmoniously with the governor and thought he had earned the old man's respect. It was not clear to anyone, least of all, perhaps, Josephine, whether or not he was actually courting her. She was certainly a different woman from others he dated while in Atlanta. Josephine wore her dark hair bobbed and the slim short dresses of the flapper, but she was the daughter of a distinguished family with strong religious beliefs and high moral standards. Dick could not have failed to note that Josephine well knew the life of a politician's wife, the sacrifices required. Her youth and inexperience, appealing to his manly instincts, meant he had to be entirely circumspect in his approach, and he was. Members of both families could only suspect the two were developing strong feelings for each other.

As the legislative session ended, Dick Russell was on good terms with almost all legislators, and beyond the capital, he was considered one of the best-known, liked, and trusted young politicians in the state. His leadership style was to stay close to the pack and to give credit to others for accomplishments. He said his primary interest was to achieve results that produced governmental action helpful to the people. This was not campaign rhetoric alone, for his record shows that he acted on these ends.

Dick Russell was aware that he had built a position of considerable power. He had confidence in this position, and friends and family alike were not surprised when he announced on 5 April 1930 that he was a candidate for governor of Georgia. Russell had his father's determination to become governor, but unlike his father, he had a better sense of timing. Or perhaps events unfolded in a more auspicious way for him. The young man—he was only thirty-two—sensed that Georgia was ready to follow someone free of old politics and factions, and he had always planned to run for governor. With the backing of his large and energetic family and a multitude of friends across the state, all dedicated to his ideals of helping Georgians, he believed he could run a thrifty but effective campaign.

Five candidates offered their services in 1930 for Georgia's top executive office. Dick was considered a third choice at best. The first two spots were expected to go to George H. Carswell, who had served in the state House and Senate and had also been secretary of state, and E. D. Rivers, who had terms in the House and Senate. Rivers was aligned with the powerful commissioner of Agriculture, Gene Talmadge. Defeated by Hardman in 1928, Rivers and others thought his time had come. Many people thought Russell was entering the race to get known, in the same way Rivers had done, and that the young man did not really expect to be elected in the first try. Although Russell's years in the state house as Speaker had given him power, a fourth candidate, John N. Holder, was chairman of the state Highway Commission and would surely attract House members who wanted highways in their counties. The fifth candidate was James A. Perry, head of the Public Service Commission.

Those who believed Dick Russell was entering the campaign for a trial run did not know him. When he entered a race, it was because he saw a need he believed he could fill better than anyone else. He was running to win. Setting forth a clear 10-point platform, Russell had three main focuses: leadership free from the influence of deals, factions, and special interest; meeting the major needs of the state, those being fiscal responsibility through tax reform, better education and highways, and government reorganization; and finally, presenting himself as a sixth-generation Georgian, a man familiar with the state's history and tradition, experienced yet young enough to lead his people on the road to conservative progress.

Russell's campaign strategy quickly became evident as he organized a grassroots approach that brought him in contact with thousands of voters on farms and in small towns. Almost immediately following his announcement, he began traveling the state, going into towns and walking down Main Street, shaking hands with everyone he could find, while giving a short speech about his candidacy. Mechanics did not even have to get out from under the cars they were working on if they would just listen to him. He sought out the farms and worked late into the night, sometimes waking people up to give his speech. Amazed and gratified, he found that under all circumstances voters listened, asked questions, and made comments. His love and admiration for the people of Georgia continued to grow.

From both his father and his mother, Dick Russell, Jr., had acquired a genuine interest in other people. With his father and mother, he shared a remarkable memory, not only for facts and dates, but for people—where they came from, who were their kin, and what their dreams and accomplishments were. From his school days throughout his legislative career, Dick had met many people from all over the state, and his ability to recall and make these encounters personal served him well. In addition, he remembered his father's friends, met campaigning or in the legislature, and could make those connections as well. This social strength was a tremendous asset to him in his person-to-person campaign. Another strength was his indefatigable energy and an enormous capacity for work, again inherited by blood and example, from his parents. Quick-witted, he was able to make people laugh, but he was also well-informed and able to make them think.

Eager to show that he was free from the usual political machinations, Dick made the decision to move his campaign headquarters from Atlanta—the traditional site for all such races—to Winder. This decision not only showed that he was not part of the Atlanta cartel, but it also saved renting costs. His brother Rob acted as campaign manager, and Uncle Lewis returned from Florida to add his expertise. By summer, student brothers Fielding, Edward, and Alex were called into service from time to time. Sister Carolyn worked in the Winder office that summer as she prepared to attend Agnes Scott College in the fall. The youngsters drove the candidate to speech-making venues, put up campaign posters statewide, stuffed envelopes, answered phones, and wrote private letters to their own friends. Richard senior's brother Edward, who had spent thirty years working for the post office department in Washington, DC, took a month's vacation and came to work in the office. The energetic young brothers marveled that Uncle Ed could sit at a desk for four or five hours without stirring.

Dick Russell, Jr. made appearances in towns and cities across the state, and he had no trouble drawing a crowd. He or his father had friends everywhere who were eager and able to organize a Russell meeting. His early training in school and the constant honing of oratory skills in his work had made him an excellent and entertaining speaker. The age of electronic communication was beginning to dawn—his mother had thrilled to hear Hoover's inaugural ceremony described on her new radio in 1929—but the entertainment factor in politics was still important. People went out to stump meetings for information and for fun. With an enviable ability to relate to almost any kind of audience, Dick Russell was soon a topic of conversation among Georgia voters, whether they were lawyers, bankers, farmers, or mill workers. Perhaps the toughest test for him was learning to use the new medium of radio to reach Georgians. After he gave his first talk over radio station WRHA in Rome, Georgia, a friend told him that the reception was so good that he could hear his papers rattling as he shuffled his notes. Russell replied that those noises weren't papers because he had had no notes. They were his knees knocking.

Relationships in the large Russell family unit were bound to become complicated. Dick was indeed in a favored position as the eldest son, and his career and ambitions were assumed to have priority. Nevertheless, when emergencies arose, he was expected, and he expected himself, to step in to help. In early February 1930, the family received alarming news: Edward had been injured in a wrestling match and was paralyzed in a hospital in Raleigh, North Carolina. Dick dropped everything and drove his mother to Raleigh. During the six weeks she remained by her son's bedside, Dick wrote frequently to say he would come for them whenever Edward's doctors thought it safe for him to travel. Edward's arms were paralyzed, and after he gradually regained their use, he came home for a few weeks to recuperate. He returned to school, hoping to graduate with his class in June, which he did, with the understanding that he make up the missed work in summer school at the University of Georgia. His brother understood that his time to campaign was limited that summer. In the family, "one for all and all for one" truly meant the street ran both ways.

Dick watched with pride as Edward finished his missed work at summer school, and when Jeb announced that he felt called to enter the ministry and wanted to attend Columbia Theological Seminary, the older brother called him aside with a very personal question. Dick understood that religious devotion was important to his mother and her sister Pipey in extraordinary ways, exemplified in their lives of service to those around them. Pipey had often been Jeb's principal caretaker. Dick also had heard countless times the story that his father's mother had dreamed Richard senior would become a Presbyterian minister, and how the boy's decision at the age of fourteen to study law instead had broken her heart. The stand of the Methodists against Richard senior during the 1911 gubernatorial campaign had produced mixed emotions in Dick about organized religion in general. As the elder brother, he felt compelled to discuss Jeb's decision with him.

As they stood on the front porch of the house while the rest of the family gathered for supper, Dick said, "Jeb, I am interested in your decision to study for the ministry. That is a noble goal. But I want to ask you if you are absolutely sure about it. That's not something to do because you think someone else wants you to do it. Are you sure that is what you want?"

Jeb, who admired and loved his older brother, marveled at his interest and caring. He assured Dick that he genuinely felt called to this work.

"All right, then," his brother said, "you go to it. We just don't want any hypocrites in the family."

This theme of sincerity was a deep one with Dick Russell, Jr. You had to mean what you said, and what you did should reflect your beliefs.

Sister Patience became engaged to Hugh Peterson early in the year, and a wedding was planned for 24 June 1930. The Russell daughters favored their parents' anniversary for their own weddings whenever possible. This wedding was surely a delight to Dick, but it meant he lost an able and willing campaign worker. His loss was Hugh Peterson's gain, literally. Peterson planned to run for Congress in Georgia's First District, and Pat would prove as good at politicking as her more experienced husband. Although Pat was not on hand in the Winder office, Hugh was editing the *Montgomery Monitor* in Mount Vernon and kept up good news on his new brother-in-law. In Savannah, where Dick's sister Marguerite and her family were now living, she and husband Jim Bowden worked constantly for south Georgia support.

The campaign featuring five candidates was bound to get hot, and not just from Georgia July and August temperatures. In the beginning, Dick Russell had carefully avoided getting into personalities, but as the primary got closer and he suffered from harsh attacks by the others, he showed he could give as good as he got. His wit was often biting and memorable. He told one group that if Holder's "promises were pavement, the highway system of Georgia would be the modern wonder of the world." He said some of Carswell's charges were despicable, even by Georgia political standards, and challenged Carswell to a debate. Like candidates running against his father in '06 and '11, no one wanted to debate Dick Russell, Jr.

The speaking schedule Russell kept up was demanding, but he also relied on backers throughout the state, and these did not let him down. In this first statewide race, he did not have, nor did he ever have, anything that resembled the usual political organization held together by favors and jobs. What some were pleased to call an organization was, in reality, a league of friends and supporters bonded by their belief that

Dick Russell, Jr., would be good for Georgia. Russell and his supporters pushed the idea that he was independent, committed to public service, and experienced enough to implement the needed changes. He was not bound by political debts to job holders and factions, not "tied hand and foot" to special interests that had controlled the state for years. Instead, he was the people's candidate, without an expensive Atlanta headquarters, without a slush fund financed by special interests, and he had sought, with the help of friends and others interested in good government, to show the issues to the voters. With the statewide support of many representatives and senators from the legislature who declared he was a man of his word, Dick Russell was convincing more and more Georgians to mark his name on the ballot.

Although the campaign strategy was to remain on the offensive and to issue regular statements claiming that Russell was well ahead, the youthful candidate sometimes had to defend himself against curious charges. Some newspapers supporting other candidates tried to make nepotism an issue, writing that the Russells were trying to establish a political dynasty. Georgia had supported Dick senior out of her state treasury for nearly fifty years, and it was too much to expect her to do this for Dick junior. The younger Russell called these charges "irrelevancies." His father's being chief justice of the state Supreme Court had nothing to do with the governor's race, and he believed voters would recognize this accusation as unfair and senseless. He proclaimed that he was proud of his father and hoped his father was proud of him.

Another charge involved, indirectly, Dick's mother. Some Russell opponents tried to convince voters that he was too young and presented his bachelorhood as a handicap, saying there would be no woman to carry on the social duties of the office. Dick replied with humor to these accusations. He said that he met the constitutional age requirement and he was getting older as fast as he could. As for a woman in the Mansion, he promised that when he was elected, a Mrs. Russell would be with him to greet visitors at the governor's residence. Because his name was more and more often linked with Josephine Hardman, many believed he was contemplating marriage, and this romantic picture enhanced his attractiveness.

Dick Russell might have intended to propose marriage to Josephine, but certainly there was almost no time for courtship. He admitted many years later that he had fallen in love with her. All his life he would remember times they went dancing, nights he wished would never end. They made a handsome couple, and those who saw them together were struck by how suited to each other they seemed. As he campaigned for governor, Dick might have, indeed, dreamed of seeing Josephine beside him in the Governor's Mansion.

In the meantime, Governor Hardman came out in support of George Carswell, and in a newspaper campaign ad, the Carswell camp attached the governor's name to a card that made, according to Dick Russell, "an unprovoked and misleading attack" upon him. Russell was incredulous because the claims were of misdeeds that he knew the governor would know were false because of how closely they had worked together for four years. He wrote a three-page defense to Hardman, sounding hurt and puzzled: "If you really wrote that card, it was a blow beneath the belt for you know I did everything possible to make your administration a success, not because I belonged to your faction but for the welfare of all the people." Russell asked Hardman to refute the card, but surviving records show no reply to the young candidate's letter. Having run for governor in his fifties twice and been defeated, Hardman finally had been elected in his seventies. It would not be surprising if he thought Russell much too young for the office.

Rumors began to fly that Russell was courting Josephine in hopes of gaining more votes because she was part of the established network. This became the straw that broke the courtship's hopes. Whether such a rumor angered Josephine or Dick more cannot be known, but it had unhappy consequences. Josephine would not be courted because of her father. Dick Russell, Jr. would have no one believe that he would court a woman for political reasons. The couple broke off their relationship, but without quarrel. They wanted to remain friends.

Dick Russell, Jr. could be entirely practical where politics was concerned. He had broken up with Josephine, but when he said that he could promise a Mrs. Russell in the Mansion, he was absolutely sincere. He had no doubt that his mother would become Georgia's First Lady.

On election eve, 9 September, Russell reviewed his campaign and his position on the issues in a fifteen-minute radio address in Atlanta. Then he went home to Winder to await the voters' decision. There was heavy voter turnout on 10 September, and, as the Russell camp had predicted, Dick Russell, Jr., received the most votes, popular and county unit, with George Carswell a close second. In a hotly contested five-man race, this was the outcome the team had hoped for: a runoff. It was set for 1 October 1930, three weeks away.

Dick Russell launched his runoff campaign in Valdosta, going for the E. D. Rivers territory of south Georgia. John Holder announced that he would support Russell, but Dick reiterated that he would make no trades or combinations. Rivers came out for Carswell to counter the Holder/Russell pact, a development which Carswell felt assured his victory. Hotly denying any such alliance with Holder, Russell threw himself into campaigning as if the race were very close. More and more newspapers came out for Russell, and at Russell rallies two and three times a day all over the state, it was soon evident that Russell was on a roll that would not be stopped. On 1 October, Georgia voters gave Dick Russell, Jr. an unprecedented majority vote, the largest in any guber-natorial race in the state's history. He carried 126 of the 151 counties and tolled a popular vote of 99,505 to Carswell's 47,157. His biographer, Gilbert Fite, called it more than a landslide. It was, Fite wrote, a political earthquake.

Although a situation not even worthy of note in this era in the South, Dick Russell was elected by the white voters of Georgia. When Benjamin Davis, editor of a black newspaper, the *Atlanta Independent*, seemed to be supporting Russell in the primary and the runoff, calling him the candidate of the people, the Carswell camp immediately tried to discredit Russell among white voters. Russell was not a rabid racist but was a reasoned white supremacist, believing white and black societies must be strictly segregated. Although he genuinely hoped that black people would achieve better lives within their own society and wished them no ill whatsoever, being a political realist, he took no chances with having the white voters consider him liberal on this matter. He categorically denied that he had sought black support and charged that the "Carswell crowd" had hired "this negro" to come out for him in an attempt to discredit him with voters. His father had always considered it inappropriate and unbecoming for elite Southern leaders to raise the race issue for political gain, and, agreeing with this stance, Dick wanted to dismiss the controversy as quickly as possible. Relatively unimportant in this contest, the question of race relations was destined to become more demanding in the future career of Dick Russell, Jr.

Winder and Barrow County planned a massive victory celebration on 3 October, and between five and ten thousand people thronged the streets of the county seat by the evening, ready to welcome their hero home. Four bands paraded the torch-lit streets. Flags and banners flew and emblazoned store windows. It was a euphoric moment, especially for the family who had endured two gubernatorial campaign defeats and the hostile disapproval of their fellow Barrow County citizens a few years earlier. Judge Russell spoke to the crowd, almost overcome with emotion, and declared with characteristic humor that he "at least furnished the candidate." Lewis and young Rob were introduced as having been essential to the victory. Dick junior, holding his mother's hand, declared her "the best sweetheart I ever had." The crowd called for Ina to speak, but she was too shy. Surprised by local support of her husband's election to chief justice eight years earlier, her son's gubernatorial victory left her speechless.

The new governor kept his remarks brief, giving credit to others for this happy outcome and acknowledging his responsibilities to serve a government for the people. Then he spent hours shaking hands with the crowd.

Four days after the runoff results were in, the *Atlanta Journal* rotogravure section ran a large photo of the Russell family at home in Winder. Judge and Mrs. Russell sat surrounded by their six daughters and seven sons. In the middle of the picture, directly behind his parents, stood Dick Russell, Jr.[8] No footloose bachelor image was being presented. Here, instead, was his family, as surely as if he had had wife and children. Carolyn had started her studies at Agnes Scott College in Atlanta in the midst of the election hoopla. Edward also had started his studies at Columbia Theological Seminary. Fielding was finishing a Master's in English at the university, although Papa had hoped he would become a doctor. Alex, who enjoyed science and math, said he'd take up that banner. With no children at home in Winder, Ina was able to move

---

[8] This photo was likely made in 1926 when all the family was reunited following Richard senior's Senate race.

to Atlanta to preside in the Governor's Mansion, but she viewed the prospect with some dread. Her preferred residence would always be the homeplace in Russell, Georgia.

It would be nine months, however, before Dick assumed the governor's mantle, for the inauguration of a new governor took place in June after the previous summer elections. In the meantime, Governor Hardman called a special session of the General Assembly for 6 January 1931, to deal with the state's worsening financial plight. By the end of 1930, the Great Depression was creating havoc, even in a state that had long struggled with hardship and poverty. Poor farmers by the tens of thousands battled a boll weevil infestation while cotton prices plummeted. Business failures in Atlanta, Savannah, Augusta, Macon, and other cities created long lines of the unemployed. Tax revenues disappeared to the point where Georgia was unable to pay obligations to schools, charitable institutions, and veterans' pensions. On 6 January, Hardman explained to the legislature that the state had nearly $7.5 million in unpaid appropriations.

During the sixty-day session that followed, the governor and the legislature could not agree on how to meet the financial crisis, and bitterness and acrimony resulted. As Speaker of the House and governor-elect, Dick Russell encouraged harmony and somehow managed to maintain a neutral position, hoping to avoid controversy started by a lame-duck governor.

Family events went on with regularity. In January, sister Mary Willie nearly died in childbirth, and her baby was stillborn, causing anxiety and grief to his parents. Sister Ina in Washington had been going to law school at night, and she earned her degree and passed the bar in Georgia, Virginia, and the District of Columbia. She planned to attend the inauguration ceremonies, arriving by a new-fangled mode of transport: an airplane. Pipey went to her well-earned eternal rest in February 1931. Her obituary gave her credit for helping to raise the governor and his siblings. This passing left Aunt Annie watching feebly at the gate. Because Ina would be moving to Atlanta in June, the family worried about how to care for this cherished Old Guard and right-hand woman. Another Dillard woman, a niece of Ina's and Annie's, stepped in to care for Annie in her final days.

Dick Russell, Jr.'s, fame as the youngest governor in the country and the eldest son among so numerous a family attracted national attention to the patriarch in a way that his son found distressing. Margaret Sanger, an ardent and talented promoter of birth control education nationwide, challenged Richard senior to a debate on birth control and he accepted. Although he had no previous public record of supporting anti-birth control measures, the fee of $250 was too tempting to turn down. Carolyn was at Agnes Scott, Edward at Columbia Theological Seminary, and Alex would soon enter the Emory University School of Medicine. Dick junior was horrified when he heard about the debate. He declared that he would have rather given his father $250 than have him participate in such a spectacle. There was unusual tension between the two, and for a while, Richard senior claimed he would not move into the Governor's Mansion with his wife. Ina, in her usual quiet way, went about her own plans to move, and the judge finally came along.

The inauguration of his son to the office of which he had dreamed of occupying himself, while laced with bittersweet moments, was gratifying to Richard Russell, Sr. As chief justice of the Georgia Supreme Court, it was his duty to swear in the governor. Ina was seated on the podium. To a father and son who loved and respected each other, as these two did, this had to be a moment of acute satisfaction. The photograph of this historic event appeared in newspapers all over the nation.

Following the ceremony, the Governor's Mansion was the scene of a warm reception to which Dick Russell, Jr. had invited hundreds by handwritten notes on Speaker of the House stationery. His mother and sisters, aided by brother-in-law Gordon Green, made punch for 3,000 guests. Russell and Dillard women served, along with a few other longtime women friends, including Hettie Langley. They needed every drop of punch as nearly 3,000 people moved through the receiving line while the temperature hovered at 95 degrees. This event demonstrated how Dick Russell intended to run Georgia government. There would be no waste, frivolous expense, or unnecessary show. Times were too hard. Everyone would be asked to pitch in.

It was not the Russell way to emphasize the gloom and discouragement of the times anymore than it was characteristic to ignore hardships. In his inaugural address, Dick junior said that the deepening Depression had made people hopelessly disheartened, engulfing them in a tide of pessimism, but he called on Georgians to respond with courage and self-sacrifice. Particularly in government, people must forget petty factional politics. He promised to balance the state budget and to exercise strict economy. The perennial questions of education, road construction, and government reorganization were at the center of his assessment of what the state government must handle. Reflecting the general independent attitude of Americans, he also encouraged farmers and others to produce as much of their own needs as possible in these hard times.

Although he would, by a stroke of fate, serve as governor of Georgia for only eighteen months, Richard B. Russell, Jr., had extraordinary success with his vision for state government. His shared history with the legislature and ability to compromise made his leadership effective in getting people to forget politics and look to how the crisis could be solved for mutual advantage. His work ethic decreed that he spend long hours at the job, and many nights the lights were on in the governor's office long after others had gone home. His executive secretary, Isaac Hay, grateful for the job, nevertheless found the eight-in-the-morning to eight-sometimes-nine-at-night work days long, yet had to admire his boss. Dick Russell, Jr. did not ask others to make sacrifices he wasn't willing to make himself. He led by example.

Governor Russell shocked everyone when he suggested that a worthwhile means of saving would be to lower the pay of state employees by five to ten percent. By law, the governor's salary could not be changed in this way, but he promised to return the same percentage of his own pay to the state coffers. The legislature refused to go along with this measure, but Russell was able to balance the budget through other strict economic policies. The Budget Act passed at the controversial session called by Hardman in March 1931 had established a budget bureau and named the governor as director. Governor Russell took full advantage of his authority to squeeze state agencies in order to be able to pay Confederate veterans' pensions, keep all the schools open, and maintain a highway building program. At the end of Russell's eighteen-month term, the state had met its current requirements and had paid close to $3 million on previous unpaid appropriations. Never before had a Georgia governor had the legal means to exercise such tight control over the state budget nor the inclination to do so.

Dick Russell, Jr., had a reputation for fair decisions that became enhanced while in office. Most politicians suffered from their constituents' bitter disillusionment. Yet Russell had a way of explaining situations that people judged as honest. Once during a demanding legislative session, Isaac Hay was worried when a group of farmers showed up, determined for a showdown with the governor. As executive secretary, Hay, trying to protect his boss, explained that the governor was unavailable—he was, in fact, at lunch, one of the rare times when he had left the office. The farmers refused to budge, and their anger and frustration did not make a reassuring sight.

Hay escaped out a back door and went to find Russell. He explained to the governor that there was a large group of farmers in his office and that they were "het up." His advice was to stay away and let them eventually give up the wait. He reiterated that the men were "het up."

Russell told him to go back and tell the men he'd be there presently. When he arrived a short time later, he allowed the men to talk, listening intently as they vented their frustrations. Then he told them honestly what might be done about their concerns and what could not be done. Hay was amazed to see the men calm down and eventually walk away quietly, satisfied that their governor was doing the best he could for them. Dick Russell, Jr., would never forget the plight of farmers during these hard times.

Russell considered reorganization of state government a high priority, and he pushed ahead with these plans, giving the ball to his friend and now brother-in-law Hugh Peterson. The Reorganization Act consolidated all of the old administrative agencies into eighteen new departments, boards, and commissions. A tax commission to consolidate tax collections was established, and state purchasing was also centralized. One of the most significant changes was the abolition of twenty-five boards of trustees that had governed the various institutions within the university system. Richard senior was chairman of the Board of Trustees of the University of Georgia at this time, and so not only had the governor volunteered to cut his own salary, but he had also put his father out of a job. To replace these twenty-five boards, an eleven-person

Board of Regents was established that would serve Georgia well for decades to come as her higher-education system expanded.

Russell was as severe with personal expenses as with other state funds. At home in the Mansion, he retained a cook and a chauffeur, who also served as gardener, as part of the expected gubernatorial grandeur, but he insisted on close accounts of food and other household expenses. Ina was the perfect match for him in this attitude after years of making the judge's salary go such a long way provisioning her large family. Dick's sister Carolyn, studying at Agnes Scott College, visited her parents often, and she mourned that Dick would not let them spend anything extra. Happy to have reliable servants, Ina did not complain about economies. Her Thanksgiving Day meal, reported in the newspapers, featured simple Georgia products like black-eyed peas and coleslaw. Isaac Hay, who handled details of Mansion fiscal affairs, came to love and admire Ina as together they tried to find ways to keep expenses low yet maintain the dignity of the official state home without mentioning spending to the governor. Hay often served as driver—and knew that the governor liked to drive himself—so that Gus, the chauffeur, could have some time off.

Russell's successful record attracted national attention, and as a youthful, energetic, yet dignified and effective leader, he was credited in the *New York Times* with restoring Georgia's political and financial solvency. Nothing pleased Dick Russell more than feeling he made Georgia look good. His achievements had increased his love for his state and its people, and his work vividly underscored his conviction that Georgia was the place he wished to serve.

Perhaps the most telling attention he attracted was from national Democratic leaders. Franklin D. Roosevelt was governor of New York and a part-time resident of Georgia as well, because he came frequently to Warm Springs, Georgia, for therapy in his battle with polio. Russell was an early supporter of Roosevelt for president, and in fall 1931 the two men met several times, either at Warm Springs or in Atlanta. A group of Georgians, including Hugh Peterson and Dick Russell, invited Roosevelt to a south Georgia possum dinner, and the New Yorker accepted. It was later claimed that Roosevelt also went on the possum hunt, showing he had remarkable physical vigor in spite of his polio.

Once, Roosevelt dined with the family at the governor's Mansion when Dick's ten-year-old niece Jane Bowden was visiting. Jane was shocked that Governor Roosevelt drank the juice out of his fruit cocktail cup, an action her mother had told her was bad manners. Figuring it was okay to do so if Governor Roosevelt had done it, Jane promptly drank her own juice. Having his nieces and nephews visit with his mother in Atlanta was a delight to Dick Russell, as he embraced his family, which was growing larger and larger. It was no surprise that Franklin Roosevelt took an immediate liking to Dick's parents, and his discussions of current events with Judge Russell were lively.

This easy acquaintance of Roosevelt and Russell would result in Dick Russell's receiving an invitation to make a seconding speech for Roosevelt's nomination at the Democratic Convention in summer 1932. By that time Russell was embroiled in a totally unexpected political contest, and his speech at the national convention would boost considerably his chances of winning it.

As 1932 began, Georgians looked with affection and favor on their young governor. It was the custom for a popular governor to be given a second term without serious opposition, and Dick Russell, Jr., knew that the office was again his for the asking. Everyone assumed that he would offer for reelection. Then, on 18 April 1932, William J. Harris, senior United States senator from Georgia, died of a heart attack in Washington. This sudden, shocking, and saddening death of a man prominent in Georgia politics for the past twenty years changed the political landscape dramatically. Governor Russell, who would appoint the interim senator until an election could be held, had a decision to make and quickly. Who would run for Harris's unexpired term, which would finish in 1936? Should Russell run for the post? This might be his best chance for many years to become Georgia's advocate in Washington, a job he would relish. It was also a job with much more future than the governor's chair, which could last only two more years.

Old friends of Judge Russell wrote to entreat the governor to appoint his father to the post, thus making good another dream of the old man. The power he had to gratify his father must have seemed less than a blessing at this time, but with proper respect to the fallen servant, Dick Russell said that he would make a decision only after Senator

Harris's funeral. Although he regretted not being able to help his father fulfill a dream, Dick never gave serious consideration to appointing Richard senior. Realizing that his position was perhaps stronger than it could ever be again, the son chose to run for the office himself. To appoint his father would damage his own chances, perhaps irreparably, and he knew his father would not want that to happen. It is doubtful they ever conferred on the matter, but what is certain is that Richard senior would have wanted his son to go for the job.

Dick Russell, Jr., had a well-honed sense of timing in the political arena that did not fail him. This was his moment to run for national office. He was only eighteen months beyond his smashing political victory over a strong field of opponents. He had achieved much in the one legislative session of his governorship and had earned credit as the leader of these accomplishments. His image was that of a winner. His network of enthusiastic friends throughout the state remained ready and eager to help. If he were reelected governor for a term that expired in 1934, he would have a two-year layover before a national senatorial election in 1936. There were few political opportunities in that two-year period. His realistic nature clearly told him: the deadest thing in Georgia politics is a second-term governor. The time to grasp opportunity was now.

On 25 April, Dick Russell, Jr. announced that he had appointed John S. Cohen, publisher of the *Atlanta Journal* and Democratic National committeeman from Georgia, to serve as interim senator and that he, Russell, would seek the unexpired senatorial term at an election set for 14 September 1932. Cohen declared that he would not seek election to the office.

On 26 April, Charles Crisp, dean of the Georgia congressional delegation, declared for the office. Crisp, from Georgia's Third District, had served honorably and well in the House for twenty years, and many felt that his election to the Senate would be a logical promotion. Almost all the major newspapers in the state supported Crisp, and if Dick Russell had listened to the dire predictions from the press, he would have withdrawn his candidacy. Instead, he surveyed his own strengths, rolled up his figurative sleeves, and went to work. His friends and family went to work with him.

In the lively campaign, each candidate tried to make himself look more senatorial than the other. Crisp, with his Washington experience, had the advantage here, and after making his announcement he went back to Washington, underscoring his reputation as a hardworking public servant. Russell, with his youth, his reputation for serving the entire state (as opposed to one congressional district), and his undeniable charisma, began to outdistance the congressman fairly early. Russell opened his campaign with a radio address in Atlanta that once again emphasized his determination to keep faith with the people. He wanted to be elected to the Senate to speak the voice of Georgia in Washington. Then he set out to examine Crisp's record in Congress.

Because the Hoover administration was being tarred with all the feathers causing the Depression, Russell did not find it difficult to associate Crisp with many of the nation's problems. Government waste, skyrocketing government expenditures, and taxes that favored the rich were stuck on Crisp. Russell's own program called for currency inflation to create credit, reorganization of the national government, and stricter immigration controls. Russell regularly struck a strong isolationist stance, in keeping with the Monroe Doctrine, a view popular with many Georgians following the Great War.

Leaving the broadcasting room, Russell headed for the main streets of Georgia towns and cities once again, making speeches and other visits three or four days a week statewide. He hired Mark Dunahoo of Winder, a recent high school graduate, to be his driver, saying he was unable to pay much, but that if he were elected, Mark could go to Washington to work. In spite of another tempting opportunity in these tough economic times, Dunahoo decided to bet on Senator Russell, and the two set off on a rigorous campaigning schedule.

By July, Crisp was being urged by his people to come home and stop this young whirlwind of campaigning vigor. The Russell campaign "machine," while loosely organized, had matured. The people in it were loyal, and having seen the fruits of victory gave them more reason to believe in their man. They were ready for the challenge of this race. As usual, on the home ground, Uncle Lewis and brother Rob made up the managing team, and other family members came and went throughout the campaign. Although Russell tried to show that they were working on a shoestring budget, in keeping with his image as the people's candidate, he was, in fact, well-funded by contributions of friends, at least comparatively so. He had about $12,000, donated by Atlanta businessmen who were his friends. In the governor's race, he had spent less than $5000, all but $600 of which he furnished himself. In keeping with Russell tradition, however, waste was carefully curtailed.

Russell positioned himself with Franklin Roosevelt as the New York governor emerged as the strongest contender for the Democratic presidential nomination. Images of Russell and Roosevelt in Georgia in the preceding two years appeared in photos or stories in newspapers throughout the state. About six weeks before the Democratic Convention, Russell and other leading Georgia Democrats visited Roosevelt at Warm Springs and, no doubt, discussed the presidential campaign. Although Roosevelt did not endorse Russell, Russell received an invitation to make a seconding speech at the national convention. Dick Russell appreciated Roosevelt's approach, for the Georgian made it a rigid practice not to support others when he was campaigning himself. It was too potentially damaging to become connected to another campaign, and this wise strategy was never abandoned in any Russell race.

Only three major daily papers in the state supported Russell: the *Augusta Chronicle*, the *Atlanta Journal*, and the *Columbus Ledger*. National publications also favored Crisp, including the *New York Times*, the *Washington Post*, the *Washington Herald*, *Collier's*, *Time*, and several others. When the *Atlanta Constitution*, a Crisp paper, reported these endorsements, Dick Russell turned this urban support to his advantage by charging that Northern papers backed Crisp because he was under the influence of the power trust and other special interests. Georgia voters would not be told how to vote by outsiders, he contended. Increasingly, Russell presented himself as a progressive in contrast to a reactionary, and he won the battle of popular perception by showing himself to be the representative of the average man against big vested interests who sought to control the government.

On 20 August, Ina Russell was walking down a main street of Atlanta when she heard a newsboy crying an extra: *Georgia's governor in car crash in south Georgia*. Her heart almost stopped, but by the time she was writing to his siblings the next day, she was calmed and reassured. On his way to Dublin for a speech, Dick had barely escaped death when

Dunahoo swerved the car off the road to avoid a head-on collision. Thrown through the windshield, Dick Russell, Jr., lost four front teeth and sustained cuts and bruises. After attention from a local dentist, he went on to the Dublin speech and another in Alamo. He arrived home in Atlanta about 2 A.M. His mother and sister-in-law Sybil were waiting up for him, and they woke Rob when Dick arrived. The four sat up a long time talking about the accident. Dick joked and showed three teeth he'd picked up from the floor of the car. His supporters liked to claim that this escape showed he had been plucked by a divine hand to represent Georgia in Washington.

Not free of mudslinging on either side, the campaign deteriorated at times into the ridiculous. Once Crisp claimed that it would be better to send a married man to Washington because, with a wife, he, Crisp, would be better cared for. A single man could just run around loose up there. Although ridiculous in the extreme, this charge would have an ironic outcome as Dick Russell's Senate career progressed.

It was likely difficult for Crisp or anyone else to grasp how devotedly the Russell family fort was manned and womanned. Ina wrote to her daughter Pat in Ailey, Georgia, a few days before the election in order to recount life on the campaign trail in north Georgia. Pat and Hugh were waging a battle for the congressional seat for Hugh in the First District:

> William came Mon. and added one more strong arm (or two I should say) to our wheel. The boys seem like *young folks* to me, yet they are working like *men*...everyone gets up early and if they do not, real early, the 'phone rings and its uncle Lewis wanting to know the whys & wherefores. Every one cheerful and full of vim. Virginia [Fielding's wife, married the year before] is so sweet and sensible. All this life is so new to her. You know how Sybil has always been so pleasant about turning over Bob [Rob] to such work and never making a complaint, even when she is left alone....

Dick Russell had good women in the family, both sisters and sisters-in-law, who stood behind him as faithfully as did his brothers.

Right up to Election Day on 14 September, Crisp supporters and his newspaper support nationwide predicted he would win. Georgia voters, however, backed their young horse and sent Dick Russell, Jr. to Washington with an overwhelming victory. Russell received 162,745 popular votes and 296 county unit votes to Crisp's 119,193 popular and 114 county unit votes. The at-home Georgian had succeeded in identifying his opponent with the forces in Washington that had pushed the country to the brink of economic ruin, and when the November election sent Franklin Roosevelt to the White House, it was the turn of the Democrats to show whether or not they could clean up the mess.[9]

Ina Russell rejoiced in her son's success, but the joy of victory for Dick was tempered with regret because Hugh Peterson did not win his congressional contest. Fortunately Pat had seen her mother live graciously through many defeats and so knew how to encourage her husband for another try.

Part of Dick Russell's reorganization of state government involved a constitutional amendment moving the governor's inauguration to January, instead of the June date established in an era when winter travel was difficult. Thus his term was shortened by six months, but after his election to the Senate, he had four months to remain as governor of Georgia, and he carried on the usual administrative duties, while also making speeches for Roosevelt prior to the November election.

The family gathered, numerous and joyous, at Christmas in the Governor's Mansion, a special time of family reunion for Ina and Richard senior. Richard senior made a speech, as usual, that left the family in tears. Uncle Lewis added to the emotion with words of his own, and Dick witnessed both the family man and the bachelor surrounded by lifelong love and support.

In light of these changes, Ina and the judge moved to an apartment on Piedmont Avenue rather than returning immediately to Winder. With Alex, Edward, and Carolyn in school in the Atlanta area, Ina felt it would be prudent to stay near these three children as each finished his or her studies. Dick left his personal car with them so that Alex, Jeb, or Carolyn could drive their parents when needed. There was no question of not

---

[9] With a one-party system dominant in Georgia politics, a primary victory was tantamount to a general election win.

returning to Russell in the summer. The old homeplace would remain home to Dick Russell, Jr. when he was not in Washington. There was no place on earth that he would rather be.

On 10 January 1933, the senator-elect appeared before a joint session of the state legislature for a farewell address, expressing confidence in the resilience of his beloved state in spite of hard times. In the evening, he and a large group of relatives and friends boarded the train in Atlanta for Washington, where on 12 January, Dick Russell, Jr. was to be sworn in as Georgia's junior United States Senator.

The Russell family gathers to christen the twins, Fielding and William, sitting on their parents' laps, about 1908. R. B., as Richard, Jr., was then called, is about ten years old. He is standing straight against the wall, wearing a bow tie, beside his sister, Mary Willie.

Dick Russell, Jr., poses with lawyer-friend-cousin Joe Quillian and an unidentified infant, in 1922, as he is beginning his Winder law practice.

Family portrait, about 1926. Front row, l. to r. Patience Elizabeth Russell, Mary Willie Russell Green, Ina Dillard Russell[, Jr.], Carolyn Lewis Russell. Second row, l. to r. Alex B. Russell, Harriette Brumby Russell, Ina Dillard Russell, Richard Brevard Russell, Sr., Margarite Russell Bowden, Walter Brown Russell. Third row, l. to r. Fielding Dillard Russell, William John Russell, Richard Brevard Russell, Jr., Robert Lee Russell, Edward [Jeb] Russell

Richard Brevard Russell, Jr., Speaker of the Georgia House, at his desk, about 1927.

Georgia's youthful Governor Russell meets with New York's Governor Roosevelt at Warm Springs, Georgia, about 1932.

Above, new Senator Russell cuts watermelon for a family gathering in 1933. Mother Ina is on his right, his youngest sister, Carolyn, is on his left.

Below, in 1936, Dick Russell's Senate campaign against Gene Talmadge was sometimes funded by donations of bales of cotton.

Above, Senator Russell helps a Georgia farmer plant pine seedlings, perhaps near Winder, December 1938.

Below, Pat Collins and Dick Russell out on the town in 1938, as rumors flew about their romance. Although the marriage did not take place, Pat saved this photo for seventy years.

Chairing the Congressional Investigation of American bases overseas, Senator Russell is shown here with Captain Henry Myers, also from Georgia, pilot of the *Guess Where II*, the Liberator aircraft that transported the five senators around a wartime world.

In 1945, about a month after World War II ended in Europe, Senator Russell was reunited with his brother Alex in France when the senate again sent as investigative committee to the war theater. Alex, a doctor, had been serving with the 107th Army Evacuation Hospital in Europe since early 1944.

Above, looking unsuitably dressed for barbecueing, the Russell men pose for a publicity photo with their mother in 1947. L. to r. Rob, Fielding, William, Ina, Dick, Walter, Jeb, and Alex.

Below, those who really cooked the barbecue: unknown, Rich Davenport, Jesse Davenport, Carabell Teasly, holding John Russell, Modine Thomas, Grant Thomas, J.R. Teasly, unknown.

This portrait, gift of President Truman, is inscribed: "To Hon. Richard Russell with kindest regards from his good friend and great admirer, Harry Truman"

Senator Russell comes home in mid-winter to celebrate with others of the clan his mother's eighty-third birthday, February 18, 1951.

Above, Russell was often invited to lunch at the White House with president Eisenhower. In this photo: Eisenhower, center, front row. Georgia's Walter George is on the President's right. Senator Russell is the first man on the row, left.

Below, Senators Russell and Talmadge confer with President John Kennedy about a Lockheed aircraft project, 1962.

Above, Senator Russell at home in Winder, Christmas 1957, with his sister Ina Russell Stacy, who acted as official hostess for him after 1955.

Below, Dick Russell and his life-long companion, Harriet Orr, at a Washington nightclub, ca. 1958.

Senator Richard Russell makes a final point to President Johnson as the senator leaves one of their many White House meetings, ca. 1966.

Above, senate leaders count the electoral college votes after the 1968 election. Dick Russell is on the left at the back. (Corbis)

Below, senate leaders with new President Richard Nixon, inauguration day 1969.
L. to r. president pro tem Richard Brevard Russell, senate minority leader Mike Mansfield, Nixon, senate majority Leader Everett Dirksen

PART III

1933–1971

With Six Presidents in the
Greatest Deliberative Body in the World[1]

FRANKLIN DELANO ROOSEVELT: 1933–1945

"No man in public life for generations has so completely possessed the affections and confidence of all classes of our people and all sections of our nation."
—Richard B. Russell, Jr. on Franklin Delano Roosevelt, 1932

1933–1940: New Deals and Fair Deals

Shortly after noon on 12 January 1933, Walter F. George, senior senator from Georgia, escorted Dick Russell, Jr. into the chamber of the United States Senate for the swearing-in ceremony. Vice President under Herbert Hoover, Charles Curtis administered the oath of office. Russell, because he was filling an unexpired term, could be sworn in before the 4 March Presidential Inauguration date that would begin the next Congress. The new Georgia senator would thus gain seniority over other newly elected officials. Seniority in the Senate was often the key to important positions.

As he had done when he took the oath of office as governor of Georgia, Dick Russell, Jr. put his left hand on his mother's small, well-worn Bible to take the oath: "I do solemnly swear that I will support and defend the Constitution of the United States against all enemies, foreign and domestic; that I will bear true faith and allegiance to the same; that I take this obligation freely, without any mental reservation or purpose of evasion; and that I will well and faithfully discharge the duties of the office on which I am about to enter. So help me God."

---

[1] In Dick Russell's understanding of the American system of government, the three branches served alongside each other. Thus he would point out that senators did not serve under a president, but *with* him.

Although originally the oath was strictly oral and consisted of only fourteen words—"I do solemnly swear that I will support the Constitution of the United States"—beginning during the Civil War, senators were obliged to speak and to sign an extended oath that included specifics regarding defense of the Constitution. By 1933 the written requirement had become part of the ritual, and each senator signed an individual page in an elegantly bound oath book.

When Dick Russell completed the oral and written oath, several senators offered their congratulations. The press was eager to photograph Russell with Robert M. LaFollette, Jr., senator from Wisconsin, to emphasize Russell's extreme youth. LaFollette, at thirty-eight, had been the baby of the Senate. Dick Russell, Jr. had just passed his thirty-fifth birthday.[2]

Family and friends in the gallery beamed at the proceedings, but the senator's parents were not among the well-wishers. The summer of campaigning and the move from the Governor's Mansion had taken its toll on Ina and Richard senior. In spite of an intense desire to go with the group, Dick's offer to pay for the trip, and the chance to see their other children in Washington, neither felt strong enough to travel for their son's swearing-in ceremony. Ina sent her Bible.

Nothing the Russell family did, however, could be considered short on people. This was a family who knew how to rally, and rally they did at the US Senate on 12 January. Rob, Sybil, and Uncle Lewis travelled with the group from Atlanta. In Washington, more family was waiting. Sister Billie, her husband Gordon, and Ina junior had been in the Washington area since the end of World War I. Sister Harriette, and her husband Ralph Sharpton had recently moved to Washington after Ralph had lost his job in California. They were living with Ina junior while Ralph looked for work. Ina junior and Harriette had met Dick on the morning of 11 January when his train arrived in Washington, and they were with the Greens and three of their children at the Senate for the swearing in. Richard senior's brother Edward had been living and working in Washington since the early twentieth century, and he and his

---

[2] Constitutional age requirement for senators is thirty, but the term "senator" comes from the Latin for "old," and much older senators were the norm. As of 2009, the average age of a United States senator was sixty-three.

wife Susie would not have missed this milestone. The new senator's uncle Rob, career naval officer and young Dick's boyhood idol, was also retired in the Washington area, and, although in poor health, he no doubt was also in attendance. Even without his parents, Dick Russell felt strong family backing as he began this new adventure. One longtime Washington resident reported to Ina and Richard back in Atlanta that he had never seen so many present at a ceremony of that kind.

Following the swearing-in, Senator Cohen, Dick's interim appointee, gave a luncheon for the Georgia congressional delegation, to which many of Dick Russell's friends and relatives were also invited. Seeing the elevator marked "For Senators Only," Russell rang its bell and prepared to board as the door opened. The young elevator operator scolded him. "You can't ride on this elevator. It is for senators only."

Almost as surprised as the operator, Russell answered, "I am Senator Russell from Georgia."

Red-faced and stammering, the young man apologized over and over. Those with them were impressed at how Dick Russell's graciousness finally reassured the operator that everything was all right.

Seeing the throng of friends and family assembled in his honor in the historic Senate dining room, flush from the oath-taking, the new senator experienced not pride but its opposite. His voice filled with emotion, he expressed his awe and humility at having come "to the greatest deliberative body in the world, from the greatest state in the world whose people are the best...in the world...surrounded here by many of the best friends I have in the world." Those friends knew that he was absolutely sincere. No one who knew Dick Russell well ever doubted his modesty.

Dick's mother, having received written accounts of the day from her daughters as well as from the senator himself, wrote to say how much pleasure it gave her to think of his sharing that momentous occasion with his sisters. She could picture how happy Harriette, Ina, and Billie were among that gathering of male leaders. It was good fortune that, as a family man lacking a wife, Dick Russell, Jr., had sisters whom he could join as he left home for the first time.

Because Dick Russell, Jr., had decided to run for the Senate at the sudden death of Senator Harris, it is unlikely that he had, at that time, a clear idea of the functions of this unique legislative body within the American system, but it is certain that he studied its philosophy and history thoroughly as he campaigned and in the interim following his election. He studied also the Constitution of the United States, Revolutionary and post-Revolutionary American history, and other documents such as the Federalist Papers. He learned the rules of order of the Senate and considered how these could be used to Georgia's advantage. In a sincere desire to be a respectable "Voice of Georgia," Russell did not go to Washington unprepared.

Dick Russell's keen political mind understood that in creating a system of checks and balances, the Founding Fathers intended the Senate to check not only the executive branch but also to balance the House of Representatives, its partner legislative branch. Fearing too much democracy that could deteriorate to mob rule, the framers of the Constitution created a body whose members, in the beginning, could be appointed, not elected. More than 100 years would pass before senators were chosen by popular vote. The way senators were chosen was left up to the individual states, and the Senate itself was a reassurance to states that all would be equally represented in this arm of the federal government. No matter how small, each state would have two senators. In the House, the larger population centers had the most strength, but in the Senate, everyone was on equal footing. As this unique institution evolved, the personality, wisdom, compatibility, and leadership of individual men became what counted most. The Senate tradition was to foster friendship while encouraging ardent debate and thoughtful consideration. Although it was not unknown in the first hundred years of congressional record for fistfights to break out in both branches of Congress, the Senate was considered the calmer, more dignified of the two houses. Dick Russell, Jr. formed a deep and lasting respect for this original American institution from the beginning.

The Senate was also a place for the discussion of states' rights, established as the intended stronghold against feared federal usurping of power that lay, from the beginning, with state governments. Southerners, fewer in population, had had to learn to grow effective senators, especially following the Civil War and the humiliating defeat of their homeland and its subsequent occupation by Union troops. They had had to wrest back their states' rights, they felt, following Reconstruction. It is likely that all Southern senators in Dick Russell's day arrived in Washington on the defensive, anxious to protect their states from insult and injustice. In 1933 there was a vivid sense, by Southerners at least, that the South was still being treated like the stepchild of the Union.

Americans in the twenty-first century might struggle to understand the divided concept of the rights of states versus the powers of the federal government because we have for three generations seen the federal government decide how we educate, where and how we build roads, how we employ, who we allow to vote, and how much old-age pension we receive. Both at the state and the federal level, we tolerate much more governmental interference than any of the Founding Fathers, from Hamilton to Jefferson, could have envisioned. Yet in the beginning, these very questions of education, local travel and trade, voting rights, and care of the aged and infirm had been designated to the states. At the time Dick Russell, Jr. went to Washington, the all-pervasive presence of the federal government in the daily lives of the citizenry was only about to step onstage as the New Deal of Franklin Delano Roosevelt got underway. Expecting government to extricate us from the problems of daily existence was not the American way. The predicaments of the Great Depression, however, dictated a new view of governmental responsibility.

Dick Russell, Jr. brought to Washington well-entrenched Southern ideas of independent states. After all, Southerners had believed they had the right to secede. As governor of Georgia, however, Russell had seen hardworking people lose their jobs and homes in the deepening financial crisis. The stories he'd heard from these responsible citizens in letters and in firsthand encounters on the streets of Georgia towns and cities, as well as at the door of the Governor's Office and Mansion,[3] had prepared him to support President Roosevelt in innovative federal programs that would put people back to work and get money circulating again. Nevertheless, the new senator was determined to be a clear representative for Georgians above all else. In a daring move, he requested to serve on the Senate Committee on Appropriations, the most powerful committee in the Senate because it controls the purse strings. Normally a new senator

---

[3] During Ina Russell's tenure as mistress of the Governor's Mansion, she sometimes provided meals for men on the road who stopped there to ask for help.

could not have any hope of being on Appropriations, but Russell decided to ask because Senator Harris had been on this committee.

Senator Joseph T. Robinson of Arkansas, majority leader, was in charge of designating committee assignments. Robinson was startled when he questioned Russell about his committee preferences and learned that he wanted Appropriations. As the elder statesman and fellow Southerner, Robinson explained to the brash recruit that a senator usually had to have at least four or five years Senate experience before he could expect to be on Appropriations. Although Dick Russell was certainly familiar with Senate tradition, he did not back down. Senator Harris had been on Appropriations, he said, courteously but firmly, and the people of Georgia expected Russell to fill that place. He'd rather not have a committee assignment if he could not have Appropriations.

Robinson, a kind and gentle man, a reputed true "Southern gentleman," was also known for a fairly wide ornery and combative streak, and he could have squelched this upstart from Georgia. However, Huey Long of Louisiana was at the same time causing trouble in Democratic ranks with radical ideas far out of line with Roosevelt's and most other Democrats'. Robinson, fearing that Dick Russell might possess a radical and independent spirit similar to Long's, decided to comply with his request. It would be years later before Russell understood what had made Robinson give him this coveted committee assignment, but he early recognized what a stroke of good fortune it was. In addition, the Georgian received appointments to committees on naval affairs, immigration, and manufacturing.

Russell benefitted from another stroke of good luck when he was chosen chairman of the Subcommittee on Agricultural Appropriations because Carter Glass, chair of the Appropriations committee, did not want "Cotton Ed" Smith of South Carolina to have it. Russell was thus in a position of influence where agricultural legislation was concerned. Because most senators had large agricultural constituencies in the 1930s, Russell's fair handling of this legislation soon helped him build up obligations from many senators.

Contrary to being a fiery, showy senator of the Huey Long variety, Dick Russell, Jr. made a conscious decision to be a Senate workhorse rather than a show horse. While some senators addressed the nation about an issue, such as the poor and the disadvantaged in these

Depression times, hoping that popular opinion would force Congress to act on the matter, others preferred to work within the institution. Rather than give interviews to reporters, write articles, or give talks on the radio, these senators worked behind the scenes, quietly negotiating, calling in obligations, and suggesting compromises. Never having been one to get far out in front on an issue, Dick Russell was a natural in this latter approach. Equally important, this was the way judged most senatorial, and the young man soon gained a reputation as being unobtrusive but hardworking, someone who could be relied upon, a man not given to making rash promises or to breaking those he had made. His gift for friendship and his ability to compromise, traits both heredity and environment bestowed on him, made the United States Senate the ideal political arena in which Dick Russell, Jr. could serve and excel.

Several other abilities stood the new senator in good stead as he began his career in Washington. His penchant for reading history and for serious study of legislative proposals soon made him one of the most informed senators in the body. Early in his tenure, Russell told his former driver and friend Mark Dunahoo, who was now on the senatorial staff, that he was dealing with his homesickness by memorizing the Senate rules of order at home each evening. Russell reputedly read the entire *Congressional Record* daily, and often could be found at work on Saturday or Sunday, reading old *Records* for information regarding legislation or Senate rules and history. A rapid reader with an exceptional memory, he believed in knowing what he was talking about and gained the respect of fellow senators with his diligence. Although Russell was a skillful debater, he made few speeches on the Senate floor in his early years, preferring to build personal relationships to gain influence. His father and his mother had shown him the value of this way of life, and the character of the Senate itself made this approach highly suitable.

Another factor that helped Russell in his first years in Washington was undeniably his single status. Contrary to Congressman Crisp's assessment that a bachelor would drift wildly about in Washington, Dick Russell, with no immediate family obligations but with a determined goal of becoming an outstanding senator for Georgia, spent more time on Senate work than most of his colleagues. An eligible bachelor, good looking, courtly, and refined, he frequently received invitations to social functions. Washington hostesses often asked him particularly to escort a dignitary's wife at special dinners, where the custom was for couples not to sit together, and he sometimes agreed. More often than not, though, he refused social engagements. His invitation file held many more regrets than acceptances.

In January 1933, Dick Russell had left for the first time the haven his mother and father had provided for thirteen children. At the age of thirty-five, in spite of several years away at school and one trip to Europe, his home had been under Ina Dillard Russell's roof. As governor, he had taken his mother with him to Atlanta, and she had been willing to remain his feminine stability because she perceived he needed her. Setting up his own place in a large city was not easy for him. Unable to think about anything as permanent as an apartment, he chose rooms at the Hamilton Hotel on K Street. It was customary for senators and representatives of that time to live in hotels because Congress was in session generally only half the year. The Hamilton, built in the Roaring Twenties, was a prestigious address, and a common one for members of Congress. By living there, Dick would give Georgia a cultivated image without undue expense, since he did not have rooms all year long. The Hamilton was close to the Capitol, so he could walk to and from work. He also had cleaning services and lounges in which he could entertain friends for drinks, important features for a bachelor. Nevertheless, he was undeniably homesick. Dick wrote to his mother that although many considered Washington nothing but a sprawling Southern town, he had been unable to find grits to his satisfaction in any restaurant or cafe.

Fortunately, family was not far away. Ina junior had her own apartment on Connecticut Avenue, and in 1933 sister Harriette and husband Ralph lived with her until Ralph found work. Sister Billie, as consummate a homemaker as her mother, lived in nearby Alexandria, Virginia, with her husband and four children. Dick was especially fond of his eldest sister, perhaps because she reminded him in spirit of his mother, and he was always welcome at the Greens'. In 1934 Hugh Peterson was elected to Congress from Georgia's First District and sister Pat, another homemaker *par excellence*, joined the Russell clan members in Washington. In typical family tradition, the women organized frequent get-togethers at each other's homes for meals and fellowship, and thus Dick Russell had family for nurture and solace. He could eat the best grits and fried chicken in the world at both Billie's and Pat's. Knowing how much he treasured this family time, Billie was acutely disappointed when he sometimes said he could not come because he was working in his office on the weekends, studying old *Congressional Records*.

When Roosevelt launched his New Deal in March 1933, Dick Russell, Jr. was one of his staunchest backers. The two men had a short but cordial history from their time as governors and Roosevelt's association with Georgia at Warm Springs. Not friends, they were, however, colleagues who shared a deep concern for their country and wanted to do what they could in their respective positions to improve their staggering world. From his Southern background, Russell was likely to oppose too much intervention by the federal government, yet Roosevelt's brand of progressivism was acceptable. Defined as an expansion of federal powers to serve the people and to regulate predatory interests without calling for fundamental institutional change, the Roosevelt program seemed to Russell necessary and reasonable. In later years he would say that he was a liberal in bad times and a conservative in good times, a position, in his view, too obvious to be questioned.

The Georgian made it clear that he was not a New Deal insider. He enjoyed telling the story of how one night about midnight the phone rang in his hotel room, and when he answered, someone said, "This is Franklin Roosevelt." Not quite awake and not recognizing the voice, Russell replied, "Oh, yeah? And this is the Pope," and hung up the phone. A White House staffer phoned a few minutes later to tell him he had hung up on the president. Mortified, he apologized, explaining he thought it was a prank call, and prayed the president to forgive him.

Russell did not need to be close to Roosevelt personally to vote for most of his program during the famous Hundred Days of the New Deal. The Georgia senator voted for the Emergency Banking Act, for relief, for the reduction of federal salaries, for the Agricultural Adjustment Act, for establishing the Tennessee Valley Authority, and for the National Industrial Recovery Act. He strongly favored setting up such programs as the Civilian Conservation Corps, and although it pained him to agree to reduce payments to veterans, he did so because he thought an overall reduction in government spending was the best Congress could do at the time.

There was no dearth of critics of the New Deal. They charged that the president was becoming a dictator and that his programs were radical, un-American, and communist. Russell defended the president against these charges, claiming that the present must be reconciled to the requirements of the future. It would take decades, of course, but he believed that these momentous changes would be judged beneficial to the nation. His mother, following his work daily by reading Atlanta papers and by listening to radio broadcasts, agreed with Dick's assessment. She wrote to him that she sympathized with the difficulty of knowing what to do when things were happening so fast, but "...changes have to be made & right now seems to be the time & then adjust for the good of all." His mother's understanding and wisdom continued to guide and sustain him.

Because Congress adjourned in June, Dick Russell, Jr. was able to spend a good part of the year back in Winder or traveling to speaking engagements in Georgia. Not entirely free of official responsibilities during this time, in September 1933, he joined a group from the Naval Affairs committees of the House and Senate to inspect a number of US naval bases. They left Norfolk, Virginia, and travelled to the west coast via Haiti and the Panama Canal Zone. This was the first time that Dick Russell had been west of the Mississippi River. Busy with inspections and lavish entertainment, the novice senator nevertheless found the highlight of the trip to be watching the operations of the aircraft carrier *Saratoga*. As a boy, he had idolized his uncle Robert, a career naval officer, and as a young senator, he judged witnessing the naval takeoff and landing of seventy-four planes the most spectacular sight he'd ever seen. Childhood war games that acknowledged a country unable to defend itself, later mature reading of history, an awareness of current events following the Great War—all these had marked Dick Russell to be an adamant and determined advocate for national defense.

Russell's seriousness about his work did not prevent his having women friends, and his appointment books show he had frequent dates. The situation remained as it had for women dating him at the time he ran for and served as governor. Women friends had to be willing to let his work take priority, and many of them did. Because he was such an eligible bachelor, well-known Washington hostesses tried to set him up with friends. He liked to tell of one such social icon who cornered him one evening and demanded why he was not married.

"Well," he said, thinking himself witty, "I've been looking for a girl too proud to see her husband work and rich enough to prevent it."

A few days later the woman phoned to say she had found him just such a woman and would pair them at an upcoming dinner party. Chagrined to have been taken seriously, Russell stammered his regrets. He was forever convinced that the famed hostess never forgave him for not being willing to try her choice.

In 1934 Josephine Hardman, recently graduated from Rome's Shorter College, married Linton M. Collins, a Miami attorney about Russell's age who came to Washington to work in the Roosevelt administration. Showing the depth of their friendship, Josephine invited Dick Russell to meet her husband, and thereafter the two men became good friends. Linton Collins was always glad when they could get Dick to share a meal and conversation in the Collins home. Collins would go on to a career in government and in law, ending up as a United States justice on the Federal Court of Claims with Dick Russell's help in guiding Lyndon Johnson to make the appointment.

By 1937 Dick Russell was enjoying the presence of more family in Washington, and between sisters and sisters-in-law, he often had an escort who did not provoke gossip. His brother Fielding, teaching English at Georgia Teachers' College in Statesboro, had been accepted for doctoral studies at George Washington University. He and his wife, Virginia, and two young sons moved to Alexandria to live with Billie and Gordon and their four children when Fielding began his studies. The Russells were good at making room for each other. Dick helped Fielding secure a part-time job, first as a Capitol guide and later with the US Post Office, so that the little family was able to move to their own apartment.

As he had often invited Billie or Ina junior, Dick invited Virginia to attend a White House reception with him. She was a strikingly good-looking young woman, one sure to turn heads, but there would be no unpleasant gossip about his love life when she was identified as his sister-in-law. Virginia's husband, glad for her opportunity, managed to get up money for a corsage for the occasion. Hugh Peterson, Sr., Georgia congressman and husband of Patience Russell Peterson, fearing the Fielding Russells could not afford a corsage, had ordered one sent to Virginia as well. And as her escort, Dick also brought a corsage, leaving Virginia perplexed as to whose flowers she should wear. This was the kind of family unity that Dick Russell treasured.

In 1934 and 1935 Dick Russell, Jr. continued to support Roosevelt's programs, yet he gained a reputation for independence as he helped affect compromise on important legislation before the Committee on Appropriations. In spite of reservations about a few aspects of the New Deal, Russell remained an enthusiastic supporter. On the other hand, Georgia's governor, Eugene Talmadge, had emerged as a fierce critic of Roosevelt and his policies. Russell was up for reelection and Talmadge had to vacate the governor's office in 1936. Hugely popular in the home state, the ambitious Talmadge was clearly gearing up to unseat Dick Russell in Washington.

Russell continued to make numerous speeches in Georgia, taking the pulse of his constituents on the New Deal. A special thrill for his family came on 10 June 1935, when he made the commencement address at Emory University. His brother Alex received his medical degree that day, and the proud parents were in attendance to see two sons shine. They heard the senator defend New Deal's social and economic programs against charges that they were threatening individual liberty. He declared that if the president and Congress had held to a limited concept of government, the people would have enjoyed only the liberty to starve in peace.

Eugene Talmadge, in the meantime, spoke loudly (and ungrammatically) against welfare, big government, and the farm program. Well-educated and capable of refined exchange, Talmadge chose to appear to the common people of Georgia as a stereotypical Southern demagogue, using colorful but coarse expressions and wearing red suspenders to appear a veritable "man of the people." As governor, Talmadge was heavy-handed in asserting authority and had called out the National Guard on more than one occasion to enforce his will. In 1935 he made a nationwide address over CBS in Washington declaring that the New Deal was an extravagant, wasteful boondoggle and "the largest dole system ever known in the world." By 1936 he was trying to organize southern Democrats to block Roosevelt's renomination. He was especially enraged by the Roosevelt administration's soft attitude toward the possibility of placing blacks—or "niggers," as Talmadge took pride in calling them—in high political office. Talmadge's overwhelming reelection in 1934 had shown that many Georgians agreed with his tactics.

Dick Russell, Jr. however, was sure that most Georgians were devoted to President Roosevelt and that it would be political suicide to oppose him. Although he clearly agreed with Roosevelt's major policies, he also believed supporting them was good politics in Georgia. He continued to align himself as closely as possible with Roosevelt and the New Deal.

Everyone close to Russell knew that the biggest political battle of his life was looming. His mother wrote to him on 26 January 1936:

> With my meager knowledge and understanding of things, I can foresee tough times, but we can face 'em, can't we? Prepare now, *every* day, in getting ready for anything that might come—and I believe that would be by handling things as they come day by day in our most conscientious and painstaking way. To do this, we will be ready to handle the *crucial* times. You remember what you said long ago when you came home so sick, from a hunt down at Farm Hill. We must all be ready for the crucial times.

Following his mother's precept and example, Dick Russell did his Senate work conscientiously and painstakingly day by day.

Governor Talmadge launched his campaign for the United States Senate in McCrae, Georgia, on 4 July 1936 at the most lavish barbecue in the history of Georgia. These barbecues, on a smaller scale, would continue throughout the campaign, and state workers and equipment were blatantly used to provide various aspects of the gatherings. At McCrae, the huge Fourth of July crowd roared its approval of "Old Gene" as their choice to go to the United States Senate. There was no doubt that he was the idol of tens of thousands of rural Georgians.

Ready for crucial times, Richard Russell, Jr. did not quail before this tough opponent. Dick threw himself into his own campaign with his usual vigor and determination. He continued to support Roosevelt, and his friends and supporters organized statewide speaking engagements, as they had done for his previous races. In addition, they used every other means of publicity to spread the views of their candidate—speeches, fliers, posters, advertisements, form letters. Both candidates would also use the radio extensively. Dick Russell's people even distributed fliers from airplanes. The Russell camp held to their creed of not getting mixed up in other races, and they did their best to portray Talmadge as an erratic, irresponsible demagogue who would be a disaster for Georgia in Washington.

Although early reports were not encouraging, Russell kept to his themes. Talmadge supporters distributed a small booklet entitled, "What Senator R. B. Russell Did in the United States Senate." Inside, the booklet was blank. In speech after speech, however, Russell stressed what he had done for farmers, senior citizens, labor, veterans, and others. He could point to tangible proof: federal money spent in county after county since his election for roads, waterworks, and a new auditorium.

It was encouraging to the campaign to find people eager to contribute small amounts to the fight. Most of the gifts were for $1, $2, or $5. A few were for $10 and the rare ones for $50 or $100. A grateful Russell acknowledged each gift and closed his note by saying it would be a hard fight, but the outcome was not in question. Other contributions were sometimes made at rallies in the form of farm products, especially cotton bales. Dick's mother was touched by these offerings. She noted in her diary that at the rally at Warm Springs, twenty-six bales of cotton were donated, "one of them ginned the year Dick was born [1897]."

Although Senator George did not openly endorse Russell, the popular senior senator, not a consistent Roosevelt supporter, did give the president high praise for the New Deal to leading state Democrats, implying support for Russell as well. The message was clear: if Georgia hoped to continue to benefit from efforts to pull the country out of its Depression, the state would do well to back Roosevelt.

A seasoned campaigner, Russell nevertheless found the hard feelings and bitterness that the campaign generated as the summer wore on unlike anything he had experienced. Fights regularly broke out at rallies between Talmadge and Russell supporters, and Russell himself received threats of violence. He wrote his first will during this campaign. When he was accused of being one of the New Dealers who favored black rights and social equality, however, Russell kept his composure. While vigorously defending his positions as a "Deep South" Southerner, he did everything he could to avoid the common approach of "nigger baiting." The Russell family was one in which the word "nigger" was considered a form of despicable disrespect. Russell pointed out that Talmadge's tactic of accusing him of sympathies with blacks was "what every candidate who is about to be beaten does. He comes in crying nigger."

When word got out that Talmadge was being accompanied by national guardsmen in plain clothes, people recalled Talmadge's frequent use of force as governor, and the word "dictatorship" was suggested as applying to his reign. The *Atlanta Constitution* editorialized that the use of the military *à la* Talmadge had not occurred in Georgia since Reconstruction. Russell, well-known for polite but biting sarcastic remarks, saw the chance to turn these reports of body guards to his advantage. The Winder American Legion had organized a drum and bugle corps of thirty Winder High School girls, dressed in red and black (the school's and the University of Georgia's colors), to attend the senator's rallies. At their first appearance, Russell introduced them as "thirty of the prettiest and [most] talented girls in Georgia, and I'm going to make them my official body guard." Such a spoof made Talmadge look pompous and, more important, shifted his stance from offensive to defensive.

When both candidates were invited to speak at a huge rally and barbecue in Griffin, Georgia, on 26 August, the Russell camp was chagrined to learn that Talmadge was assigned the preferred last spot on the program. In political debate when there is no chance for rebuttal, the last speaker in joint appearances has the advantage. Undaunted, Russell prepared a speech that would effectively knock out the governor before he had a chance to speak. First Russell's "body guards" entertained the crowd of 40,000 with several rousing marches just before his speech. Then Russell mounted the platform and proceeded, in his best oratorical style of sarcastic humor and fact, to shred Talmadge's platform, showing that there was nothing in the governor's proposals for farmers, workers, senior citizens, widows and orphans, nor anything of a humanitarian nature. Charging the governor as an outright liar, he left copies of the *Congressional Record* on the platform to prove that he had voted for bills that Talmadge claimed he had voted against. As a final blow, the senator tacked a list of fifteen questions to the podium, questions he said Talmadge should answer when he spoke, about how he proposed to help farmers by cutting their federal payments, how he could reduce the national budget to $1 billion, and how government could be funded if the income tax were eliminated, as Talmadge insisted. The crowd roared their approval. When Talmadge tried to speak after the lunch break, the crowd's demands that he answer the questions left his usual bombastic performance weak and disjointed.

Talmadge biographer William Anderson wrote of this day: "Gene had been drawn and quartered—his style and stomping, his demagoguery and showmanship all pared away." Listening to her son speak on the radio that day, Ina Russell felt proud as the crowd roared their approval of Senator Russell. "Splendid speech," she wrote in her diary. In the *Atlanta Constitution*, Ralph McGill wrote that it was the greatest campaign speech Russell had ever delivered.

The Russell homeplace was again the center of much activity as various family members came and went, working on the campaign throughout the summer. Judge Russell, famous locally for his love of moving dirt, had spent the past twenty years landscaping his grounds with a shovel and wheelbarrow and the infrequent aid of his seven sons. When Talmadge claimed that, while governor, Dick Russell, Jr. had paved the sidewalks of the little settlement of Russell using state funds, a delighted cry of glee rose from the family. Someone, probably William and Alex, painted and posted on the highway a tall sign which read: "$10 Reward to Anyone Finding Paved Sidewalks in Russell." To Ina and Richard senior's amusement, sidewalk search parties arrived from time to time, but no paved sidewalk was ever found.

As Election Day neared and pundits predicted a nail-biting finish, Ina Russell remained her son's steadying feminine influence. She spent her summer cooking and preparing sleeping arrangements for family and other campaign workers who landed at Russell, rejoicing in all reunions of family and friends. On 2 September, with the election one week away, she wrote in her diary: "A very busy pleasant day—things went well in the home. Nothing seemed to be lagging or hard to manage. We listened to speech made by Talmadge at Thomson Ga.—nothing to it but gall & venom. Went to Commerce to hear Dick speak. Big crowd, nice & orderly. 3 bales of cotton given to Dick." Ina was clearly proud of the differences that emerged between her courtly son and the rampaging Talmadge.

On 9 September 1936 Georgians went to the polls and proved the pundits wrong, reelecting Richard B. Russell, Jr. to the US Senate by an overwhelming majority. Russell received 256,154 popular votes to Talmadge's 134,695. These returns translated to 378 county unit votes for Russell and only 32 units for Talmadge. Georgians clearly preferred Dick Russell's style in Washington. His mother wrote in her diary: "A wonderful day & will linger long in our memory."

The next day the citizens of Winder again celebrated with a gigantic reception as 7,000 people converged on the little town in a pouring rainstorm to congratulate the senator. Besting an opponent of the strength of Gene Talmadge was the headiest political brew Dick Russell had yet tasted. Even having been elected governor by a landslide did not equal this pinnacle. Speaking to the crowd that evening, Richard Russell, Sr. said that this one-sided victory was perhaps the happiest moment of his life, since by it the judge felt dignity and democracy for Georgia had been saved. Hearing the aged patriarch, his own father, express such a feeling was humbling to the young senator. His love and admiration for his state and its people deepened. With sincere humility, he tried to express his thanks.

A few weeks later Dick Russell, Jr. met Eugene Talmadge on the streets of Atlanta, and the two men shook hands. Talmadge smiled and said, "Dick, you and I have a lot of friends in Georgia. I guess they are just better friends of yours than they are of mine." Politics being politics, that might have been the best explanation of Russell's triumph. Years later Herman Talmadge, Gene's son, wrote that his father could have beaten Russell but could not beat Roosevelt. While that assertion smacks of sour grapes, it is certain that Dick Russell, Jr. felt as a sacred mandate in his heart of hearts the faith that the people of Georgia had in him to represent them with dignity. His determination to serve them well grew in proportion, but the specter of demagoguery in the person of Gene

Talmadge would continue to dim Russell's political horizons for a decade to come.

Until Congress reconvened in January 1937, Dick Russell, Jr. had time to relax at home and to hunt, a treasured activity since boyhood, with his brother Rob on the homeplace or with brother-in-law Hugh Peterson, Sr., in Ailey. Family changes were afoot as his youngest brother, Alex, married his nurse sweetheart Sarah Eaton on 28 September 1936. The couple moved in with Richard senior and Ina as Alex started medical practice in Barrow County. Brother William also decided to come home and try to farm his father's land because most of the tenants had gone. Dick knew that his parents were growing increasingly frail and was comforted by family members close by to care for them. From the beginning of his time in Washington, he had sent a monthly check to his mother for her personal use, a habit he would continue to the end of her life. He was a bachelor, yes, but he welcomed family responsibilities.

As he began to work on the home farm, William Russell showed a special ability to get along with black tenants. William had high hopes for a young couple who came to live and work there, Modine and Grant Thomas. Grant was industrious and dependable on the farm, and Modine, although only in her late teens, was proving capable in the house, learning to cook and to clean to Ina's satisfaction. Ina Russell also got along well with black servants, perhaps because she respected their work as much as she did her own. Over many years, the black women who had lived on the farm had come to her with problems, and Ina had sheltered in her home at least one such woman from an abusive husband.

Thus when Modine got into deep trouble during a Saturday night ruckus, both William and Ina were eager to help. The charge was perhaps as serious as murder resulting from a knife fight, for Modine had a formidable temper. Yet Modine's own wounds, stitched up by Dr. Alex Russell, proved to them that she had been equally attacked. Dick Russell, Jr. wanted to help everyone in this predicament. All of his people were good judges of character, and he knew they had faith in Modine's. The senator requested the charges be dismissed against the young black woman and for her to be released from jail. Modine came back to Russell and continued to work under Ina's tutelage.

Dick Russell once tried to direct his mother's teaching program with Modine. At breakfast one summer morning when he was home, he frowned when Modine came to the table with the coffee pot in hand and asked, "Miss Ina, you want yo' coffee het up?"

Ina nodded and thanked Modine for the hot coffee she poured into Ina's cup. When the black woman had gone out, Dick said, "Mother, don't you think you could teach Modine to talk better than that?"

His mother considered the question only briefly, then answered, "No, son, I can't. I'm too old, she's too old, and besides, I did want my coffee het up." Several grandchildren visiting for the summer never forgot this retort and how it made even their stern uncle laugh.

Back in Washington, each for second terms, Roosevelt and Russell continued to agree on many of the New Deal programs, but Georgia's senior senator, Walter F. George, always a reluctant Roosevelt convert, was falling away. George had opposed Roosevelt's nomination in 1932 and had not favored New Deal legislation unless he could see that it clearly would benefit Georgians. In addition, George was a supporter of big corporations like Coca-Cola and Georgia Power Company and thus did not approve when Roosevelt's plans meant higher taxes for wealthy businesses and greater regulation for utility companies. When the Supreme Court struck down some of the New Deal programs, Roosevelt introduced a plan to reorganize the court early in 1937, hoping by a major judicial reorganization to get some younger blood on the court. The Roosevelt plan called for the addition of six justices to the Court. Walter George became a highly vocal critic of this plan, agreeing with other critics that the president was seeking to "pack" the Court and that he was threatening a sacred American institution.

Dick Russell, Jr. found himself between a rock and a hard place. While he agreed that the conservative justices had blocked some programs he felt were needed to strengthen the country, the junior senator could not support any measure that assumed the Supreme Court could be affected by party politics or political pressures, even for Roosevelt. As was his wont, he met with other Southern/conservative senators and tried to come up with a compromise. This group of senators

met with Roosevelt and offered that they would support the addition of
two justices to help with the court's heavy case load. This seemed
reasonable to them, but Roosevelt turned them down.

Dick Russell wanted to keep a low profile during the acrimonious
fight over the president's court bill in order not to emphasize his
disagreement with him. When Richard senior and Ina came to
Washington in May 1937 in order for his father to attend the annual Law
Institute, Dick was chagrined to read an interview in the *Washington Post*
with Georgia's chief justice that Richard senior agreed with the president
on the court plan. The son was irritated with his outspoken father, who
never seemed to take into account how his remarks might stir up trouble.
Not surprisingly, Richard Russell, Sr. was warmly welcomed by President Roosevelt at a White House reception. Georgia's junior senator
managed to fend off probing questions from the press, keeping his head
down, but he joined sixty-nine other senators who voted to recommit the
controversial bill to the Senate Judiciary Committee on 22 July,
effectively killing the measure.

In spite of the tensions associated with this parental visit, Dick
Russell, Jr. was pleased to see his mother and his sisters Ina junior, Pat,
and Billie embellishing the scene of a White House reception. The
women of the family were quite at home there, and he was proud of
them. In addition, his sister Margo and her husband, Jim Bowden, and
his brother Rob and wife, Sybil, were on hand because of the Law
Institute and another honor that was coming to the family.

From Washington, the pleasant family reunion continued in
Camden, New Jersey, where the USS *Savannah* was to be christened. The
Bowdens lived in Savannah and were well-known and active in their
community. Dick Russell, Jr. thought it appropriate that their fifteen-
year-old daughter, Jane Mayo, be invited to be the ship's sponsor, and so
the family was elegantly entertained by the shipbuilders. At a banquet
on the evening before the launching, Richard senior nearly choked to
death on a piece of meat. His sons Dick and Rob had to escort him from
the party, and he ended up in hospital for surgery to remove the food.
Richard senior was shocked that the doctor's bill was $500, but his son
Robert assured him this was the going rate. Everyone gave thanks for
their continued time with the beloved patriarch. Ina felt the gratitude for

this happy outcome put the hoopla surrounding the ship launching in proper perspective.

About a month later, the unthinkable threatened to happen. Although the family might have expected that Ina, seven years his junior, would one day have to live without Richard, no one had envisioned that she might precede him in death. In June 1937 Ina suffered a stroke, and although she recovered, she never regained her amazing energy. She had to proceed carefully, and for the first time she had full-time household help. Modine Thomas became a faithful cook and housekeeper. Ina Russell was the first woman in her eldest son's life, and the older he grew and the more women he met, the more he admired and respected her accomplishments in living so graciously with his father's many political campaigns and in rearing her many children to responsible adulthood. He was glad to pay for her to have help, and he was grateful to his sisters-in-law Sybil and Sarah, who were also on hand to help, living next door on either side of the Russell homeplace.

In fall 1937 Senator Richard B. Russell, Jr. of Georgia, as a member of the Battle Monuments Commission, was sent to Europe to dedicate battle memorials on the various battlefields where American troops had been engaged in World War I. Only a few days after returning home, he wrote in a letter to all his brothers and sisters:

> As a representative of the government of the United States on this solemn mission, I was thrown with many of the officials of France and England and associated with a class of people I had not known or met on my previous trip there as a tourist. We were royally entertained, not only at dinners and luncheons given by our own embassies and the various veterans' organizations, but also in the smaller communities recaptured by our troops from the Germans, where the people still remember and appreciate the brave Americans who brought the war to a speedy end.

It is typical of his character that Dick Russell was most impressed with the common people he met in the villages and believed that if they were in charge of the governments of France and England that they would be seeking to repay the war debts owed to the United States.

Unfortunately, according to Russell, "all the governments of Europe are [so] busy in expensive preparations for the next war, which most of them accept as inevitable, that they will probably never pay these just debts. May they serve as a reminder to keep us out of the next one."

Dick Russell was still of an isolationist mind, and he believed that privately and publicly a just debt should be paid. Another lifelong belief is expressed at the end of this letter, which he typed himself on his office typewriter and which was intended to make the rounds to every family member:

> I send my affectionate regards and best wishes to every member of our family circle, as wide as it is, and express the earnest hope that it will continue to increase in quality and numbers. I am exceedingly proud of every one of my fine nieces and nephews and hope that their parents will overlook no opportunities to instill in them the principle of the old French expression, noblesse oblige, which I first ran across when in about the fifth grade. (Pardon moralizing and advice. I get this way sometimes.)

As an eleven-year-old boy, Dick Russell had resonated to his first lesson in the aristocratic ideal of noblesse oblige,[4] and it is key to his character that he saw himself immediately as one to whom much had been given. The Russells had little in the way of material goods, yet the boy understood that nobility had to do with character, not money, and with a willingness to share the riches of intellect and education. He did not let early success in politics cause him to forget both sides of that equation. He worked hard to give as much as he received, and he thought this lesson worth passing on.

Because Walter George had openly fought the court plan and Roosevelt had other differences with George, the president decided it was time to get him out of the Senate and out of the executive hair. Believing he had enough power in Georgia to unseat George, Roosevelt decided, against advice to the contrary, to promote an opponent against the senior senator when he came up for reelection in 1938. Eugene Talmadge was making another run at the Senate, but obviously

---

[4] Often translated as "To whom much is given, much is required."

Roosevelt could not support this New Deal opponent, so he called Dick Russell to the White House and asked for his help in choosing someone to unseat George. The president promised Russell all the campaign funds he would need to elect another candidate to the US Senate from Georgia.

Roosevelt's presence and his personality, coupled with the respect due his office, made Dick Russell break out in a cold sweat as the president talked, but Roosevelt had not taken the true measure of the man he was propositioning. Russell was a man who had always made it a point not to get involved in other people's races. In spite of the presidential arm-twisting, he was clear in his refusal. "Only one senate seat in Georgia is my responsibility, Mr. President," he said, and he stuck to that position, even though he felt the presidential cold shoulder for many months after that.

To make matters worse, the opponent the Roosevelt camp chose was Laurence S. Camp, an old, valued, and trusted political friend. Camp was an early Russell supporter for Russell's first step up in the Georgia House to Speaker Pro Tem in 1923 and had helped manage aspects of Russell's campaigns for both governor and senator. Camp was in the crowd of Georgians who travelled to Washington to see Dick Russell sworn in on 12 January 1933. Nevertheless, Russell told his friend that he would have to keep silent and did. George easily defeated both Talmadge and Camp in the September primary. Georgians were satisfied to have a senior senator who was experienced yet conservative toward new deals and a junior senator who was willing to bend with the changing times. They had their bases covered.

When Dick Russell, Jr. trounced Eugene Talmadge in 1936, it made national headlines. The *New York Times* predicted that Talmadge's defeat was a sign that Southern demagoguery was on its way to extinction. Although there was reason to rejoice that Georgia so clearly supported Roosevelt and the New Deal, it was also true that Dick Russell, Jr. walked a razor's edge in appearing moderate regarding expanded federal power in economic policies yet archly conservative regarding changes in race relations in the South. Anti-lynching bills introduced in Congress in the years before World War II were a source of unusual stress for him. Russell abhorred lynching as the horrible crime that it was, and he feared it represented too well the specter of mob rule that his study of history underlined as the principal ghoul haunting democracies. Yet Russell was alarmed by the possibility of federal intervention in race relations. He saw anti-lynching bills that seemingly no one could object to as the first step in federal domination in the South regarding race questions. Following anti-lynching would come federal intervention in elections and then the abolishing of segregation on interstate public transportation, including eating facilities, accommodations, and restrooms. Also, there would be an attempt to enforce social equality in schools, hospitals, colleges, and other public institutions. Russell saw the striking down of state laws that prohibited interracial marriage as the worst development of all. Miscegenation haunted him more than anything else. He knew that members of the Communist Party had circulated ideas for breaking down "white supremacy," but in the Thirties he did not fear that "the colored people of the South" had fallen for such propaganda.[5]

It is worth noting that in the 1930s, "white supremacy" did not have the strong negative emphasis that it earned in the 1950s because of vicious acts of violence. Before the days of opinion polling and the rise of the influence of mass media, it is certain that many, perhaps the majority of, Americans believed in the inherent inferiority of the black race without wishing blacks ill. The brutalities and atrocities that black people suffered at the hands of a minority of white individuals were not part of the national consciousness, as they are today. An overall feeling that race relations were "not as bad as all that" allowed the violations of civil rights to continue. When the despicable treatment of black people in myriad aspects of American society became commonly known, there would be a change, and it would produce all the effects that Russell

---

[5] Fielding Russell, a rather mild-mannered man studying for a doctorate in English literature in Washington, wrote in the family letter about how anti-lynching debates affected him: "For one unaccustomed to senatorial debate, the anti-lynching filibuster was a genuine thrill. In fact, by the end of its first week I was ready to again secede from the Union. As it continued, I became feverish, began muttering in my sleep. On the first vote to invoke cloture I carried a razor, on the second I sneaked into the gallery with a razor and a pistol...." Although clearly exaggeration and humor was used for effect, this is a fairly accurate account of how most white Southerners viewed national attempts to meddle in their race relations.

feared. During his early career, however, Dick Russell, Jr. felt that his view was essentially benign and even progressive, because he supported segregation while genuinely encouraging black individuals to rise within their own sphere. The demagoguery of the South, on the other hand, regularly preached putting black people down in every way and did not condemn violence against them.

There is no doubt that Dick Russell, Jr. had a real affection and regard for the black people with whom he worked, they in their sphere and he in his. His willingness to stand up for his friend Arch Barnes, his aid to Modine Thomas, the respect he earned from the black staff at the Governor's Mansion in Georgia, and the strong relationships he had with various black workers in the nation's Capitol building during his entire Senate career attest to that fact. One of his first acts after coming to Washington was to secure a job on the cleaning staff at the US Post Office in Atlanta for a woman named Millie who had worked for him at the Governor's Mansion.

Believing the segregated way of life in the South as being inherently better than anywhere else in the country, Russell took it as his role to educate Northern senators (conservatives were his prime hope) that the South should be left alone to handle its racial problems. His reasoned and polite but passionate explanations of how federal interference violated states' rights were well-received in the Senate prior to World War II, and it is likely he believed he had succeeded in educating some leaders from outside the South. The star of civil rights was on the rise, however, and while World War II eclipsed it, after 1946 it would glow with greater and greater intensity until at long last the position taken by Russell and others in the South would stand muted in its shadows.

The year 1938 turned out to be a time of radical change in the life of Dick Russell, Jr. and in the life of the Russell family, in more ways than one. While his work in the United States Senate went on normally, and Georgia's junior senator continued to fight to support farmers, build up the nation's defenses, and search for ways to make government largesse fairer to the smaller earners, his personal life took a sharp turn. Dick Russell, Jr. fell in love.

Although Dick did not enjoy the formal Washington social scene and avoided it when he could, the social events he attended faithfully were those of the Georgia Society. Each year this group gave scintillating dinners, dances, and parties to unite Georgians living and working in Washington. Sometimes Dick liked to invite a sister, niece, or sister-in-law as his escort for these evenings, because then he could be free to wander around and do a little politicking. At one such event in 1937, though, he was guest of honor and so went alone. During the evening he was introduced to Pat Collins, a Georgia woman who had graduated second from law school at Emory in 1931, the only woman in her class. In addition to being highly intelligent, Pat was young, slim, vivacious, and pretty. Dick Russell, Jr. always had an eye for a pretty girl, and he took a few minutes to chat with Pat when she was introduced. What he learned was not comforting. Although Pat Collins had been working in Washington about two years by this time and had never met Senator Russell, she had a grudge against him.

Pat had done legal aid work in Atlanta in the years following her graduation from law school, but she had not found a firm that would take her on, thanks, in general, to the Great Depression. When the chance came for a government position in Washington, she questioned Smythe Gambrell, an Atlanta lawyer for whom she had done legal work, and he encouraged her to interview to work as a lawyer in the Department of Justice. He warned, however, that she would have to have "political clearance." Pat had not ever voted at that time, did not consider herself a Democrat or a Republican, in fact, and had no idea what "political clearance" was. Mr. Gambrell explained that she had to have the approval of her senators but added that he knew George and Russell well and for her not to worry about that part. He would take care of it. Pat did not worry.

Pat's interviews resulted in the offer of a job with the Department of Justice in 1935. Smythe Gambrell wrote to the two senators asking for her political clearance. Walter George replied with a cordial approval, but much to Mr. Gambrell's surprise, Dick Russell wrote that he could not endorse Patricia Collins. "Do you know Dick Russell?" a surprised Gambrell asked Pat.

"No," Pat answered, "I've never laid eyes on him, nor has anyone in my family had any dealings with him, as far as I know."

Gambrell did not understand the letter from Russell, but he wrote again and finally received a sort of grudging endorsement that enabled

Pat to have the job, especially in light of the gracious letter from Senator George.

Thus when Pat Collins was introduced to Dick Russell, Jr., who no doubt made a courtly remark about being proud to have such a pretty Georgian working in Washington, she couldn't resist. She quipped that yes, she was working in Washington, no thanks to him.

Looking at the decidedly attractive Collins, Dick Russell could not believe he would have done such a thing as fail to support her. As a guest of honor at the soiree, the center of attention, women vying for his ear, Russell had time only to ask why she had said that, and to hear her brief explanation of the withheld endorsement letter. Pat heard him say he didn't remember anything about it before he was swept away by the crowd. Well, at least she'd had her say.

Dick Russell did not forget Pat Collins or her report. A few days later, he called her and wanted to talk about this letter. It turned out that coinciding with her arrival in town, his administrative assistant, Leeman Anderson, who ran the office, had advised him not to give endorsements to people he did not know personally. Always somewhat indifferent to such protocol matters, the senator had allowed Anderson to introduce such a rule. Now he tried to explain this situation to Pat, and if she could understand and forgive him, he'd like to take her out. Pat excused him willingly, but the matter would remain a source of humor and teasing between them.

After Dick Russell had become governor at such an early age, the cynic in him wondered whether women were interested in him or in his office. Now, as Dick and Pat were seen together more and more on the social scene—they liked to go dancing at the Shoreham or out to eat in some of Washington's better restaurants—he began to feel he had met someone who cared about him for himself. Anyone could see how attractive Pat was, so he liked to introduce her to friends as "the smartest girl I've ever known." She had a challenging job, and she understood the complexities of law and government, which she could discuss in lively fashion with any lawmaker. Intelligence was a characteristic Dick Russell appreciated. It pleased him to have a woman so pretty and so smart as his girl. He sometimes called her up with a matter puzzling him, legislative history, for example, and he would ask her to look up old statutes in the Justice Department library, tasks she was happy to complete thoroughly. In addition to these matters, Dick Russell also told Pat his more intimate thoughts about things that happened in the Senate, his estimates of people, and his thinking about the future. He swore her to secrecy about these things, saying, "I haven't said this to a soul, and I don't want you to talk to a soul. I'll swear I never said it if you do tell it." The two became confidants and real friends.

Dick's courtship tactics did not change, in spite of the fact that he felt he had met a woman well worth courting. He continued to work long hours and to call Pat at the last minute for dates, and she accepted this pattern as part of his personality and his work ethic. Sometimes Pat would go down to hear the Senate in session. She had always found lawmaking fascinating, but now that she was seriously dating a senator, she was more interested than ever. Although Dick seldom debated in those years before World War II, she was pleased to see him on the Senate floor. Dick would look up and spot her in the gallery and send word for her to have lunch with him, or, if it was late, to go out for dinner at the end of the day.

Pat was on hand for some of the 1938 anti-lynching debate that had so stirred Fielding Russell. Although Dick Russell was not a leader of the Southern coalition at that time, all Southern senators were deeply involved in the defense of states' rights that the bill seemed to challenge, and a Southern-led filibuster blocked the legislation. On dates, Dick confided in Pat his fears that the changes to come in race relations would damage both black and white people.

Dick learned that his sister Ina, also a lawyer working in the government[6], had met Pat earlier and liked her very much. It was reassuring to Dick that Ina liked his sweetheart. It is doubtful that he asked Ina outright what she thought of Pat, but Ina was pleased with his choice and saw nothing but good on the horizon should they marry. Ina junior likely would have told him her opinion without being asked.

Whether Ina's judgment at this time could be considered reliable might have been in question, for after nearly twenty years as a Washington career girl, she was in love herself. For years Ina had answered queries as to why she was not married with the reply that she had not met a man for whom she would give up her name or her job. At

---

[6] Ina junior worked for the Veterans Administration.

the age of forty-two, she finally met a man she liked enough to consider marriage. When she met Jean Stacy, she felt she might be able to change her name for his. Giving up her job would not be necessary, at least not in the immediate future. Jean was a captain in the Army, stationed near Washington. In January 1938 Ina accepted a diamond engagement ring from Jean Stacy, and their wedding was set for 4 June 1938, in Washington. Dick and Pat enjoyed going out with Ina and Jean. Afterward they would end up at Ina's apartment for late-night breakfast. Pat sometimes visited Dick's apartment. She found his rooms were neat and rather bare, a true bachelor's dwelling, not a home.

In February, Ina senior fell ill again and spent almost a month in the hospital at Emory. Dick was comforted by reports on her condition from his sister-in-law Sarah. Expecting her first child in March, Sarah spent much time with her mother-in-law in the hospital to help with her care. On 16 March, she and Alex gave her a grandson, Alexander Brevard Russell, Jr. As a doctor, Alex had some special privileges in the hospital and so was able to take the new grandson to see his grandmother in her hospital bed. When she said that she had feared she would not see him "discover America," her doctor son predicted she would see the boy reach his sixteenth birthday.

Encouraged by this prognosis, Ina recovered, and she and Richard senior travelled to the capital for Ina junior's wedding. Richard senior was so feeble he was unable to escort his daughter down the aisle. Thus Dick became her escort for this sacred occasion. Another family wedding was scheduled for 15 June 1938. Brother Henry Edward, called Jeb, the thirteenth child, was to marry his college sweetheart on that date in Vidalia, Georgia. Ala Jo Brewton was Hugh Peterson's first cousin. Ala Jo and Jeb had met while both were working on one of Hugh's congressional campaigns, but Jeb had had to finish his seminary training to become a minister, and Ala Jo had been determined to finish college at Georgia State College for Women. Jeb was now the pastor of a Presbyterian church in McDonough, Georgia, and Ala Jo had just completed her degree.

Love was in the air. One evening, as Dick and Pat were chatting over the family weddings, Dick said, "Well, when are we going to get married?" Pat was amazed that he did not consider asking her first if she would marry him, but she was so much in love that all she could do was ask when he had in mind. Dick thought a summer wedding would be fine for them. Congress would be adjourned, and they could go to Georgia for the 3 July family reunion and announce their plans. Then they could be wed on 15 July. Pat was surprised but pleased. Neither of the pair appeared to worry about a honeymoon trip, where to live, or how to make their home together.

Although Pat was a devout Catholic, the couple did not see religion as a barrier to their union. Dick, having grown up under the tutelage of a person as deeply spiritual as Ina Russell, was comfortable with a woman to whom religion was important. He was still a Methodist and had no objections to almost any Christian doctrine, but formal religion had little importance to him. Prejudice against Catholics in the South was prevalent in this era, but Dick Russell had not let fear of public opinion regarding religion sway him in his choice of staff, having had Catholics working for him as governor. It is unlikely that he would have let such fear govern his choice of a wife. There was, however, a deep-seated family aversion to control by the church in personal or political matters.

When Richard senior had run for governor of Georgia in 1911 and the Women's Christian Temperance Union criticized his stand on alcohol so vociferously, Methodist and Baptist churches climbed on this bandwagon with flags flying. The result within the family was that Richard senior had left the Methodist Church and although raised a God-fearing and church-going man, he had not gone back to church for nearly ten years. Although Ina did not want to leave her church, she felt that she could not attend a church that would not accept her husband, and so she too had abandoned the Methodists. Dick knew that his mother valued her church life, and he understood the sacrifice this choice had meant for her. The family joined the Presbyterian church in the 1920s, and Ina wrote her children how happy it made her to sit once again in church with Papa, holding hands. During all this time, she had encouraged the older children to make up their own minds about which church they would attend. Dick and his sisters Billie, Ina, and Pat all chose to stay in the Methodist church.

At the time of the family reunion, Pat Collins and Dick went to Atlanta in early July to tell Pat's father about the engagement and impending marriage. Pat's mother was ill in a sanatorium at this time and there was never a question of anything but a private wedding. Pat's father, delighted that his daughter had snagged the state's most eligible bachelor, gave his blessing to the union readily. They decided on 14 July for the wedding, and Mr. Collins, a former newspaperman and friend of Ralph McGill, editor of the *Atlanta Constitution*, said he would write the engagement for the paper, to be released on 14 July. Inexplicably, Dick made only one request: that Pat not be identified as a lawyer in the newspaper announcement. Then the couple went to visit Pat's priest.

Pat was a member of Sacred Heart Catholic Church in Atlanta, where Father McGraff was pastor, and he granted the couple an interview on short notice. While Father McGraff was deferential and respectful to the senator, the priest made it clear that Dick would have to formally agree not to interfere with his wife's religion and to raise their children in the Catholic faith. This injunction came as a shock to Dick, and he felt ill-disposed toward it, but he did not say much about it that afternoon. In love, longing for the traditional union, Dick and Pat agreed that they could work out the religious rules to their satisfaction. They continued on their way to Winder for the family reunion.

By this time everyone in the family was married except Dick, William, and Carolyn. Grandchildren numbered nineteen. Because family reunions meant so much to their mother, everyone made the effort to attend, and it was a lively and large gathering of the traditional Southern variety. Ina was no longer able to supervise the kitchen for such a gathering, but daughters, daughters-in-law, and Modine cooked piles of fried chicken while watermelons cooled in washtubs full of ice water on the back porch. Caramel and coconut cakes, coleslaw, fresh sliced tomatoes, and potato salads adorned the kitchen. Family photos and even an early film show everyone smiling, energetic, and happy. After lunch at long tables in the pecan orchard, all were herded to the front porch for a photo that appeared on Sunday in the rotogravure section of the Atlanta paper. Three generations of Russells fill up the broad front steps. Dick is seated beside his mother, holding Mary Ina, the youngest grandchild, his beloved Rob's youngest child, only three months old.

Although news of the Russell-Collins love affair had gotten out in the family, Dick and Pat's coming announcement caused a stir at the clan gathering as everyone rejoiced with their brother. Pat felt a little self-conscious as Dick introduced her around as "the girl I'm going to marry," but she felt welcomed and accepted. Dick introduced his brother Jeb as the man who would perform their marriage ceremony, and Pat understood that if she were to marry Dick Russell, she would have to do it out of her church. She was so much in love that she decided she would not let the Catholic Church govern her choice of a husband.

The evening wore on with storytelling, laughing—the Russells loved good jokes and could tell them—and visiting. Pat marveled at how many people came and went on the front porch, in the living room, and in the dining room of the house, adults and children. Old Judge Russell sat in a rocker in the midst of all the activity, saying little, watching. Dick took his bride-to-be to meet his father and the three of them sat together talking. Or rather Pat and Dick talked. The judge did not say much, just looked at Pat with a kindly little smile. They told him about the meeting with the priest, and Dick mentioned the need to sign a paper promising to raise the children as Catholics and his objection to it. He said he wanted his children to make up their own minds about religion. Dick walked away a time or two, and then the judge asked Pat a few questions, listening attentively to her answers. When his son came back, he said quietly, "Dick, if you ever marry this girl, you're going to sign that paper."

The judge and Mrs. Russell went off to bed earlier than the children and grandchildren. The youngsters played a rousing game of Capture the Flag, chasing each other among the trees and shrubs in the dark yard, while the adults sat in the rockers or porch swings on the wide veranda, laughing and talking. Pat felt at home in spite of being a stranger to everyone except Dick and Ina junior. Well into the morning hours, they went to bed, Pat finding a bed with Carolyn in a room with several children. Pat slept soundly and woke late, surprised and a little embarrassed. When she went downstairs, she found Ina Russell making breakfast for the engaged couple in the kitchen. Dick had slept late as well, and the others had already eaten.

Mother Ina noticed that the pair did not eat much and commented on this fact. "Well," Dick said, humor in his voice, "Pat's in love and I'm not hungry." His mother laughed at this statement. Pat knew that mother and son had a close relationship, but she did not feel any animosity from her mother-in-law-to-be nor any lack of pride in his chosen one from Dick.

After breakfast, Dick drove Pat back to her home in Atlanta, but he said he was going to take a room at the Winecoff Hotel and have Maier and Berkele Jewelers send over some rings for her to choose from later in the day. When Pat joined him at the hotel, there were three trays of rings waiting for her. Dick had heard her say she liked a square-cut emerald and there were several of these but also many diamonds in traditional engagement settings. They went through the rings together, and Pat finally chose one, although she thought it was too expensive. Dick wanted her to have the ring she wanted and was not worried about the expense. Nevertheless, with his frugal nature, he would have been pleased at this awareness of the value of money in his bride.

Perhaps it was the expense or perhaps it was some other nameless thing bothering her, but Pat decided not to accept the ring that evening. It was only ten days until the wedding. They might as well wait until then to buy rings. Dick sent Pat to Washington on the train the next day, and he went back to Winder.

Back in Washington, Pat continued to prepare for the wedding, buying her wedding dress and other clothes. Yet she could not fail to recognize that deep down she felt hesitant. She had a friend who was a priest living at a Capuchin monastery near Washington, an old friend of her parents as well. She called Father Kirk and told him everything. Father Kirk invited her to spend a few hours in retreat at the monastery, and she did that. While she was there, the priest helped her to list on paper the advantages and disadvantages of this marriage. Then he went away to let her reflect in solitude. Later he told her that he had every priest at the monastery in chapel, praying that she would make the right decision. No one ever said what he thought would be the right decision. Pat left the monastery after several hours, still undecided, but within a day or so, she had made up her mind: She could not be married outside her church. She called Dick and told him of her visit to the monastery and of her decision.

Meanwhile, Dick had felt a certain reticence building. It grieved him to note that Ina senior did not "fall in love" with Pat Collins. When Ina said she had fallen in love with a prospective in-law, she meant she had a good feeling about him or her. About Pat Collins she had reservations.

Pat's people were from Brooklyn and Newfoundland before that, having moved to Atlanta when Pat was about twelve. Ina senior detected quickly that the young woman lacked a certain gentleness expected in Ina's idea of Southern women. As far as is known, Ina senior hinted at problems only with one question: Do you love her enough to accept that because she is Catholic, you might never be elected again to a statewide office in Georgia?

In the fever pitch of marriages and marriage plans during that at-home weekend, Dick Russell had seemed undeterred by thorns in the relationship. Sensing his mother's caution, he felt unsure. When the call came from Pat saying that she had been to see a priest again and that she could not leave her church, he was sympathetic but hurt. He had thought all was settled. In his experience, a wife might disagree with her husband, but in the end she abided by his wishes. This had been the pattern he had seen over and over with his mother and father. Ina Dillard Russell made her opinions known regarding political campaigns, educating the children, and building their homes, but she left the final decision to her husband and lived graciously with it.

Perhaps deep down Dick had not realized that few women in his modern world had been taught such a way to live the role of wife, and certainly not a young woman brave enough to go to law school and then to Washington to work in the Justice Department. To Dick it seemed a foregone conclusion that as a wife Pat would become compliant, but he was not one to risk the conflict that would result if she were not. Knowing how important her faith was to his mother and how she had suffered in the years when she did not attend church, Dick was loathe to ask Patricia to accept a way she found uncomfortable spiritually. To his sister Ina he likened it to asking Pat to cut off her arm. Nor did Dick Russell see himself accepting an injunction ordering his children to be reared as Catholics.

The couple phoned each other several times over the next two or three days, but neither could give in. In a mutual decision, they decided to call off the wedding. A hurried call was made to Ralph McGill at the paper, asking him to omit the article scheduled to run on 14 July. The editor was barely able to achieve this removal in time.

The couple was deeply in love, and each was hurt by this failure of their marriage plans. On 11 July, Dick Russell requested by telegram transportation to Panama via Army transport ship, leaving from Charleston, South Carolina. When he boarded the troop ship *St. Mihiel* on 18 July, a Charleston *Evening Post* article reported that the Georgia solon was unaccompanied and that he gave no special reason for the cruise.[7] Gossip about the impending union was certainly out, thanks to the engagement ring tray delivery to the Winecoff Hotel, but now the story had changed and no one was able to find out any details.

Dick wrote Patricia often from his escape to work and heal, letters of tenderness and affection, letters she would save for nearly seventy years, but he would never mention marriage again. When he returned to Washington a month or so later, the couple continued to see each other, but less frequently. They finally broke off completely because Pat felt remaining objective was too difficult. Unlike many couples deeply in love, they had let their heads rule their hearts, and bitterness did not gain a foothold in their continuing regard and respect.

The family was sympathetic to both people enduring this emotional ordeal, but Dick was like his mother in not revealing his feelings. Little was ever said about this painful broken engagement. He told his sister Ina that he would never ask another woman to marry him. Perhaps the irony of being a popular and pursued bachelor who couldn't get the woman he wanted to marry him did not escape him, and he was unwilling to risk that crucible again.

The grief of a failed love affair for Dick was soon eclipsed by a much greater sorrow. On the evening of Saturday, 3 December 1938, Dick Russell, Jr. was at a banquet in Coral Gables, Florida, as part of a congressional delegation touring Florida. An emergency phone call from his brother Rob interrupted the festivities to inform the senator that their father was dead.

Richard Brevard Russell, Sr. had worked that morning at his office in the state capitol, clearing his desk of all cases. Then he had come home

---

[7] Dick Russell would certainly have spent time on official matters during this trip. The US took a ninety-nine-year lease at Avenida Balboa in 1938, and in 1939 the US embassy was established there, upgrading the consular offices first opened in 1833. With his eye always on American defenses, Russell understood that the country should safeguard its investment in the Panama Canal.

on the train to Winder, eaten a simple supper prepared by his beloved Ina, and visited briefly with his eight-year-old namesake grandson, Richard B. Russell III, Rob's third child, before retiring to bed. Within a few minutes he had stopped breathing.

Nothing in his life had so shocked Dick. The entourage of the delegation arranged for a train in West Palm Beach bound for Atlanta to be held until the senator could get to it. Racing for the train, the car in which he was riding left the road and overturned. Dick crawled from the wreck, refused treatment for an injured knee, and insisted on continuing the journey. The second car reached the train safely, and by the next morning, Dick Russell, Jr. was in Winder. His injured knee meant that he could not walk over the farm with his brothers Rob and Alex to choose the site of what was to become the Russell Family Cemetery, but he approved of their choice of a small rise, visible from the kitchen window. Forgetting her frailty, remembering only her life of loving labor, the boys felt that perhaps it would comfort their mother to be able to see their father's grave as she went about her kitchen chores.

The body of the chief justice of the Georgia Supreme Court lay in state at the capitol on Monday, 5 December. For Dick Russell, Jr., watching the long lines of people who came to pay their respects was like watching his father's life of distinguished service unfold again. Although he admired his father as a man of brilliant intellect, classically educated, deeply learned, gracefully civil, and uncommonly wise, the eldest son remembered also how his father had cherished his title of the Great Commoner. Yet this man was so far from common that in the sixteen years he served as chief justice, his son had forgotten the close contact in the early years that his father had had with the man in the road, as newspaper reporter, solicitor general, superior court judge, country lawyer, and farmer. Now as Georgians came from all over the state to their capital city, to say a last farewell—men and women, old and young, rich and poor, some clothed in Sunday-go-to-meeting finery, many in their everyday work clothes—filing past the judge's bier in an outpouring of unparalleled affectionate esteem, his children recognized the scope of their father's life of service in a way they never had before. His eldest son, following in the patriarchal footsteps, would remember this grief-stricken but proud time, and the older he grew, the more he felt that he could never measure up to his father's standard.

The *Winder News* of 8 December reported the last rites on 6 December as equally moving:

> On a pine-studded knoll overlooking his home, Chief Justice Richard B. Russell, Sr. was laid to rest Tuesday, borne there by his sons[8], joined in their mourning by other members of the Russell family, a host of state dignitaries and hundreds of "just folks".... [S]cores of farmers and mill workers in overalls mingled with the great men of the state in paying their last respects.... Messages of sympathy were received from all over the nation, President Roosevelt...leading in the tributes.

To "Dear Dick," Roosevelt telegrammed his deepest sympathy, adding that "Georgia has lost one of her great sons and I have lost a dear old friend."

As the eldest son, Dick Russell, Jr. was clearly expected to step into the family leadership role. Although all the children rallied to make sure that their mother was well cared for, it was her eldest son who claimed without hesitation the place of patriarch. Knowing his deep affection for their mother and his love of family, no one questioned his right to make suggestions first as to how they should proceed. The judge had left a few debts, not all of which could be covered by insurance settlements. Brother Rob became the keeper of the business end of selling land or rental property to cover final debts. Then everyone pitched in to help with monthly finances, but none as much as Dick.

Ina Dillard Russell had never worried about money matters. She was a consummate manager of whatever funds were put at her disposal by her husband, and her ways did not change. Grateful for all she had, whether of material or emotional wealth, she held up well under the onslaught of grief that losing her husband brought. In January 1939, however, she suffered another attack, likely a stroke, and lay in a coma in Emory University Hospital for almost a month. The family despaired for her life, but one day she awoke, ready to go on with life without her partner of forty-seven years, ready to support their children and rejoice

---

[8] Six of the Russell sons served as pallbearers. Because of his knee injury, Dick was unable to fulfill this honor. It was his privilege to escort his mother.

in their successes as long as the God she believed in so faithfully should choose.

An outcome of this illness was that Rob and Dick suggested their mother write a will. Richard senior's will, written only three days before he died, had left everything to his wife. Having received this advice from her two learned lawyer sons, Ina got around to writing a will about a year later. By this time Carolyn and William were living at home, William farming and Carolyn teaching at Winder High School. Ina decreed that the homeplace be left to these two children because they did not have homes of their own nor comfortable incomes. Her decision did not sit well with the other children, especially the two lawyers, and they said so. Mildly amused, Ina said she thought it was up to her to do what she chose with the property. Then she asked what would happen if she did not have a will. Everything would be divided equally among your children, they answered, according to Georgia law. "Very well then," she said. "I will not write a will at all and you will have the chore of dividing it up when I'm gone."

In 1940 the Russell family gained another Judge Russell when Franklin Roosevelt appointed Robert Lee Russell, Sr. to the Federal Court of the Northern District of Georgia. For the confirmation of this appointment in the US Senate, Senator Walter George sponsored the new judge. Richard Russell, Jr., wanting no charge of nepotism to taint Rob's appointment, did not even vote during the confirmation process. Both as a brother and as an American, Dick Russell was pleased when Rob became a federal judge. His mother wrote him that it seemed natural to have another Judge Russell.

Following his father's death, Dick Russell went back to Washington and took up his work as Georgia's junior senator with renewed inspiration. The New Deal was winding down, and the world was gearing up for a war that would be more horrible than the wildest imaginings of even the most pessimistic historians. All eyes were turning from domestic to foreign problems. Yet Dick Russell did not forget that the farmers of the nation, and especially of his beloved Georgia, were not faring as well as other elements of society, nor did he forget that he was their advocate. A fierce patriot with a realistic vision of what was likely to happen in Europe, the Georgia senator struggled to balance gaining or retaining programs giving aid for farmers with expensive defense projects in the years leading up to America's involvement in World War II.

Each year Russell spent long hours getting the agricultural appropriations bill passed by arranging weeks of hearings, meetings with House leaders, and then conferencing with Senate leaders. These efforts required his now well-honed skills in negotiation and compromise. His reputation for integrity continued to grow as his fellow senators learned over and over that he could be counted on to make judicious and predictable decisions based on what he said he believed. Russell was willing to take unpopular stands as he moved agricultural appropriations bills through the Senate while trying to meet the demands of the Bureau of the Budget to lower expenditures. When he had to refuse numerous requests to fund favorite projects here and there, he sometimes doubted if any member of the Senate would speak to him when the appropriations bills were finally passed, because he had, in the name of economy, eliminated requests for research facilities, wildlife stations, and money for the study of plant and animal diseases.

American defense was a high priority with Dick Russell, Jr. ever since his work on the Committee on Naval Affairs from his first years in Congress. Always an isolationist, the Georgian did not want the United States to become involved in Europe's quarrels again, but if it did, he wanted to be ready. He made clear in speeches from the early 1940s that the coming conflict would be "a war of machines.... Raw courage alone cannot prevail.... The frontline of modern-day war extends from the fighting front to the assembly line."

Through the years Russell had been slowly building defense expertise. Congress adjourned in August 1939, but following Hitler's invasion of Poland in September, President Roosevelt called the legislators into extraordinary session to deal with the European war threat, a session that lasted into November. In January 1940, Congress reconvened with a busy schedule to consider the largest peacetime defense program to that point in American history. His unshakeable belief in the superiority of Anglo-Saxon culture sustaining his resolve, Russell's patriotism rose to noticeable early heights. From 1939 onward, he supported aid to Great Britain and backed the Selective Service Act of 1940 that gave the United States more armed men ready to fight.

In addition, Russell and Senator Overton, of Louisiana, had attached an amendment to the Selective Service Act of 1940 giving the president the power to draft factories/businesses needed for the war effort. Early in his public career, Russell had been appalled at the huge profits that were made out of war, and he had become convinced that if wars did not make money, the cause of peace would be promoted. In support of his selective service amendment, he said, "To achieve complete preparedness we should make available to the national defense the wealth, the industry, and the genius of America, as well as the vitality and lives of American manhood." He added that he hoped further legislation would make certain that "no vast fortunes are created while men are drafted at a dollar a day." Although the amendment suffered some setbacks, similar measures eventually were put into place.

In order to be ready for every possibility, Congress did not recess for the 1940 elections. Russell supported Roosevelt's decision to run for a third term, declaring it was not the time to switch horses to the untried Wendall Wilkie. Russell, who gained a reputation as a workhorse from the beginning, perhaps did not find the extended sessions Congress now worked a particular hardship. He missed having time to spend in Winder at the family home and in other parts of Georgia, but the call of duty had no onerous tone for Dick Russell.

1941–1945:
Making War and Planning the Peace Offensive

When the Japanese bombed Pearl Harbor on 7 December 1941, Dick Russell was as surprised as anyone else at the "infamy" of the attack. Sincerely supporting an isolationist stance, Russell and others had been shoring up American defense systems while trying to promote peace where it seemed possible. In his belief in the wisdom of the Founding Fathers, Dick Russell was sure that it was best for the United States to keep out of global conflicts except where they unquestionably affected our country. It would take the full-scale conflict of World War II to show him that withdrawal was no longer possible. Having continued long hours at work, having studied the defenses of his native land and pondered ways she could be made more ready for the conflict, Russell was prepared for a lead role in Congress during the struggle that began officially for the United States the day Pearl Harbor was attacked.

Indeed, boyhood dreams of fighting would come true for Dick Russell, Jr. in an unexpected way during this worldwide conflict. The senator got his chance at direct wartime service to his country when in July 1943 he found himself at the head of a Senate committee to visit the United States' worldwide military installations. Early in 1941 the Senate had established the Special Committee to Investigate the National Defense Program, better known as the Truman Committee (headed by Harry S. Truman, D-MO). The early purpose of this committee was to ensure that defense dollars were carefully spent. While Dick Russell, Jr., was overwhelmingly in favor of defense spending, he was also tight with the public's purse strings, and he supported the work of this committee, which likely saved as much as $3 billion at this critical time.

These early and wise ways of looking at military preparedness had made Russell, in spite of his relatively junior status, a natural selection as head of an investigative congressional committee that ultimately formed in 1943 to visit far-flung American bases to ascertain whether or not money was being well-spent. In spite of the successes of the Truman

Committee, the idea of extending investigation of military bases to overseas might have been judged too dangerous, too impractical, and too wasteful of the time of military commanders in the field. Nevertheless, by 30 June 1943, the Army had agreed that it could provide transportation and take care of no more than five senators for such a trip. The senators chosen in addition to Russell were Albert B. Chandler (D-KY), Henry Cabot Lodge, Jr. (R-MA), James M. Mead (D-NY), and Ralph O. Brewster (R-ME). Dick Russell, Jr., skeptical of congressional jaunts of any kind, was not thrilled to be made head of this group. He had hoped to spend the congressional summer recess in Winder, but he accepted the appointment and began preparing for the departure of 25 July.

Many of Dick's family were actively involved in the war effort by this time. As a family man, he was pleased when brothers, brothers-in-law, and nephews went into military service. His brother-in-law Jean Stacy, a career Army man, was sent to England by summer 1942 and remained there until late 1944. Gordon Green, sister Billie's husband, also career Army, had been working for twenty years on small arms inventions and held several patents. Under the Selective Service Act, brother Alex, a doctor, had been drafted in January 1941 to serve for a year. This duty was extended immediately and indefinitely when Pearl Harbor was bombed. Unmarried, brother William joined the Navy in early 1943 at the age of thirty-six and ended up in the Pacific. His twin, Fielding, the father of three, tried his best to join, but his weak eyesight and asthma kept draft boards turning him away repeatedly. Walter joined the Army at the age of forty and made the military a second career, staying nearly twenty years. Brother-in-law Jim Bowden, who had lost his trigger finger chopping wood as a young man, had been denied service in World War I. Now a bank executive with skills the Army needed in the paymaster division, Jim asked to join again, at the age of forty-seven. He was told that if he could survive basic training, he would be taken into the Army. Bowden completed basic training and served throughout the war in the paymaster corps as a finance officer, rising to the rank of lieutenant colonel.

The senator was undoubtedly almost as distraught as his brother Rob when, in 1943, Rob's son Bobby ran away and joined the Marine Corps at the age of seventeen. Neither man felt it was right to do anything to get him out once he was in.

Sister Carolyn married Ray Nelson in February 1942, and Ray, a Presbyterian minister, was called into the Navy as a chaplain.

One family member, the wife of his father's brother, John, asked Dick Russell, Jr. to help her keep her draft-age son and only child out of service. The senator's reply infuriated the matriarch. "It's my job to get them in, not keep them out, Aunt Addie," he said. For years thereafter the nephew dreaded seeing his aunt arrive for a visit at the homeplace.

Dick Russell had moved from the Hamilton to the Mayflower Hotel some years earlier, but when the hotel's employees went on strike, he left his rooms there and moved into his sister Ina's apartment. With Jean Stacy stationed in England, these arrangements suited the siblings for personal and practical reasons. They got along well, and each was keen to save money by combining living expenses. Because Pat Collins and Ina were good friends, and Pat and Dick still dated occasionally, the weekend breakfasts at Ina's apartment remained a pleasure.

Dick and Pat were each dating other people. In late 1941, Dick Russell wrote in his daybook that he had met Harriet Orr, noting that she was very nice. Within a week, he had asked her out. Harriet was also in a government job, working as a secretary for the Department of the Army. Dick Russell's daybook shows that during the next few months he dated Pat, Harriet, and Letitia, each about once a week. Having given up the idea of marriage, Dick seemed content to have several women to fulfill the duties that one wife would have been expected to achieve.

To prepare for the military inspection tour, Russell had to receive a variety of vaccinations, and in another preparatory move, he gathered names of Georgians at military bases he might visit. He planned to ask to meet these soldiers, sailors, and Marines and then to let their families know about their circumstances. This became a lifelong habit with him, one much appreciated by family and servicemen alike. Although his mother was not one to complain nor express worry, Russell knew that anxiety was keen among women left at home, and if there was some little way he could relieve some of that, he wanted to do it.

The touring senators had to be outfitted as soldiers. In addition to taking business suits for dress occasions, they were supplied Army clothes to wear when visiting field operations or flying over enemy territory. Should they be captured, the Army wanted to be sure they were treated as prisoners of war, not as spies. Each man was provided with a "dog tag," helmet, compass, knife, booklets on jungle survival, and emergency rations. The "admiral of the Oconee," who had not left Athens during World War I, knew this historic trip was as close to the real thing as he would ever get.

On 24 July 1943, Russell lunched with President Roosevelt, who was intensely interested in the project and at the same time worried about the senators' safety. One stretch of the journey involved a 3,200-mile flight across water, and the president needed to be reassured by Secretary of War Robert P. Patterson that the four-motored converted Liberator bomber in which they flew could make this distance with fuel to spare. When the Liberator, named *Guess Where II*, took off the next afternoon from Washington National Airport, it was a delight for Russell to discover that the pilot was a Georgia man, Captain Henry Myers. It was typical that Dick remembered as much about Henry Myers—perhaps more—when he recalled the trip as he did about meeting the king and queen of England.

The *Guess Where II* flew over Labrador, Greenland, and Iceland with only fuel stops before landing in England, where they were to stay about ten days. They had dinner with the king and queen and visited with Prime Minister Churchill and Anthony Eden, the British foreign secretary. To Russell, however, the highlight of this part of the trip was spending time with the Eighth Air Force, talking with the men about their service and assuring them of support from home. One of the ideas Russell would take back was that of establishing "tours of duty" of known duration in order to give the men hope for respite.[1]

On the morning of 7 August, the senators arrived in Morocco and were met by General Arthur Wilson, General Eisenhower's representative. Eisenhower had written Russell earlier that urgent military matters would prevent his welcoming the senators in person. No one was offended. From the beginning they had wanted to make sure that the committee's work did not interfere with military exigencies.

Their first big event was a dinner with the pasha of Marrakech at his palace. Although Dick Russell had been to Versailles and other palaces in Europe, he found this royal abode unforgettable for luxury. At dinner,

---

[1] Although a given in today's military climate, this was a novel idea in 1943.

Senator Russell, as head of the committee, was seated on the pasha's right. He wrote to his mother that he thus suffered from the Arab custom by which the host reaches into the common dish and serves the person sitting to his right. The guest is obliged to eat what is served him. Dick came away feeling like a stuffed pig. The pasha was impressed that the Southern gentleman was able to sit so long on the floor with legs folded, conversing pleasantly. The other senators had been obliged to get up and walk around. The Arab ruler had not seen many Americans able to do as Russell had done. Complimenting his guest on his manners, the pasha presented the Georgian with an ornate saber and case when dinner was finished.[2]

A tourist detour was taken to Casablanca on the Atlantic before the senators toured important cities and military installations along North Africa's coast. On 11 August 1943, General Eisenhower entertained the group at a dinner in Algiers, giving them a chance to talk about military matters. As always, Russell made it a point to talk with ordinary soldiers in order to get their views. He posed with soldiers from Georgia for photographs that were later sent to the men's hometown newspapers.

As an ardent proponent of Anglo-Saxon culture, Russell saw nothing to admire in North African cities. He wrote home that Arab cities were indescribably filthy, and he did not believe that an American could survive there for more than two or three days, even after receiving as many shots as he had. To himself he made notes about the squalor and mixed races. The stark contrast with American life made him grateful for his heritage and deepened his resolve to preserve what he saw as the superior American way. When their plane flew over the fertile crescent between the Tigris and the Euphrates rivers, mythic site of the Garden of Eden, Dick Russell was moved to write to his mother that the region must have greatly deteriorated (it had), and anyway, for him, the Garden of Eden was his homeplace in northeast Georgia.

After visiting Cairo, the party went on to Basra and Abadan on the Persian Gulf, then flew on to Karachi, New Delhi, and Assam, in

---

[2] When the saber was bequeathed to a niece after the senator's death, Mary Willie Russell Green added to the story by telling how she had heard that the pasha cut the saber from the uniform of a soldier standing guard that evening in a dramatic display of his approval of the senator's conduct.

northeast India. From there they flew to China, where their work involved meetings with Generals Joseph Stilwell and Claire L. Chennault, as well as with Chiang Kai-shek and other Chinese officials. A pleasant interlude for Dick Russell was dinner with Madame Chiang Kai-shek, whom he had first known when she was a student at Wesleyan College in Macon. The senator, thinking he was paying a compliment, told the general that seeing his lovely wife again made Russell regret his own single status. Immediately he sensed that the general was neither amused nor pleased. Nevertheless, Madame presented him with an exquisite Chinese bowl at some time in their friendship, and it remained a prized possession all his life.

In notes he scribbled to himself, Russell had nothing good to say about the Chinese, however, and he evidently let his prejudice against the Japanese have full sway. When someone proudly offered him—a soldier?—the severed ear of a killed Japanese sniper, he accepted the object. When he arrived back in Winder he would show the ear to his doctor brother who was embarrassed by it, not knowing how to respond.

In India, Russell judged that morale was low among American troops because they did not have enough to do. On the other hand, he found morale high in most places they visited, and his conviction that American military forces were doing their job well was strengthened. The most shocking revelation for him was realizing the enormous difficulties of transport and supply. In China, for example, he despaired of being able to supply General Chennault. In this global conflict, the hard facts of any conflict were intensified almost beyond belief. He did not doubt that American forces would prevail, but he understood that the way would be long and arduous. When he returned home, he warned against overconfidence.

From China the committee flew to Calcutta, where they stayed an extra day because of engine trouble. Whether this was before or after the only truly frightening incident of the trip is not known, but there was one white-knuckle moment. Flying over Burma, the plane suddenly began to lose altitude, free falling, as far as an inexperienced flight man like Dick Russell could tell. Ice might have collected on the wings or the plane might have encountered a wind shear that disabled its flying ability. They plummeted in darkness for what seemed an eternity before the plane began flying again. Back home, Dick Russell reported that those seconds or the minute that passed before the plane flew level again taught him more about prayer than had forty years of attending church.

The *Guess Where II* made the long flight from Ceylon to Carnarcon on the west coast of Australia without incident. This was the first time anyone had flown nonstop over the vast Indian Ocean in a land-based plane, and this was the leg of the trip that had worried President Roosevelt. In Australia the committee visited several installations and moved on to General MacArthur's headquarters in New Guinea. Russell was impressed with MacArthur's understanding of how the conflict was developing and wished he could have had recordings of the general's lengthy discussions. Then the Liberator made its way across the Pacific, reaching Washington on 28 September, sixty-five days after leaving.

Nothing could express how glad Dick Russell was to be home. He told a reporter that he would not go again for $50,000 but that he would not have missed that trip for a million dollars.

Back in Washington it seemed that any trouble associated with the trip was going to happen on American soil. Russell announced, as the committee had agreed, that a report would be forthcoming, but until the Senate was informed in executive session, findings would be kept secret. To his chagrin, a week before the scheduled secret session, Senator Lodge gave his account of the trip from the Senate floor. Although clearly Lodge had violated an agreement among the committee members and Russell felt his behavior was irresponsible, the Georgia senator would not criticize a colleague in public. There was nothing Russell could do except regroup and try to regain control of his committee. After the executive session, his colleagues quoted him before the formal report was prepared, when proceedings still should have been kept secret. It was particularly embarrassing to see his criticisms of American Allies appear in national papers.

Russell then prepared a ten-point statement on the group's findings and had it inserted into the *Congressional Record* on 11 October. On 28 October, Senator Russell appeared before a well-filled Senate chamber to give his own personal report. His report and the previous statement represented roughly the same conclusions. As a fact-finding mission, the trip had certainly shown the country that American troops were well-supplied and cared for, and it made clear that a postwar foreign policy ought to be established as soon as possible. Dick Russell had been impressed, even alarmed, by the relief and assistance that many countries were expecting from America following the war. The nation would need foreign policy leadership that was tough and dedicated to national interests. Although he understood perfectly that America's age-old isolationist stance could not be maintained in this era of rapid, ever-improving sea and air transport, he wanted to be sure that American interests came first.

Russell believed that it was going to be necessary for the security of the United States to maintain many of the military bases abroad "purchased with the blood of American boys," and he spoke emphatically in favor of demanding control of these bases when the war was over. This was also the conclusion of the committee, and critics soon countered with charges of imperialism. Russell denied that this was imperialism, but whatever you chose to call it, he said, it was a realistic assessment of what would be necessary for national security in the future. These criticisms did not bother Dick Russell. He was sure that his observations were sound and in the national interest.

Regarding his embarrassment over his remarks critical of Great Britain and Russia, Russell defended himself appealingly. On 10 December 1943, the *Washington Times-Herald* carried a cartoon showing the Capitol Dome and the Washington Monument in the background and Uncle Sam surrounded by schoolchildren in the forefront looking at a sign that read, "In the words of Senator Russell: We have come to a pretty pass if a citizen of the United States cannot support with wholehearted devotion the cause of his own country without subjecting himself to the charge that he is anti-British or anti-Russian." Wholehearted devotion to the American cause remained a hallmark of Dick Russell's record in the complicated period following the end of World War II.

Dick Russell's wartime work benefitted his state enormously. He had success in helping expand old federal facilities in Georgia and in bringing new ones to the state. Fort Benning, near Columbus, Georgia, greatly enlarged its training operations and would become the principal center for infantry training following the war. A large air depot was completed south of Macon in 1942 that would become Warner Robbins Air Force base. Shipbuilding at Savannah and Brunswick gave jobs to thousands. Bell Aircraft established a huge bomber plant that opened in Marietta in 1943, later to become Lockheed. All such facilities stimulated Georgia's economy for decades and still do.

Wartime changes giving black workers more rights directly affected Georgia because of the millions of federal dollars Russell funneled into his state. There simply were not enough white workers to take the many jobs that opened up, and the result was that black individuals began acquiring skilled jobs, deteriorating the status quo that had maintained the Southern way of life Dick Russell revered. It is impossible to think that he did not realize this, but he also understood the need for work and his ability to provide jobs for all Georgia's citizens, black and white, through these facilities. His faith in Georgians as a whole overrode his fears of racial integration.

As an agriculture advocate, as the farmers' friend, no greater champion in the US Senate than Dick Russell emerged during the Depression and war years. One of the most lasting pieces of legislation that he fostered, the only one that he wished ever to receive credit for, was the school lunch program. As early as 1935, Russell had seen the wisdom of having the United States government buy surplus farm products to feed American school children. This brilliant idea helped farmers and education, two of Russell's favorite causes. Although the idea was not terribly difficult to promote, funds to allow its continuance had to be found year after year. Wartime demand for farm commodities pushed prices up for farmers, and full employment and good wages during World War II made some leaders consider dropping the school lunch program. As chairman of the subcommittee on agricultural appropriations, Russell kept working to increase funds for the program. In July 1943, for the first time, Congress passed legislation making a specific appropriation for school lunches, and by 1944 school lunches were being provided for 3.8 million children. Dick Russell kept working to pass permanent school lunch legislation, but none of his efforts for permanency were successful before the war ended.

Throughout the war years, Dick Russell's pride in the achievements of the American fighting man grew, and the senator believed American soldiers deserved greater recognition. His world view now included the grim realization that America would carry a heavy responsibility in the postwar world in maintaining future peace, and he gave much thought to fulfilling this responsibility while ensuring the well-being of Americans. Distressed on his trip to hear nation after nation talking as if America had an unlimited supply of money and goods from which others could dip, he continued to promote the idea that postwar plans must not lose sight of American interests.

Dick Russell had had no serious opposition for reelection in 1942, and the presidential election of 1944 was rather quiet, in spite of the historic significance of a fourth term for Roosevelt. Although the president was clearly ill, Americans were unwilling to contemplate changing leaders. The end of the war in Europe appeared more and more likely as Allied forces marched across France almost into Germany following the invasion of Normandy in June 1944. When Hitler launched a surprise winter offensive in December 1944, the Allies were caught off-guard, and American forces were overrun, with thousands of US soldiers taken as prisoners of war. For a few days it seemed possible that Germany might maneuver into a position strong enough to gain bargaining for something besides the unconditional surrender demanded by Great Britain, Russia, and the United States.

The encounter that became known as the Battle of the Bulge was in its darkest days for Americans when Congress adjourned on 19 December 1944. Returning to his Winder home for Christmas, Dick Russell was worried, both nationally and locally. He knew that his youngest brother Alex, a doctor in the 107th Army Evacuation Hospital, was somewhere near the borders of France, Belgium, and Luxembourg, where the battle was raging. It would be almost a month before the country breathed a sigh of relief as Allied forces held and were once again pushing back the Nazi armies. The Russell family learned in a brief V[ictory]-letter from Alex late in January that the 107th had been very busy but had escaped any lasting damage from the invading forces.

As 20 January 1945, approached, it was decided that this was no time for parades that would waste precious gasoline nor would the usual luxurious and self-indulgent parties following an inauguration be appropriate. Consequently, the ceremonies, usually staged in Congress, were planned for the South Portico of the White House. This would be a short, simple ceremony with few people in attendance. The official crowd of legislators and invited guests stood in the snow below the porch, and across the river the general public watched while Roosevelt delivered his fourth inaugural address. Not until later would it become known that the president's failing health was another consideration in this decision. Harry Truman, a colleague of Dick Russell's for ten years in the Senate, was sworn in as vice president.

Dick Russell invited his niece Jane Bowden, a recent college graduate, to attend the inauguration as his guest. Jane noticed that the president was whisked away as soon as the ceremony was completed, but Congress was invited to lunch at the White House. Jane admired the way Mrs. Roosevelt shook hands with everyone in her husband's place.

Roosevelt attended the Yalta Conference in February 1945 to discuss with Russia and Great Britain how to deal with Germany following surrender. In later years Dick Russell felt that the president's ill health accounted for some of the decisions made there. In the spring, with the end of the war in Europe anticipated almost daily, Roosevelt decided to go to Warm Springs, Georgia, to regain some strength. On 12 April 1945, late in the afternoon, Americans across the country began to hear on their radios the devastating news: Franklin Roosevelt had died of a cerebral hemorrhage at his Georgia residence at Warm Springs, known as the Little White House.

Like his countrymen, Dick Russell gasped at the painful void left when this courageous leader fell. Words were inadequate to express what needed expression, but Georgia's senator tried: "In this critical hour of human history, there is no way to measure the magnitude of loss the cause of civilized society has sustained by the passing of President Roosevelt."

HARRY S. TRUMAN: 1945–1952

"Power is a heady wine and if a man partakes of it for a while down there at the White House, most of them lose their humility. I've never seen any of them keep it for very long; [nevertheless] the man [Truman] developed tremendously in the Presidency."[3]

—Richard B. Russell, Jr. on Harry S. Truman

---

[3] Richard B. Russell on Harry Truman, "Georgia Giant" documentary.

The nation and the world mourned the passing of a great American president, but the wartime work of governing proceeded inexorably. Richard Russell and Harry Truman had served together for ten years in the US Senate, with Russell having only two years' seniority on Truman. Their desks on the Senate floor were near enough for them to speak often, and although Russell would not have said they were close friends, they had always been cordial. In Congress Dick Russell heard Harry Truman, now the thirty-second president of the United States, ask, with sincere humility, for prayers of support as the banner of the fallen commander-in-chief passed into his hands. Russell's vision of patriotism included strong but thoughtful backing of the president, and he stood ready to do his utmost for a man he knew to be modest but capable. Having worked with Truman closely on military oversight matters, and impressed with Truman's sincerity in this momentous change, partial to anyone who had a farming background, Russell might have been more optimistic than many about the new president's ability to carry the flag forward. By early May 1945 the news from Europe was so good that President Truman prepared his "victory in Europe" speech even before the European war was declared officially over on 7 May 1945. There was still the war in the Pacific to finish, but surely the worst was over.

On 25 May 1945, another group of United States senators set off for the European and Mediterranean theaters of war to investigate conditions there. As temporary chair of the Committee on Appropriations, Dick Russell recommended himself as the representative from that committee to join this group. Intensely interested in how the postwar policies would unfold, he wanted to be involved in such matters as redeploying troops in the Pacific theater, assigning surplus war supplies, assessing battlefields and port facilities, and discharging troops.

The senators arrived at Orly, France, on 26 May, and after two days of official functions and relaxation in Paris, they went on to Normandy, where so much hard fighting had occurred the year before. Russell managed to get in touch with Alex Russell, who was serving in a general hospital in northern France at the time, and had him come to Paris. The brothers had a joyous reunion. Although Senator Russell had to have dinner with the American ambassador to France, leaving his brother to dine with Senator Harry Byrd and his son, they were reunited later for a sortie to the Follies Bergères.

Russell asked that his brother accompany them as they went into the heart of Germany, where the senator saw firsthand the devastation of ordinary towns and cities that this monumental conflict inflicted on European civilization. Not immune to the conqueror's pride, they also visited Hitler's retreat at Berchtesgaden. To Dick Russell, however, one of the most memorable moments occurred only a little while after they crossed into Germany. In a roadside field, he saw an older woman pulling a plow guided by a young boy. The conquering senator from the United States got out and went to question the pair, through an interpreter. He learned that they were grandmother and grandson, trying to plant their spring garden. This witness of common people determined to affect overwhelming circumstances stayed with him.

This congressional visit was judged much more frivolous than that of the earlier committee, though Russell spent more time with military leaders than most of his colleagues. In addition, Russell and Senator Burnet Maybank (D-SC) tried to make a trip into Russia, eager to learn more about the ally about whom they knew so little. Russell had learned that the Russian embassy in Paris had approved the committee's visit, having cleared visas for the party. Six senators, however, declined to make "a quick friendship" visit to Russia, and when Russell and Maybank indicated that they wanted to visit, the Russian government refused to approve only two senators' visas. When the Russian diplomatic services stalled, the Georgia senator returned to the States. Surprised by the lack of diplomatic sense the Russians displayed, Russell had hoped to cement better Russo-American relations with more contacts. Now he felt that Moscow was more suspicious than friendly. In the end, Dick Russell did not claim that the nation gained much from this congressional postwar trip.

Sometime during this trip, Dick received alarming personal news. His nephew, Robert Lee Russell, Jr., a Marine corporal and eldest child of his brother Rob, had been wounded during the battle of Okinawa, which began 1 April and ended 21 June 1945.[4] The island, less than 400 miles from the main island of Japan, was taken in order to have a strong place

---

[4] Okinawa would, in fact, become the last battle of the war.

from which to launch the invasion of the Japanese homeland that everyone believed it would take to end the war. Young Russell, a radio operator, suffered a serious chest wound, victim of Japanese sniper fire. Reports from Navy doctors and from his brother Alex assured the senator that it was a familiar kind of wound for which treatment was optimistic.

No one could predict in summer 1945 how long the war in the Pacific would continue, and Dick Russell wanted to be sure that the Japanese were punished to a degree that would leave no doubt they were totally defeated. He urged unconditional surrender and trying Emperor Hirohito as a war criminal. Following the Potsdam Conference, in late July the United States and Great Britain issued an ultimatum of unconditional surrender to Japan, which included getting rid of its military leaders, an American military occupation, and disarming. These demands were rejected by Japan, and on 6 August 1945, the first atomic bomb was dropped on Hiroshima. The next day Japan claimed to accept the Potsdam Declaration, but ignored the demand for unconditional surrender and retained its emperor.

From his home in Winder, Russell wired the president to continue carrying the war to the Japanese until they begged for unconditional surrender. Truman and Russell were far apart on their approaches to a defeated Japan. Truman replied that he knew Japan was a terribly cruel and uncivilized nation in warfare, but he could not agree that we should act the same as they did. It was not right to destroy entire civilian populations because of the pigheadedness of their leaders, Truman judged. On that very day, however, President Truman ordered a second atomic bomb dropped on Nagasaki, and by 15 August, Emperor Hirohito announced acceptance of the terms of the Potsdam Declaration.

On 2 September 1945, the formal surrender ceremony was broadcast from the battleship USS *Missouri* (President Truman's home state), with General Douglas MacArthur, Supreme Commander Allied Powers, directing the scene. National pride was at its peak when the newsreels reached America, showing the Japanese humbly signing the parchment documents, followed, in turn, by the victorious commanders of military forces from the United States, China, Russia, Great Britain, Australia, New Zealand, and Canada.

Dick Russell was as proud as anyone, and he looked forward to his responsibility to ensure that in the postwar era, America would remain strong enough to deter those who might believe another war advisable. He was under no illusions that this would be a simple task. The fight would go on. As Russell stated, "We are now engaged in the great struggle to build the machinery for a permanent peace.... We must resolve to contribute as patriotically and as unselfishly to the peace offensive as did the men who stormed the beaches of Normandy and Iwo Jima."[5]

By the end of World War II, Dick Russell had been in Washington for thirteen years. Only nineteen senators had more seniority. His work ethic, his ability to compromise, his respect for the Senate and its traditions, his understanding of how parliamentary procedure made democracy work, and his patriotic vision for his country had earned him the respect of his colleagues. Russell's ability to keep secrets and to stand by his word had earned their trust. He was still Georgia's junior senator, somewhat in the shadow of Walter George, who had been in the Senate nearly thirty years, but Dick Russell preferred to work in the background. He was not concerned that he was known as a regional spokesman, taking up for the farmer, the school child, and the states' rights of the white South. By his understanding, this was the work he had been sent to Washington to do.

Throughout his long career, Dick Russell never lost sight of the electorate that had sent him to the post he so valued. When asked to do something for an interest outside Georgia, as opposed to what he considered best for his state or what he knew the state wanted, he was quick to point out that he was sure that Georgians had sent him to the Senate to be Georgia's voice in Washington, not Washington's voice in Georgia.

Russell was uninterested in self-promotion. At best he was suspicious of newspaper reporters, and at worst he disliked them and avoided all contact if possible. He never called a press conference to gain publicity, and it would be the late 1950s before he was persuaded to hire a press secretary. When he had time off, Dick went home to Georgia and

---

[5] Speech to University of Georgia alumni, 13 June 1946.

travelled his beloved state, making speeches in low and high places. He did not charge for these speeches, or accepted only small honoraria, in spite of the lucrative side income they could have produced. To him, this was part of his job.

When Colonel Jean Stacy was sent home from Great Britain late in 1944, ill with diabetes, Dick Russell moved from Ina junior's apartment back to the Mayflower Hotel. Still dating Pat Collins and Harriet Orr, but not exclusively, he continued to have many women friends and to visit his sisters in their homes in the Washington area frequently. These family times were precious to him, but he became less and less likely to accept invitations involving the official Washington social scene.

It was with sorrow that the whole family realized during this time that Ina Russell was no longer able to travel to Washington to stay with her daughters and give all the Russells in the area the tonic of her lively presence. After a serious illness in late 1941, she had come to Alexandria, Virginia, for a prolonged stay with her daughter Billie in 1942. Dick hosted the family at a meal in a fine restaurant, a festive gathering. Afterward an unknown gentleman stopped Billie and asked the identity of the lovely woman who had made them laugh so often. They all missed their mother's presence, but perhaps none as much as Dick. Ina Dillard Russell remained mentally as bright as ever, but her physical health continued to decline. Several times late in the war and immediately afterward, the family had hired a live-in nurse to care for their mother. Ina remained her eldest son's most stabilizing feminine force, as well as the person whose life and work he most admired.

In 1946 the family suffered two painful changes that occurred on the same day. Early in the year the family received the shocking news that Patience Elizabeth Russell, Pat Peterson's namesake and the six-year-old daughter of Alex and Sarah, was ill with a virulent leukemia. Dick Russell made a special trip home to see his niece and his brother's family in the spring. Congress had adjourned for the summer, and he was home when the little girl died on 17 July 1946. Hugh Peterson, Sr., Pat's husband, was in a congressional reelection battle on this date in Georgia's First District, and he lost the election in a race so close that a recount was requested. Brother Rob arranged for his sister to come from south Georgia to the funeral and return the next day to support her husband as votes were recounted. The close-knit family held together in love and grief, confirming again Dick Russell's admiration for the kind of people his mother and father had produced.

Just before America entered the war, the family erected an imposing obelisk to their patriarch in the family cemetery that was started when Richard Russell, Sr. died in 1938. They put down markers for the two children that Richard and Ina lost in 1905 and 1906, beside the patriarchal grave. Now little Patience would be the next family member interred there.

During this period, brother William was farming on the homeplace, and the young black couple Grant and Modine Thomas continued to live and work there. Modine had been, and would continue to be, dependable help, despite the demands associated with starting her own family. Dick Russell treasured the way the Thomases responded to the family's troubles, and he was pleased to come home to still find mules in the barnyard, fields being plowed, crops sown, and gardens growing.

This gentle working union of blacks and whites, based on hierarchy, personified the South that Dick Russell idolized, a land that some say never was, in one sense, but a land that many knew well and would/could not deny. Brother William had particularly amenable relationships with the black laborers on the farm, and black individuals throughout the county respected him perhaps more than the elder patriarchal brother and senator. Although William, like everyone else, was having trouble making a living at farming, the fact that he lived at home made it possible to keep trying. Everyone was reluctant to see land that their father had begun to farm fifty years earlier taken out of production. William was saving to buy his own farm, and Alex, living next door, had bought two small farms. Dick Russell also bought land but teased his doctor brother about making so much money he had enough to pour down a black hole by buying Barrow farms.

Although his salary of $10,000 annually was ample for the times, Dick Russell, Jr., did not change his tightfisted way with his money. Not only did he refuse honoraria for speeches, but his expense accounts for trips were miniscule. In addition, following the elections of 1942 and 1948, when he had no serious opposition, he returned money donated on a pro rata basis. The idea of keeping extra campaign money and spending it on himself in any way, as congressmen and senators were beginning to do, was beyond any idea of ethics and morality with which he could be comfortable. Although income taxes had gone up considerably in the war years, he paid his without complaint.

Dick Russell was as tight with the taxpayer's money as he was with his own, as his Washington staff knew well. The size of his staff nearly doubled in his first ten years in office, and by the end of the war his staff numbered about ten. As time went on it was recognized that he hired fewer people than almost any other senator, and their salaries might remain the same for as long as six years. Occasionally he hired a relative, but always in a temporary position, or he found him or her work in another department. It was well-known in the family that he expected more work from kin than from non-kin. Often these temporary positions were with the post office department, but Senator Russell expected brothers or nephews to finish their work at the post office and then come to his office to put in an extra unpaid hour or two.

Russell's staff worked long and hard hours. Because he himself put in such long hours, they, of necessity, did too. Ten- or eleven-hour days were common. Russell regularly worked from 9:00 A.M. until 6:30 or 7:00 P.M. and at least one staff member would stay with him in case he needed help. He enjoyed a drink of Jack Daniels whiskey at the end of the day and might be in the office until 8:00 P.M. before going out to dinner. Russell did not invite staff member to have a drink with him. He worked most Saturday mornings and often into the afternoons, and staff had to take turns working on weekends. Staff members wished he would marry so that he would stop spending so much time in the office.

In 1947 perhaps the last chance that he might ever marry evaporated when, much to his surprise, Pat Collins married someone else. Notes in his engagement books show that Pat and Dick had continued to be close throughout the war years. In early 1947 Dick was invited to Pat's apartment for a dinner with friends, to which he gladly went. Afterward he wrote that "Sal Andretta plays the piano marvelously." A few months later Patricia wrote to Dick that she and Sal were to be married. He responded that he was shocked but that he wished her all the happiness in the world and that he stood ready to do all that he could "for you and yours." Notes he scribbled trying to write this letter to his former fiancée show the pain he must have felt.

Although Dick Russell might not have made this decision consciously, by this time it is clear that he was more and more married to his job as Georgia's senator and to the United States Senate as an institution. As time went on, he understood more deeply the processes of the American governmental system, and he appreciated its unique qualities. He was thrilled and honored to be a part of governing within a body he respected as much as he did the US Senate.

Throughout 1946 to 1948, Russell of Georgia continued to fight for his school lunch program, farm legislation, soil conservation, and an increased minimum wage. He could not understand how anyone could justify reducing funds to the lunch program or soil conservation. By February 1946, following a House bill, the Senate presented its own permanent school lunch legislation, a bill that was essentially Russell's. Russell defended his measure by saying it could contribute more to the cause of public education "than any other policy adopted since the creation of free public schools." Russell was indignant when Senator Robert Taft (R-OH) objected to the cost. He stated that Congress had just appropriated $2.7 billion for overseas relief without batting an eye. Would they now split hairs over help for American children?[6] On 4 June 1946, President Truman signed the Russell-Ellender School Lunch Act into law. Senator Ellender of Louisiana had stayed with Russell throughout this long road to a national school lunch program, and it is typical of Russell that he shared the credit with his colleague.

As for farmers, Russell defended higher fixed price supports and pointed out that if allowing industry to raise prices to meet expenses was not inflationary, how could higher prices for farmers be? He warned against a serious degradation in the country's awareness of the importance of farming. To force farmers out of business would "strike a mortal blow to the soul of America," he said. "We cannot save the country and destroy the farmer."

As for postwar foreign policy, Russell was an independent thinker, unafraid to raise a dissenting voice with the Truman administration. He did not want the United States to assume too much responsibility for the economic and military welfare of the world with the resulting tax burden it would mean for the American people. He continued to advocate that the United States receive special rights to bases that Americans helped to

---

[6] The school lunch program was funded with $70 million in 1947.

build during World War II, but he was against actions that would extend American influence where the country had no clear national interest.

When Great Britain requested a nearly $4 billion loan in 1946, in spite of his reverence for Anglo-Saxon culture, Russell voted against it because he felt it would not help in a country that was losing its empire and was not equipped for the modern age. In 1947 Russell shocked everyone by suggesting that England, Scotland, Wales, and Ireland and perhaps even Canada and Australia could be invited to become states. He pointed out that such a political combination would create freer world trade and reduce economic competition. Not only that, it would result in a Navy of unrivalled power. Although no one took him seriously and perhaps he was simply being audacious to make a point, Russell had, in a sense, foreseen the advantages that would inspire the European Union.

While Great Britain was viewed as a world power in rapid decline, the question of Soviet-American relations soon became the central foreign policy issue following the war. Russell never had any confidence in Russian goodwill or integrity, although, like most other Americans, he fervently hoped the two powers would be able to live together in peace. Recognizing the increasingly destructive military power of both nations, he knew that "the alternative was too horrible to contemplate." His study of history had taught him that any nation with treasures whatsoever was in danger of some other country's trying to take them. The United States, he believed, had more that was worth defending than any other nation in the world. The Union of Soviet Socialist Republics, while also wealthy, was the most imperialistic power in the world and would have to be faced from a position of strength. Consequently, Russell supported the Truman Doctrine of foreign aid to countries such as Greece and Turkey, threatened by communist encroachments. He was highly critical of Americans who were communist sympathizers and bitterly denounced those who criticized America while enjoying the country's blessings. He suggested they go to Russia to live and said he would even contribute from his modest means to send them there.

As the Marshall Plan was being considered in 1947, Russell became part of the special congressional investigating committee sent in the fall to Europe to assess how the hundreds of millions of dollars of American aid for relief and reconstruction were being spent. The group visited

France, Germany, Italy, England, Greece, Turkey, and other countries to observe, meet with military and intelligence officers, and look at plants in Germany scheduled for dismantling.

This fact-finding trip clarified Dick Russell's views about postwar Europe. He saw immediately that the economic restoration of Germany was the key to Western European recovery. It would be impossible for the United States to keep Europe on her feet while Germany remained prostrate. Impressed as he had been on his initial postwar visit with the German work ethic, Russell discouraged dismantling German factories. Instead, he supported the Marshall Plan with the reservation that recovery depended on the willingness of Western Europeans to work hard. While the Marshall Plan of spending $17 billion over the next four years in Europe seemed at least a little extravagant to Russell, he supported its passage.

In 1946 Congress passed the Legislative Reorganization Act, which among other things reduced the number of Senate standing committees from thirty-three to fifteen. With this change, Russell lost committee chairmanship of Immigration, which was moved to the judiciary committee. His work on naval affairs would be continued on the new Senate Committee on Armed Services, however, and he retained membership on the Committee on Appropriations. By 1949 he ranked second on Armed Services and fourth on Appropriations, thereby giving him weighty positions on two of the Senate's most powerful committees.

Russell also was appointed to the new Joint Committee on Atomic Energy, and, certain that the Soviet Union would soon have an atomic bomb, if it did not have one already, he stressed secrecy and atomic monopoly. In September 1947 Russell and other members of the committee toured the country's nuclear military installations, because he wanted a personal view of the quality of security around the plants. He believed that the development of the atomic bomb was one of the great tragedies of the war and that it was equally tragic that emphasis had not been made upon using nuclear power for peaceful purposes. Given world conditions, however, he was sure that the United States must maintain the power of the atom bomb to assure peace.

During the early postwar years, Dick Russell became acquainted with a young Georgian, a 1946 graduate of the United States Naval

Academy at Annapolis, who was assigned to the budding nuclear submarine division of the Navy. James Earl Carter, Jr., or Jimmy, as he preferred to be called, was deeply involved in this new branch of the national defense, working for Captain (later Admiral) Hyman Rickover. Carter found great pleasure in being sent sometimes to Washington by his commanding officer to discuss military matters with the chairman of the Senate Armed Services Committee. That this powerful senator also was from Georgia made young Carter proud. Even when not on official business, he would stop by Russell's office to pay his respects and was warmly welcomed. Jimmy Carter never lost his belief, from firsthand experience, that men like Russell and Rickover contributed substantially to world peace through their insistence on strong national defense.[7]

In April 1947 Dick Russell fell critically ill with appendicitis, not the first time he had been so plagued. Perhaps as early as 1938 he had suffered an attack but had feared surgery to the extent that he battled the infection rather than submit to the knife. Richard B. Russell, Sr. had had a preternatural fear of surgery, since his father, William John Russell, had died following what was considered minor throat surgery in 1897, and this fear had been communicated to Dick. When he fell ill in 1938, Dick consulted with his doctor brother, Alex, who advised the surgery, but who could also comment scientifically on the body's defense mechanisms that might kick in. Dick Russell bet on the latter and withstood other attacks as the years went on. By 1947, however, there was no remedy for his besieged appendix other than surgery. Dick requested that his brother come to Washington and be in the operating room for the procedure. Alex Russell had never seen an appendix so scarred as Dick's, scars that showed the pain he had endured in ten years of battling infection.

Although Dick Russell liked to tease Alex about having purchased land in Barrow County, calling him the "Baron of Barrow," the two men were close. Dick Russell trusted his personal secrets with this brother. In 1947, while Alex and Sarah were reeling from the death of their daughter Patience, Dick invited Sarah to come to Washington and attend a White House reception as his guest. Sarah stayed with Jean and Ina Stacy and

---

[7] In this light, the legacy of national security from Dick Russell could be said to have included seven presidents.

was thrilled to meet President and Mrs. Truman. Dick Russell assumed, seemingly without question, this kind of patriarchal family responsibility and leadership.

In autumn 1947 the Russell family held its first reunion since 1938, the year Judge Russell died. Usually reunions were held on the anniversary of Richard senior and Ina's wedding day, 24 June. In 1947, however, Rob's older daughter, Betty, was to marry Ernest Vandiver on 3 September, and so it was decided that people could come for the reunion and the wedding at the same time. Dick was keenly interested in the marriages and careers of his nieces and nephews, and he was especially close to Rob's children. This was a delightful family gathering, with Ina presiding over meals and parties that were reported in the Atlanta and the Winder papers. Perhaps knowing that Pat Collins had now married someone else and that he would never have a family of his own made this family reunion dearer than ever to Dick Russell. It is certain that nothing made him happier than seeing his mother enjoying her family and the family taking pleasure in being with her. Family reunions would become more and more important to the bachelor senator as the years passed.

Russell's relationship with Harriet Orr became more important following Pat Collins's marriage, and they began discreetly to travel together. When the Robert Russell clan took a cottage at Myrtle Beach, South Carolina, in summer 1948, Dick and Harriet were often on hand. Harriet's family had a house at nearby Cherry Grove, North Carolina, and Rob's younger daughter, Mary Ina, only ten at the time, recalls that although it was never said, she understood that this woman was Uncle Dick's very special friend. When her uncle invited the family out for supper with Harriet, Mary Ina was impressed with his offer to "order whatever you want." When the child ordered the most expensive thing on the menu, a steak, her judicious father objected, telling her to choose something else. Uncle Dick came to her defense and said she could certainly have the steak if she wanted it. Pleased with this support from her parsimonious uncle, Mary Ina knew she had better eat every bite of that steak, and she did.

In 1948, Dick Russell was once again up for reelection, and once again no one stepped forward to challenge his right to be the junior senator from Georgia. Harry Truman was highly unpopular with Southern Democrats because of his insistence on confronting civil rights issues, and, not surprisingly, Dick Russell disagreed with the president on this question. During the period 1948 to 1952, Russell emerged as the undisputed leader of what became known as the Southern Bloc, a group of Southern senators determined to derail all civil rights legislation. Although there is no evidence that he sought this position, the Georgia senator earned this leadership with his understanding of the way the Senate worked and his ability to react quickly with well-organized defensive measures when Truman and others put forth civil rights legislation or ideas.[8] The perceived need to defend the traditional white Southern view of a segregated society became a heavier and heavier burden.

Russell and Truman had not been close when they served in the Senate together, and Russell had not felt that Truman was a particularly strong senator. Nevertheless, his respect for the office of the president and his dedication to the Democratic Party meant he would be as supportive as he could be in good conscience. On issues other than civil rights, Russell had backed the beleaguered president. For example, when Truman's nomination of Henry A. Wallace as secretary of commerce was highly disputed in Congress, Russell, who did not agree with Wallace on many issues, stood by the president's right of appointment. He refused to be a party to what he called a "Roman holiday" in the Senate at the expense of the office of president of the United States. By 1948 many believed, however, that Truman could not possibly be reelected, and some Democrats were looking for another nominee. Truman was even encouraged to step aside voluntarily. Dick Russell said that he would be happy if General Eisenhower would step in as a Democratic presidential exchange.

At the Georgia State Democratic Convention in Macon on 2 July 1948, only days before the beginning of the party's national convention in Philadelphia, Georgians tried to nominate Eisenhower as president with Dick Russell as vice president. Both men refused to permit their names on such a ticket. Meanwhile, other Southern extremists were talking of withholding their electoral votes from Truman should he be

---

[8] See Fite, "Russell, Truman, and Civil Rights," pp. 224-42.

nominated, and they approached Dick Russell about heading a states' rights Democratic Party. Later Dick Russell would recall sardonically that they were going to raise "almost incredible sums of money...if I would run on a third-party ticket." Referring metaphorically to the temptation of Christ, he went on, "I was taken way up on the mountain with that one."

Not seduced by the third-party prospect, Dick Russell nevertheless reluctantly agreed to allow his name to be put forward at the Democratic National Convention as a symbolic gesture of opposition to the president and civil rights. Russell was not at the convention, having chosen to stay home in Winder instead. He explained his decision this way, reflecting a lesson he had learned from his own father's varied political races, especially the much-maligned Senate race of 1926: "I was very reluctant to permit the use of my name, but decided that those who were opposed to Mr. Truman were entitled to have someone for whom they could vote."

Russell received 263 votes to Truman's 947. Alabama, Arkansas, Florida, Georgia, Louisiana, North Carolina, South Carolina, Tennessee, and Texas voted for Russell. What became memorable about this convention, however, was a speech made by then mayor of Minneapolis, Minnesota, Hubert Humphrey. Humphrey urged Democrats to get out of the shadow of states' rights and walk in the bright sunshine of human rights. When his speech continued to extol civil rights as the way forward for Americans, the Mississippi delegates and some of those from Alabama walked out of the convention.

The convention not only nominated Truman, but in response to Humphrey's eloquent plea it also included in its platform a plank in support of moderate civil rights. The states' rights Democrats felt forced to meet in a rump convention in Birmingham, Alabama, to nominate South Carolina Governor Strom Thurmond and Mississippi Governor Fielding Wright for president and vice president. Having no desire to weaken the Democratic Party, Russell stayed away from this crowd, who became known as Dixiecrats. He understood that a split among the Democrats at this time would only help Republicans and weaken Southern power in the Senate. Like everyone else, Russell expected the Democrats to lose in November, and he wanted to be strong enough within the defeated party to guide it to return to its former philosophies.

Although he took no part in the campaign, Russell did announce that he planned to vote for Truman.

When Truman was elected, along with Democratic majorities in both houses of Congress in 1948, Dick Russell was pleased. During this Truman administration, while continuing to oppose civil rights, Russell proved a staunch advocate with the president on strengthening the nation's defenses, and the Georgia senator continued to influence agricultural legislation to help farmers. Russell was almost as proud of his part in funding the Rural Electrification Administration as he was of the school lunch program. He felt great satisfaction that this legislation helped all Americans equally, whatever their color.

Russell recognized that foreign aid to Europe was necessary as the Cold War grew chillier and Russia exploded its first atomic bomb. He voted for the North Atlantic Treaty Organization but wanted to reduce America's financial commitment to it, fearing that American arms left in some Western European countries would, in the event of war, wind up in Russian hands. He regretted the communist takeover in China but did not think that the United States could have changed the outcome, nor did he see the nationalist regime under Chiang Kai-shek as reliable. It would not be worth going to war with Russia and China over Formosa.

Senator Russell was alarmed over what he called the casual manner in which Congress viewed the large deficit created by spending more money than was taken in. A principal advocate of economy and lower taxes to balance the budget, Russell often opposed various liberal programs. When he was criticized for funneling federal largesse, with unmitigated success, into Georgia, he did not see anything untoward about the situation. He had opposed the measures, he said, "but if they are determined to make the giveaway, I am going to get in the line with my little tin cup like everyone else." To his way of thinking, that he was near the head of the line made this position even more sensible.

When the Korean War broke out on 25 June 1950, Russell understood that the enormous cost of fighting "little" wars around the world would weaken the United States through deficit spending and high inflation. With the view of saving defense dollars and providing a fairer kind of military service, Russell introduced a Universal Military Training bill sponsored by nine members of the Armed Services

Committee, of which he had just become chairman. Such universal training would be much cheaper than maintaining a large standing Army, and it addressed another issue as well. It seemed unfair to Russell that men who had fought in World War II were being called up now to fight another war when there were many eligible men who had not fought at all.

The Universal Military Training bill required the registration of seventeen-year-old men who would then undergo four months of military training when they reached eighteen or completed high school. The bill was authored by Lyndon B. Johnson, a first-term senator from Texas. The bill was steered through Congress and was passed and signed by the president by June 1951, but implementation, not having been figured out, was slow. When the Korean War wound down, support for the change in Selective Service dropped quickly and the law was never implemented. Nevertheless, this legislation shows that Dick Russell was constantly trying to determine how America could afford to provide the strong defense needed to survive in the modern world.

The Korean War thrust Dick Russell, who preferred working behind the scenes, into a starring national role. On 11 April 1951, controversy over wartime policy in Korea resulted in President Truman's dismissal of General Douglas MacArthur as commander of the United Nations and US troops in the Far East. Firing a popular military hero during an unpopular war did not endear President Truman to Americans, many of whom already believed that he was, at best, soft on communism, and, at worst, grossly incompetent. Dick Russell, along with other congressmen, received heavy mail decrying the president's action. Emotions soared hot and high. When MacArthur landed in New York, more people turned out to give him a hero's welcome than had greeted Eisenhower at the end of World War II.

While some senators saw fit to make public statements in favor of Truman, the junior senator from Georgia, chairman of the Senate Armed Services Committee since 1948, sought to work quietly to survive the crisis and save the Democrats unnecessary political damage. His idea was to hold carefully structured hearings before the Armed Services Committee in executive (closed) session. He called his committee into session on 13 April and they voted to conduct an inquiry into MacArthur's dismissal. Without criticizing Truman, Russell indicated that MacArthur would be invited to testify because he was one of the "great captains of history" and that people were entitled to know the facts.

Russell was immediately contacted by Senator Tom Connally (D-TX) with the idea of joining forces with his committee, Foreign Affairs, to conduct the inquiry. Russell agreed that this would be a proper way to proceed, but he retained the right to preside. While some of the questions were concerned with foreign affairs, Russell was sure that this was basically a military matter and should be handled carefully so that no military secrets would be revealed. He felt that he had enough power and influence to direct the investigations in a way most beneficial to the country, and he was keen to retain his authority. He meant to direct a deliberate, quiet, objective investigation, avoiding what he called "a circus atmosphere" with television cameras and radio transmitters in the room. Consequently, at the original meeting he asked the members to vote in favor of closed hearings, and he received unanimous consent. Later, when public criticism of closed hearings arose, some senators changed their opinion, and Russell was not happy with their reversals. Determined to prevent the hearings from being used for personal or political gain, he opened the first session with a plea for nonpartisan conduct and a true spirit of national interest from all.

On 3 May 1951, the joint committees held the first session, with General MacArthur appearing. Following this session, Russell spoke on the Senate floor for continued closed hearings, stressing that although the American people might see and hear more from open sessions, representatives of *Pravda* and the Kremlin would also gain more information. He arranged to provide reporters copies of testimony purged of compromising military information at the end of each session, and this compromise, so typical of Russell's approach, proved satisfactory.

Russell himself opened the questioning of MacArthur with a series of questions covering a complete range of the military situation. Russell had become known in his earliest days in the United States Senate as a man who did his homework, a man who knew what he was talking about. Nearly twenty years of tough work habits coupled with a brilliant mind engaged in military matters meant that Dick Russell was, indeed, the senator best suited to direct this affair. It took three days and 320 pages for the committee to complete its questioning of MacArthur. The first day alone, MacArthur spoke for six hours. The general would never be able to claim that he had not had his say. Russell praised MacArthur for his "patience, thoroughness and frankness." Although Dick Russell was a strong supporter of the military, he also supported civil control of this powerful branch, and he was not unduly impressed by the general's bombast. During the next seven weeks the committee would call upon, among others, Secretary of Defense George C. Marshall, General Omar Bradley, and Secretary of State Dean Acheson. Satisfied with the judicious proceedings, Russell felt the hearings were an example of democracy at work.

When some of Marshall's remarks were leaked to the press, Russell was horrified to hear the secretary comment that he felt as if he were acting as an intelligence agent for the Soviet Union. Russell lectured his colleagues on the dangers such leaks posed to American fighting men in Korea and said carelessness in these matters was unforgiveable.[9] He confessed that he possessed information so highly secret that he wished he did not know it, but the senators must rise to meet the challenge of providing the people enough information to make proper decisions, while at the same time protecting the nation's security. This was a delicate balance he had become painfully aware of as he served on the Senate Oversight Subcommittee for the newly formed Central Intelligence Agency (1947).

During the questioning of General Omar Bradley, Senator Alexander Wiley (R-WI) asked Bradley to reveal the content of conversations with President Truman shortly before the outbreak of the Korean War in 1950. When Bradley declined to answer the question, Russell backed him on the grounds of executive privilege. Wiley gathered some other Republican senators of the committee to discuss challenging the principle Russell was enforcing. Russell, seeing this as choosing partisan politics instead of American patriotism, told Wiley that he was disappointed at such huddles. Perhaps because he had been working so hard conducting the hearings and keeping up his other Senate work,

---

[9] Russell had two young nephews serving in Korea at the time, both in combat units, so he was acutely aware of the personal nature of any war to the families involved.

Russell became so discouraged by these developments that he decided he could no longer preside and wrote a four-page letter of resignation on 16 May. He intended to hand the letter to the committee the next day. He explained that he had tried to keep the hearings on a high, nonpartisan plane, but when Republicans injected politics into the hearings, he could no longer preside because he would not be the ringmaster of a political circus.

Although there is no record of what changed Dick Russell's mind, something or someone did, for on 17 May he appeared as usual in the presiding chair and his letter was never distributed. Debate on allowing executive privilege continued that day, and the chairman's ruling was then brought to a vote which upheld Russell's decision by 18 to 8. Wiley's criticism did not end here, however, and he wrote to Russell charging that this failure to require witnesses to answer certain questions was politicizing the investigation as the Democrats sought to cover up their bungling foreign policy since World War II. The charge that his motives were something less than those of promoting national interests infuriated Russell, but he maintained his calm because he knew that answering these charges would allow the Republicans to use the hearings to criticize Democratic foreign policy. He did everything he could to keep the testimony confined to MacArthur's dismissal and the situation in the Far East.

The hearings finally ended on 25 June. Although Russell felt they had lasted too long, he did not want charges of whitewashing substantiated and so had not shortened any testimony. The full record of the investigation filled some 8,000 pages. On 29 June Dick Russell's picture appeared on the cover of *U.S. News and World Report* as the magazine featured Russell and the work of the committee. Throughout the hearings, Russell received favorable publicity in newspapers all over the country for his work, and the perception was that he had conducted the proceedings wisely. He had, indeed, defused what could have become a highly inflammatory situation, and Harry Truman and Douglas MacArthur were each treated fairly. Truman was grateful that Russell's skillful handling of the situation had defused the firing to the point that by the end of the hearings the public found the general's attempts to defend his insubordination and hubris tiresome. *Time* magazine voted the Truman-MacArthur affair the story of the year in December 1951.

Although the charge of partisan politics continued to be leveled at the Democrats because of the secret hearings, and no doubt Dick Russell knew he was helping his party by keeping things quiet, it is certain that the chairman of the Committee on Armed Services had as his first goal the security of his nation. The dangers of the Cold War with the USSR became more apparent to him daily, and he understood that if he did not do his job within the Senate, the country would be more threatened than it already was. His duty on this powerful committee to serve as civilian protector was one he relished.

It was decided that an official committee report would not be issued, but the committee did release a statement declaring that democracy had been served and communist aggressors warned by the hearings. By this time the country was in truce negotiations with North Korea, and it seemed counterproductive to issue anything that might hint the country was divided on the question of MacArthur's belief in a more aggressive stance. The committee passed a resolution transmitting the hearing records to the Senate, and members could include individual statements in the appendix. In spite of the disagreements that occurred, the committee passed another resolution of gratitude to Dick Russell for the "fair and very splendid" way he had conducted the work.

In his classic book on the United States Senate, *Citadel*, author William S. White summed up the importance of the hearings: "Without rejecting outright a single MacArthur military policy, without defending at a single point a single Truman policy, without accusing the General of anything whatever, the Senate's investigation had largely ended [MacArthur's] influence on policy-making. It had set in motion, by the nature of the inquiry, an intellectual counterforce to the emotional adulation that for a time had run so strongly through the country." Perhaps it was the knowledge or the fear that only he would have the will and the skill to keep the committee on this intellectual track that kept Dick Russell from resigning on 17 May.

Dick Russell began to spend more and more of his time on military matters. Not only was he passionately interested in military defense, but it was the Russell way to be certain that in positions of power he discharged his responsibilities carefully and thoughtfully. In fall 1951, at the urging of General Eisenhower, commander of the North Atlantic Treaty Organization forces, the chairman of the Senate Armed Services Committee visited American bases in Western Europe. Because Russell had recommended cutting some foreign aid to Europe, Eisenhower and Truman hoped to gain his support, or at least to soften his opposition, by showing him what was going on.

Russell returned from his trip impressed with the morale and training of American troops, and he felt that Europeans were doing more, in his opinion, than they had done previously for themselves. Nevertheless, he was adamant that they should do still more. He wanted to see most economic help related to defense purposes. In everything, Russell put the United States first, a position not always popular with men like Truman and Eisenhower as they struggled with international issues.

By this time it was becoming evident that the quiet, self-effacing Georgia senator was likely the most powerful man in the US Senate. He could have been, had he wished it, the Senate majority leader, but because he disagreed with the administration on many issues, he preferred to remain independent. In spite of repeated urgings from colleagues and from President Truman, Russell refused to accept this leadership post. So powerful was his place at the center of the Senate's inner circle of power, however, that no other senator would get the post without Russell's approval. He gave the nod to Ernest McFarland of Arizona, and for majority whip he supported his young friend from Texas, Lyndon Johnson.

Johnson and Russell had worked together occasionally while Johnson served in the House of Representatives, especially in their ardent support of the Rural Electrification Administration. After the Texan was elected to the Senate, Johnson made it a point to court the Georgia senator because he understood that here lay the way to his goal of Democratic leadership and political advancement. Johnson had also served on the House Armed Services Committee, where he had worked with Georgian Carl Vinson. Vinson, chair of the House Armed Services Committee after 1949, spoke highly of Johnson to Russell, and so Johnson, following his election in 1948, was able to win appointment to the Senate Armed Services Committee over other senators with more seniority.

Lyndon Johnson instigated the friendship that developed between these two leaders, since he knew that without Dick Russell, he could not advance as he hoped in the Senate. Given the force of the Georgian's character and his reputation for making good friends, it is certain that Johnson did not find spending time with Russell a chore, and there is no reason to doubt the sincerity or the depth of the friendship. The two made strange bedfellows, to be sure, because Russell, with his genteel family background, was a quiet, introspective, modest man, whose conduct defined the word gentleman. Johnson, on the other hand, being from a Texas hardscrabble background, was loud, brash, often ill-mannered, and blatantly ambitious for power. Yet they got along, perhaps because both revered the Senate and its institutions. Their understanding of power and how to wield it was complementary. Russell enjoyed his mentor role because he found Johnson a likely student. He hoped Johnson, coming from Texas, could serve as a bridge between the North and South on the civil rights issues, which Russell knew would continue to arise. He wanted healing for the rifts between North and South, and some deep sense of human nature made him feel Johnson was the man most likely to succeed in that arena.

During Johnson's early years in the Senate, he began to invite Dick Russell to spend evenings in the Johnson home, sensing that Lady Bird was the kind of woman that Russell admired. Although Russell had family in the Washington area and he relished visiting with them, it became a great pleasure to him to be included in the Johnson family circle, usually on short notice. The little Johnson girls, Lynda Byrd and Luci Baines, were soon calling him Uncle Dick. Lady Bird, like his sister Billie, cooked special Southern dishes for him—black-eyed peas and turnip greens with savory "potlikker" for the cornbread—which he complimented with gracious remarks that pleased Mrs. Johnson. Although a bachelor, Russell was not lacking in family, but he was moved by the Johnsons' attentions and accepted their admiration as genuine. When he was invited to spend a long vacation hunting on the Johnson ranch in 1949, he accepted and wrote following the trip of a "near perfect" time of relaxation and fellowship.

When Ina Dillard Russell was chosen Georgia's Mother of the Year in 1950, no one could have been prouder than her eldest son. He felt that no one in the family deserved more honor or recognition than did this remarkable woman. The town of Winder held a gala celebration with a parade, historical skits, and a speech by Georgia's governor, Herman Talmadge. Twelve of Ina and Richard's thirteen children were in attendance. Their son Walter, a career Army man, was stationed in Japan and could not come home. It was typical of Ina Russell that she insisted on writing Walter a long letter to let him know how much he was missed. "Your name was called several times," she wrote. Ina had to have help from her daughter Billie to write because the matriarch's eyesight was failing badly by this time. She was never averse to soliciting an amanuensis, however, and kin to serve in this capacity were never lacking. Among the congratulatory telegrams that flooded into the Russell household was one from Lyndon and Lady Bird Johnson. Dick Russell was pleased.

In 1952 Harry Truman announced that he would not be a candidate again for the presidency, though the new Twenty-second Amendment limiting presidential terms to two did not apply to him. This decision left the race wide open and hats sailed into the ring. Senate hearings on a variety of issues had made several senators well-known. In addition to Dick Russell, who had been in the public eye so favorably during the MacArthur hearings, there was Estes Kefauver (D-TN), who was conducting hearings into organized crime, the first televised Senate hearings. Unlike Russell, Kefauver had no objection to becoming a ringmaster, and his hearings turned him into a national hero. This was also the McCarthy era, with its exaggerated emphasis on communist "traitors" in the United States, and many senators had become well-known either supporting or castigating Senator Joseph McCarthy. Before Truman withdrew his name as a possible candidate, there was speculation over which party might end up with Dwight Eisenhower. Many felt that an unbeatable ticket would be Eisenhower for president with Dick Russell as vice president. Russell believed the South could be returned to mainstream politics only when a Southerner had been elected president, but he had no interest whatsoever in the vice presidential office, one without power. He had earned Senate power and could serve his state and his nation better, he was sure, in that august body.

The Democrats, after twenty years in presidential power, were in deep trouble. Like other Southerners, Russell could not support Truman's civil rights legislation, and outside the South others saw little to commend the Truman administration. The prolonged but unwon war in Korea and charges that the administration was soft on communism made the Democrats look weak. The specter of the Southern walkout in 1948 also haunted the Democrats. Without the solid South, they had scarce hope of a win. Because some Democrats thought the way to prevent another Southern bolt was to run a Southerner with a record for reason and intelligence, Dick Russell's name came more and more to the fore. Other possible candidates included Senator Robert Kerr (D-OK), a visionary oil magnate elected to the Senate in 1948, and Adlai Stevenson, governor of Illinois. Stevenson was widely believed to be Truman's choice, even though early in the year Truman had not yet announced his intention to withdraw.

Russell had no illusions about the chances of a Southerner with his decided views against civil rights legislation claiming the Democratic nomination, much less the presidency, and he said as much on various occasions when questioned about the possibility of a bid for the White House. Georgians heartily endorsed the idea of Dick Russell for president, however, and when Estes Kefauver appeared to be leading the pack by winning the New Hampshire primary, Lyndon Johnson and others persuaded Dick Russell to enter the Florida primary. Otherwise, they said, the convention was headed for another Southern walkout. Agreeing a walkout likely, Russell entered the race, hoping to avoid another party split.

In later years he said that his main objective was to keep the South within the Democratic Party by giving it someone to vote for, and that he had had no intention of campaigning seriously. Once he entered the fray, however, he found no way to withdraw gracefully. There is no reason to doubt his sincerity in this analysis.

On the other hand, it is certain that a veteran political campaigner like Dick Russell got caught up in the race. He was surrounded by people who truly thought he would make a good president, and he was sure himself that he could take on the job. Never immune to the

intoxicating wine of a political scrap, Russell must have recalled how he ·
had been able always to garner more votes than anyone expected.
Certainly it was a long shot, but he had been a long shot before. He
campaigned hard in Florida, and when he won that primary by a 56
percent margin over Kefauver, the "Russell for President" campaign
train picked up speed.

Russell travelled by train between Washington and Georgia
frequently, and it was a pleasure to arrive in Winder early in the
morning and have breakfast with his mother before driving to Atlanta.
Modine Thomas, by this time the main family cook and housekeeper,
knew just how to make the country ham, eggs, grits, and biscuit toast
that he liked. Other family members were involved in the campaign.
Rob's son, Robert Lee, Jr. (Bobby) became a key man in the organization.
As a federal judge, Rob senior could no longer be involved in politics,
and he was careful not to compromise his brother's race. That the two
conferred privately is certain. Young Bobby, however, proved energetic
and capable, although his lack of experience might have been a problem
from time to time. During this period, Bobby became friends with
Lyndon Johnson, who was also supporting the Russell candidacy.
Bobby's sister Betty was married to Ernest Vandiver, head of Selective
Service for Georgia, and "Ernie" took a leave of absence to work on the
Russell campaign. As convention time neared, someone said, "You need
a woman," and sister Ina Stacy was called upon to act as official Russell
hostess in Chicago.

In this era before numerous state primaries, candidates had to
persuade the delegates themselves, and in the run-up to the opening of
the convention on 21 July, Dick Russell spoke all over the country, from
Pennsylvania to Montana, hoping to win support. As usual, he made a
good impression, but nationally he would continue to be considered a
Southerner, and thus not seriously eligible for the presidency. In June he
went to the White House to meet with President Truman on a Korean
matter, but before they turned to that topic, Russell was surprised to
hear the president say, "Dick, I do wish you lived in Indiana or Missouri.
You would be elected president hands down." Russell knew that if he
had Truman's backing, he would have a much better chance at the
nomination, and he replied diplomatically that although they had had
their differences, both had managed to stay with the Democratic Party

and he was confident that would continue. Truman said the Democratic Party was big enough for all its conflicting elements.

Dick Russell was unable to shake the view that he was a regional candidate only, and at the convention, despite his personal charisma, Russell support fell away. Though many people worked hard during this chaotic week, the truth was that, for the first time in Dick Russell's career, he was not going to win. Sister Ina felt like a puppet jerked from one stage to another, but she was glad she could be there for Dick. The candidates' wives were amazed that Ina would perform such duties for a brother. We have to do this for our husbands, they said, but you don't have to put yourself through this. His brother Fielding, watching the convention on television, was so upset by what he saw as betrayals of delegates that he phoned Dick and said, "Why don't you just come on home and leave it to them?"

His brother's reply remained with Fielding for the rest of his life: "That's not the way it's done, Fielding. You can't get in and then just leave when times get rough." Dick Russell knew the political game had been kind to him previously. Now he would not fail to stand up and take his hard knocks. Although neither wanted to break campaigning rules, the senator and his judge brother, Robert, managed see each other for brief periods by meeting outside the hotel on the fire escape between the judge's room and Russell headquarters, which were several floors apart. They called this time "meetings of the Fire Escape Cabinet."

On the first ballot, Kefauver led with 340 votes, with Stevenson garnering 273 and Russell 268. In this era of smoke-filled back rooms, in which various power brokers maneuvered to influence the nomination, it was perhaps knowledge of the system that had made Dick Russell believe he had a chance. Yet nothing surprising happened to catapult Russell into the victor's seat. On the second ballot, it became clear that the move was to Stevenson, and by the third ballot, Adlai Stevenson became the Democratic Party's 1952 presidential candidate.

Russell was a gracious loser, stepping in behind the nominee immediately, urging support. Some people, including his sister Ina, hearing him speak in favor of Stevenson thought Dick Russell appeared relieved. Stevenson was a moderate, and most of the South felt they could live with him as a candidate. Certainly Dick Russell considered him qualified for the post, while at the same time feeling himself better qualified. Offered the vice presidential slot, Russell declined unequivocally. When he suggested Senator John Sparkman of Alabama as an alternate candidate, he was surprised that his choice was accepted. Sparkman was also Truman's choice for vice president.

At this point, no one suspected how unstoppable the Eisenhower presidential bid would be. Nominated at the Republican Convention two weeks before the Democratic Convention, Eisenhower bested a powerful opponent in Robert Taft, who had linked himself with Douglas MacArthur. MacArthur, rumored to have been a candidate himself, made a keynote address at the convention, but he was not well-received. Eisenhower emerged as the lasting national hero, and he was elected by a landslide in November, bringing a Republican House and Senate in on his coattails.

In later years, Russell, a political realist, analyzed his defeat as inevitable, but he remained satisfied that he had achieved his original goal of keeping the South in the party. He had found the experience rewarding, had not gone into debt, and felt he had fought a good fight. He had no regrets. Perhaps his mother summed it up best when she was questioned by reporters following his defeat at the convention. "I'm glad he tried," Ina Russell said.

One thing was certain: Dick Russell would never run for president again. Rejection had hurt, but the experience simply deepened in him the determination to remain a considerable force in the greatest deliberative body in the world and to represent his state and his nation with all his ability in that distinguished forum. For decades people would quote Truman's remark that if Russell had been from Indiana or Missouri, if he had not been from Georgia, the presidency could not have been denied him. Russell's reply: "I'd rather be from Georgia than be president."

Russell, cautious about military heroes in the office of president (with his knowledge of early American history, he would have excepted General Washington), held off commenting on Eisenhower before he took office. With Republican majorities in both Houses of Congress, Russell had lost his position as chairman of the Armed Services Committee, and for the first time in his twenty years in the Senate, he would have to work with a Republican president. Russell pledged to support Eisenhower in his search for world peace, and he was keen to protect the measures passed to help farmers. As a conservative

Southerner, he had no intention of helping Republicans dismantle the New Deal or the Fair Deal. With characteristic humor he counseled fellow Democrats that little could be done immediately following such a disastrous defeat. Give the Republicans time, and there would be plenty to criticize. There was no point in shooting at Republicans until people could understand what the shooting was about.

DWIGHT DAVID EISENHOWER: 1953–1960

"The confidence of the average citizen in Dwight Eisenhower should renew the hopes of every American for the future of our country. His faith in the patriotism and judgment of our people in the mass was probably greater than that of any President since Jefferson. He sought and held our highest political office without being a politician."
—Richard B. Russell, Jr.

When the Senate convened for the 83rd Congress in January 1953, Dick Russell was beginning his twenty-first year as a United States senator. During those twenty years he had seen the Republicans pursue a doctrine that dictated that the duty of the opposition party was to oppose the initiatives of a Democratic president. Now in the minority party and serving a highly popular president, as Republicans had had to do, Dick Russell developed an entirely different strategy from the Republican tactics he had witnessed for two decades.

As always, Dick Russell did not take an overt leadership position. When his name was put forth to become the minority leader, Russell instead backed Lyndon Johnson, who wanted the job and who, Russell knew, had the ability to effect compromise. With Dick Russell's endorsement, Johnson was unanimously elected, and that choice, coupled with a moderate Republican president, ushered in an extraordinary period of bipartisan politics.

For Russell and Johnson, the goal was not to oppose President Eisenhower's proposals. Instead, they would consider them and how they could be modified to meet Democratic specifications. The Democrats were split between the conservative South and other more liberal Democrats from the North and West. In addition, Republicans were far from united, claiming groups of old-line conservatives on the one hand, and moderates closer to Eisenhower's policies on the other. If the Senate were going to achieve anything, these factions would have to learn to work together.

Lyndon Johnson proved, indeed, the man for the job of compromise. Thanks to his leadership, he had men as opposite in political views as Hubert Humphrey and Richard Russell working with each other. He needed Russell to win over conservative Democrats and Humphrey to persuade the liberals, who were more likely to be impatient. However uneasy this alliance, it enabled Johnson to present a united front to the Republicans. In addition, he sometimes was able to assemble Democrats to support the president and rescue proposals that were too moderate for conservative Republicans. In the House, Sam Rayburn, Johnson's old mentor, was steering House Democrats on a similar course of cooperation, and thus the Republican president found he sometimes got along better with the opposition than with his own party.

During the entire Eisenhower years, it was not unusual for Dick Russell to be invited to the White House for a private drink with the president. Sometimes there would be a group, including Johnson, Russell, and Rayburn. Russell remembered years later with pleasure one evening when he and President Eisenhower were alone. Ike unburdened himself to the Senator in an astonishing way, revealing the strains of the office to one he felt sure would understand. Russell never disclosed the personal things the president shared, simply that the event occurred. That Dick Russell could be trusted with confidences was one of his most admired strengths.

Although there were no major legislative battles during the first session of the 83rd, by the time Congress adjourned in the summer, it was clear that Lyndon Johnson had surpassed even the optimistic predictions of his Senate mentor. At the end of the session in July, a number of senators took the floor to commend Johnson for his ability to resolve minor differences, reach consensus, and move Senate business along. Dick Russell happened to be absent for the colloquy, but when he read of it in the *Congressional Record*, he wrote to his friend that he had known he would do a good job, but "I am frank to say that I did not believe any man could have achieved as much harmony within the

Democratic Party and contributed as much to the operations of the Senate as a whole as you have done during the first session of the 83rd Congress."

Johnson replied that no other praise meant quite as much as Russell's, because Johnson could not have accomplished it without Russell, whom he regarded as one of the great statesmen of the day. Many senators at the time thought Johnson flattered Russell flamboyantly and used the good will of the older senator outrageously, but Dick Russell, who was no fool regarding human nature, accepted that ambition could also contain friendship and kept his faith in Johnson's ability to be a powerful national leader. Throughout the 1950s, Russell and Johnson had Senate seats near each other, with Russell seated just behind Johnson, and as they whispered to each other on the floor or discussed matters in the cloakroom off the Senate chamber, they were clearly at the center of formidable political power.[10]

Not long after Congress adjourned in July, the greatest sorrow of his life came to Dick Russell. The family had held its annual reunion on 24 June, and all thirteen of Richard and Ina's children were in attendance for a gala family gathering, with many grandchildren accompanying them. A photo taken on the porch of the homeplace shows a frail little woman with her thirteen adult children. Everyone is laughing. It was likely Ina herself who had cracked the joke that set them off. Dick Russell, whose brother Bill had married in 1948, was now the only one of her children unmarried, and he continued to support his mother financially and to claim her home as his. He wrote to her frequently and sent her monthly check himself, not leaving this duty to office staff. He had never thought of buying a home in Washington. His home was in Georgia, on the spot where he had grown up.

On 30 August 1953, a Sunday, Ina Dillard Russell suffered a cerebral hemorrhage early in the morning. Modine Thomas came up to Ina's

---

[10] See John A. Goldsmith, *Colleagues: Richard B. Russell and His Apprentice Lyndon B. Johnson* (Macon GA: Mercer University Press, 1998) chapters 3 and 4 for a thorough description of the Russell-Johnson team in the Senate during Eisenhower's Presidency.

doctor son's home a few hundred yards away to call for his help, but no earthly help would be needed. Ina had gone home.

All her children had known this time had to come—she was eighty-five—but they were shocked and grieved at their loss. None would feel her loss as keenly as her eldest son. She had continued to be his stabilizing female force for fifty-five years, and with his own maturity, Dick had come to recognize what an extraordinary spirit his mother possessed and what an example of moral strength and simple service her life had been. Flowers flooded into the homeplace from all over the state and the country. Helpers were kept busy late into the night trying to record them. Many were sent on to hospitals and nursing homes to be shared with others. Dick Russell was gratified at this outpouring of sympathy for the family and of admiration for the greatest person he had ever known.

Ina had decreed that her funeral service take place from her own home, where she had spent forty years, and that it be simple and celebratory. Her favorite hymn was "O, Happy Day," a song about redemption and reentry into God's kingdom, and this was the hymn sung at her send-off on 1 September 1953. Only family and a few close friends could be seated in the house, but outside, under the oaks, pecans, sycamores, and poplars that Richard senior had planted and watered by hand, hundreds were seated. They came from all walks of life to honor the life and work of Ina Dillard Russell. Flags in Georgia flew at half-mast that day.

When Ina's body was taken to the family cemetery on a knoll behind the house, a great throng, led by her senator son, followed the hearse on foot along the red dirt road. Among the crowd was Lyndon Johnson, who hated funerals, but who could not stay away from his friend's side at this time. According to Ralph MacGill, editor of the *Atlanta Constitution*, as the flower-covered casket was lowered into the earth, the family and their friends turned back to life exalted by the great dignity of this passage from an earthly life to an eternal one.

The Russell family was now left without their matriarch, but they knew she meant for them to carry on the work of the world. Ina had made Herculean efforts throughout her life to keep her family together, believing it was important that they all know and care for each other, and she had succeeded in giving her numerous brood deep family feeling. As her eldest son and unmarried, Dick Russell stepped into the role of patriarch, prepared to continue his mother's ideal of a large family in which everyone knew and cared about everyone else. Because Ina had left no will, the estate belonged to all equally. The eldest son offered to buy the homeplace and farm and continue to keep it open for the family to enjoy. The estate was thus settled with a minimum of family tension, Dick Russell was able to keep his home, and the entire clan had a place to meet and be together for years to come.

Russell's nephew, Bob junior, and his wife, Betty Ann, lived next door in the Weaning Cottage, but having just had their third child, it was decided that they should move into the homeplace, or the Big House, as the senator took to calling it in old-time Southern parlance. Before that time it was simply "Grandmother's house." The bachelor senator had to learn to share his house with a busy and boisterous young family, and he sometimes found the antics of young children bewildering. Betty Ann Campbell Russell was exceptionally easygoing, and she tolerated Uncle Dick's lack of understanding with children graciously.

About this time another burden of sorrow came to the family, one that again deeply affected Richard Russell, Jr. Judge Robert Lee Russell, Sr., now serving on the federal court of appeals, learned that he was stricken with lung cancer, and the prognosis was dismal. He had perhaps two years to live. Dick was devastated by this news. He was closer emotionally to Rob than to any other brother, as well as being closer in age and shared experience. Rob had been his campaign manager in every race before 1952, the one to whom he turned for practical help and moral support. Rob was also the only truly close friend Dick Russell had ever had, a man who knew him well and loved him. Dick had allowed no one else to become as loyal and close a friend from boyhood until now. When Rob came home from the doctor who had given him the bad news, he called his brother Alex to his home, told him what the doctor had said, and asked his medical opinion. Alex could give him no more promising picture if the diagnosis was correct.

Facing a painful death, the judge asked why he should not simply take his own life now. Alex told his brother that he understood that feeling, but "you have too many people who want to keep you around as long as possible to take that road." Confident in his sensible brother, Alex wasn't alarmed, but when he told the senator and Bob junior about the conversation, Dick Russell insisted on taking all the firearms out of his brother's house. Robert Lee Russell, Sr. died on 19 January 1955, about fifteen months after Ina Russell's death.

Having lost the two people dearest to him, Dick Russell turned even more deeply into his work as Georgia's voice in Washington. Concurrently, his family became, if anything, more important in his life and occupied his thoughts and energies more than ever. He had from the first been interested in the educational progress of his nieces and nephews, taking note of their being on the honor roll, winning an essay contest, or other achievements through congratulatory letters. He gave US savings bonds to all the newborns and sometimes also gifted small amounts of stock.

Very early in his avuncular career, Dick Russell initiated a reading challenge to his many nieces and nephews. At the age of twelve, they could indicate that they'd like to "read for Uncle Dick." If he judged their reading adequate, the boys would win a .22 rifle or $20, and the girls would win $20.[11] He chose passages from the *New York Times* or the *Washington Post* and sat beside the reader at the big family dining table to follow along. It was a nerve-wracking experience as the venerable senator continued to point out paragraph after paragraph for the reader. Those who did not read up to the mark could try again when they felt ready. Bill Russell, who later worked for his uncle in Washington, never passed muster. Mary Ina Russell Ingram, youngest daughter of brother Rob, read several paragraphs without a mistake, but then she mispronounced "adjudicate." Her uncle complimented her reading but said she would have to try again because the daughter of a federal judge had to know how to pronounce "adjudicate."

The families in Washington continued to get together for Sunday dinners and impromptu evenings at the homes of Billie, Pat, Ina junior, or Harriette. Harriette and Ralph Sharpton had settled in the Washington area after the war, and although Ralph died in 1952, Harriette remained in Washington. Hugh Peterson, Sr. had continued working in Washington as a lobbyist after he lost his congressional seat, and Dick Russell had enjoyed watching his nephew Hugh Peterson, Jr. grow up.

---

[11] One girl asked for a rifle and received it.

Bill Russell, son of Dick's brother Fielding, came to Washington in fall 1953 to work in his uncle's office while attending college at George Washington University. Bill would stay with his uncle seven years, but in the early months the young man thought he had failed and would be sent home in disgrace. University afternoon and night courses and a full day's work at the Senate proved demanding, and although Bill felt he had worked hard, at the end of his first year he received a letter notifying him that he had failed Spanish and would not be allowed to attend George Washington University the next year.

Filled with dread, Bill took the letter to his uncle's office the next day. Dick Russell was not known for being a particularly friendly person to work for, but rather an aloof employer, not given to office camaraderie. His kin felt he might have ignored them more than other staff in an effort not to show favoritism. Bill trembled at the prospect of a stern lecture and notice of termination of his employment.

He handed the letter to Senator Russell, who read it, then looked up and said, "Well, we will just have to see about getting you into the University of Maryland if they reject your appeal."

Devastated by the letter, Bill had not even noticed that he could appeal. Now he felt full of hope, validated, and, as he would define it later, blessed by grace. He made his appeal and was granted a summer to pass Spanish. In spite of his professor's estimation that he could not even speak English (judging by his Southern accent) so he mustn't expect to speak Spanish, Bill passed the class with a B and returned to George Washington in the fall. When, years later, Bill learned that he had dyslexia, he appreciated even more his uncle's ability to judge him on something besides academic achievement. Dick Russell remembered when he was a poor scholar and his own despairing father praised students who made all A's.

In March 1955 Jean Stacy fell dead of a heart attack while walking down a Washington street. This sudden shift in the life of Dick's sister Ina precipitated a change beneficial to brother and sister and the larger family as well. Ina had worked in Washington since 1918, and with Jean's death, she decided to retire. Her senator brother asked her if she would consider moving to Winder, into the homeplace, to act as his hostess there. When he wanted to see people about government matters while in Georgia, he needed a woman to help him entertain and to run his Winder home. These two had got along well together all their lives, and this living arrangement met both their needs at this time. By 1956 Ina Stacy was ensconced at the old Russell homeplace, where she would remain for ten years, giving the family and other guests a place to land and to enjoy Southern hospitality.

Modine Thomas, who had cared so faithfully for Ina Dillard Russell, continued in her work as cook and housekeeper. Sometimes Modine and Ina junior did not agree over how the house should be run, and in most instances, Modine got her way. Once, when dignitaries were visiting, Ina and Modine had prepared an excellent supper, served family style as usual, and the meal and conversation had gone well. As Modine cleared away the dishes, preparing to bring in the dessert, Ina said, "Modine, I think we'll have dessert and coffee in the living room."

Modine considered that suggestion briefly, then said, in front of all, "Now whatever give you an idea like that?"

The senator would not have dared to interfere with the two women, and dessert was duly served in the living room with coffee.

During this period, Dick Russell began to improve the family burial ground that had opened with the death of Richard B. Russell, Sr. in 1938. In 1940 the family erected an imposing fifteen-foot obelisk made of Georgia granite from Elbert County. It was inscribed on one side with Richard and Ina's marriage and the names of their fifteen children along with words from the state memorial proceedings to Judge Russell on the other. Another side was reserved for the family lineage of Richard Russell and Ina Dillard and the last for Ina's memorial. Though all her children contributed to the words chosen, it appears from notes made by Dick Russell that it was he who made the final edit. A brief enough tribute in trying to describe the long life of service of one woman to her home and family, it gives deep insight into what was important to her eldest son, who honored this woman above all other people, male and female, in his life:

"With sublime faith she walked with God and kept his commandments. To her there was no honor or station in life of such exalted dignity as that of a Christian wife and mother.

"There has never been a marriage relationship more tender and true than existed between this noble woman and her eminent husband.

"She glorified motherhood. Her devotion to her children was without bounds and blessed them like a heavenly benediction. Her love and motherly instincts were so all-embracing that thousands called her 'Mother Russell.' Even when her burdens were heavy and her way beset with trials and difficulties, she found time to minister to those in distress and rejoice with those who knew happiness.

"She met both the joys and vicissitudes of life with the serenity of a truly great soul. The priceless heritage of her character, her compassion and her good deeds strengthened and inspired her children."

Development of this hallowed family burial plot became Dick Russell's preferred pastime when he was at home. In the early 1950s, he spent hours conferring with William B. Thompson, a partner in the Barge Thompson general contracting company. Mr. Thompson continued to work with the senator voluntarily on the cemetery after its design was finished and told his friend Harry Dwoskins that he felt it was his hobby as well as the senator's. When in Washington, Russell would telephone home to learn if the azaleas were blooming or the expensive zorgia grass was growing well and being watered. Did the magnolias he'd planted near the pine woods look healthy? He was particularly careful that the workmen did not cut any trees without permission. When a supervisor insisted that a young pine near the cemetery gate needed to come down, the senator shook his head. "Don't cut that tree," he said. "It would be like taking the life of a child." His nieces and nephews living nearby had the pleasure of "running into Uncle Dick" at the cemetery or as he walked through the woods and fields around it. It was a special delight to find him under his mother's prized scuppernong vine in the autumn, for munching scuppernongs makes everyone expansive and relaxed.

As the years wore on, picturing the family cemetery as it turned into a serene, peaceful, and park-like space would continue to be one of Dick Russell's main pleasures. Using the granite from the foundation of a house his father had started but never finished, he built a picturesque wall around the burial ground. He had jonquils planted on the path from the Big House to Papa's Hill, as the family called the cemetery. His mother, an avid and talented gardener, had planted fields of jonquils on the place. In the woods between the house and the cemetery, Dick had a room built in which to store the personal papers of his growing family, with a discrete apartment attached. Shadowing this modern structure was the old mule barn, which he left standing until it collapsed of its own accord. Dick did not stay in the apartment, preferring his room in the drafty old house to the modern carpeted and kitchenette wonder that boasted heating and air conditioning. He did allow his sister Ina to redecorate some of the rooms at the homeplace, though, including adding a bathroom for his bedroom. Also during Ina's tenure aluminum siding was added to the house, but it was never centrally heated nor air conditioned. Visitors of importance would recall later how impressed they were by the simplicity of the life of such a powerful man.

As Dick Russell continued his work in the United States Senate, his reputation for honesty, integrity, patriotism, and genuine courtesy deepened among his colleagues. When Pulitzer Prize-winning author William S. White published *Citadel: The Story of the U.S. Senate* in 1956, he noted the integrity its traditions had given the Senate. White named Richard Russell as "a senator's senator," one who understood and honored the workings of the institution, and this label would stick for the rest of his life. Through his twenty-three years in the Senate, Dick Russell had come to revere more and more the unique legislative body, and although he did not seek nor enjoy publicity, he was pleased to be identified as a worthwhile example of Senate service.

As chairman of the Senate Armed Forces Committee, Russell's intense determination to keep America strong for the Cold War influenced the country's defense spending and, while preferring peace, her reputation for being "armed and ready." When critics accused him of turning America into an imperialistic power by keeping foreign bases, Russell did not apologize and continued to insist on maintaining American strength in those places where American lives had paid the price for freedom. He was careful to study all the information on military projects that came before the committee, and his support of the military was not mindless.

As the years passed, it is not surprising that this support through influence over the military budget endeared Russell to the military in all branches. When the senator asked if an Air Force plane might be flying to Georgia when he needed to go home, a plane always was going. The runway at the Winder airport was long enough for a fighter jet to take off and land, so Dick Russell almost always arrived at home in this way or even on a larger transport plane. Before the Watergate scandal, this kind of perk was considered reasonable. Russell was careful that no one other than he and staff members be transported in this way, though once he took a young niece whose father was a career Army man to join her parents. The Robert Russell, Jr., children recall at least one plane flying low over the homeplace to signal it was time to drive to the airport to pick up Uncle Dick.

Dick Russell's power in the Senate regarding military matters worked directly in favor of his native state. During most of the 1950s, Georgia's Carl Vinson was chairman of the House Armed Services Committee, and Russell was chairman of the same committee in the Senate. The two men were so effective in bringing military dollars into Georgia that a joke went around the nation's capital that if one more military project were given to Georgia, the state would sink into the Atlantic Ocean. Such a remark was once made in Russell's presence, during a meeting of the Armed Services Committee, with a fellow senator saying that he should perhaps not vote for certain money because then Russell would be sure that the funds would go to Georgia and his beloved state might disappear below the ocean. Russell replied sardonically that his distinguished colleague could be sure that the senator from Georgia would do everything in his power to get funds for Georgia if they were approved.

When the Eisenhower administration moved toward economy by closing military bases, Russell successfully fought closings in Georgia at Moody Air Force Base (Valdosta), Fort Gordon near Augusta, and Hunter Field, near Savannah. By 1957/1958, there were fifteen defense establishments in Georgia. Thanks to Russell's ability to get money for building, the millions spent on construction at these bases made closing them more and more impractical in the Cold War world.

Russell's love of farmers and support for agriculture continued unabated, sometimes bringing him in conflict with President Eisenhower and others who were, in Russell's opinion, careless about how much agricultural life meant to America. Dick Russell understood that the world had turned from an agrarian base to heavy industry, but that did not justify, to him, failing to ensure that those who stayed in farming received a fair share of the national wealth through government subsidies. His genuine admiration for those who tilled the soil to feed the rest of the world, especially the kind of small farmer he had known in the South, had made him a true friend of agriculture from his earliest days in Washington. Russell's position as second in seniority on the Committee on Appropriations in the 1950s enabled him to help farmers in various ways, one of which was by financing agricultural research. It was no surprise that he saw that Georgia received funds for a poultry research lab and also for research on peanuts and paper pulp. He also continued to promote soil conservation and was active in getting funds to build such reservoirs as Lake Lanier and Lake Hartwell.

Russell's colleagues knew of his interest in agriculture and soil conservation, and his power on Appropriations helped senators on both sides of the aisle. Consequently, many of them owed him favors, but he seldom asked for anything. Nevertheless, his courtesy and genuine interest and concern for others' projects made him a general favorite. Russell did not seem to care whether he was popular with his fellow senators, but he tried to conduct himself in ways he knew would earn respect.

Throughout the Eisenhower years, Richard Russell and Lyndon Johnson continued to work well together. The bipartisan atmosphere in Congress had perhaps never been better as moderates in both parties worked well with a moderate president and a wheeling, dealing senate majority leader who knew how to get things done.[12] Russell was literally behind Johnson as the majority leader steered legislation with unheard-of speed through the sedate Senate. At Johnson's arrangement, Russell's desk was positioned directly behind Johnson's front-row seat on the center aisle. Thus Johnson had the immediate advice of the Senate's premier expert on rules and procedure as well as that of a trusted counselor on policy.

The two senators weathered McCarthyism without undue damage. The Democrats did not want to turn Joe McCarthy's issues into partisan ones, fearing that would unite the Republicans behind him. Many Republicans became disenchanted with his heavy-handed, crass methods, embarrassed by them, in fact, but all senators were reluctant to

---

[12] Johnson became majority leader in 1955 when the Democrats regained the majority in the Senate.

censure another senator, particularly a committee chairman, so the parties worked out a way to censure so that the country would be served well without party politics taking over. Russell and Johnson helped to create the format that was used.

In 1954 the Georgian and the Texan united again to prevent American intervention in Indo-China when the French asked for help. The two senators succeeded in showing President Eisenhower that there was no congressional support for American involvement in Vietnam, especially since other European countries, specifically Great Britain, were ill-disposed to contribute. They believed Korea had been lesson enough in what could happen when the United States tried to police Asia.

Although Dick Russell had a well-earned reputation for working long hours—indeed, for putting the Senate above all else in his life—no one worked harder than Lyndon Johnson. He was the first to arrive at the Capitol in the mornings and the last to leave. In July 1955 the overload became too much, and he suffered a heart attack. He was forced to take time off to recover, and with the help of an understanding and caring wife, the tough Texan did recover, though he would be out of action for the rest of the year. He was well enough to visit Dick Russell at his home in Winder in December.

President Eisenhower also suffered a heart attack in September, and although he, too, was recovering fully, there was question as to whether he would run again in 1956. This uncertainty spurred the Democrats' hopes, and three senators were priming for the run: Estes Kefauver (TN) Bob Kerr (OK) and Stuart Symington (MO). Johnson himself might have considered a bid at this point, but when Congress opened in January 1956 and it was clear that Eisenhower would be the Republican candidate, the Texan went back to building an outstanding legislative record. With Russell willing to have his Southerners jump through Johnson's hoops, Johnson continued to add to his string of successes. To many legislators it seemed that Johnson exploited his friendship with Russell to enhance his own reputation, but later observers have concluded that Russell had an agenda of his own in building the image of the majority leader from Texas, who was more a Westerner than a Southerner, a man who could both lead and compromise.[13]

The 1956 congressional session proved difficult for Southern senators as the country geared up for judicial administration of the 1954 *Brown v. Board of Education* Supreme Court decision making segregation in schools illegal. In 1896 the Supreme Court had declared, in the *Plessy v. Ferguson* ruling, that segregation was legal under the doctrine of separate but equal. This had been the law for the whole of Dick Russell's life. Now it was reversed. As the leading senator from the white South, Dick Russell directed the drafting of a statement, which became known as the Southern Manifesto, protesting the decision. This manifesto was signed by all senators from the states of the failed Confederacy except Senators Kefauver and Gore from Tennessee. Russell and Johnson agreed, however, that Johnson should not sign in order to strengthen his position as a Westerner, and because Johnson was the leader of all Democrats, not only those from the South. This clearly national position would be essential should Johnson decide to run for the presidency.

Exactly when Lyndon Johnson decided to run for the presidency is debatable, but his favorite-son effort in 1956 is not likely the time he would have chosen. A combination of Texas and national politics pushed him into the race, in a turn of events that meant again that he and Dick Russell would partner to derail a major party split that could have resulted in another walkout, this time of Texas delegates. Adlai Stevenson secured the nomination on the first ballot, but no one else would have been any more likely to defeat Dwight David Eisenhower, who was reelected in another landslide in November.

For the next three years, Dick Russell would be called on more and more to stiffen Southern resistance to changes in the civil rights laws, which he called civil wrongs, against a changing national tide. When he refused to sanction a filibuster against a voting rights bill in 1957 because he did not think he had the support to sustain it successfully, he and Johnson worked together to amend the bill to soften it to Southern objections. Representing the first civil rights legislation to pass the Senate since the Civil War, the bill lost most of its teeth by this time, but Johnson saw it as a wedge for future action and praised Russell for his

---

[13] See Goldsmith, *Colleagues*, 46–55.

compromise. Writing to his friend, Johnson said: "The country recognizes your skill and brilliance. I hope it will also realize that your statesmanship did more to heal old wounds than any other thing."

Georgians back home, so proud of their national defense senator, gave scant credit for statesmanship on this question. Russell received many angry letters from constituents accusing him of not keeping his word to fight for them. About this same time, Arkansas governor Orval Faubus, up for reelection in 1958, challenged the integration of Little Rock Central High School, and although he was unsuccessful in that, he won reelection. Russell had shouldered this "white man's burden" willingly in the 1930s when there was scarcely more support for civil rights anywhere in the country than in the South. Now he understood that sentiment had changed dramatically and that change must come. He did not, however, have the luxury of changing his position, whatever he might have felt privately. The voters who put him in office were demanding he fight to the death. If he did not, he could be sure they would turn him out of office, a thought he could not bear.

How high his hopes were for an eventual Johnson presidency that would ease the way for changes cannot be known, but one thing is certain. Reaction to the 1957 Voting Rights bill showed Dick Russell that his constituents were still the *white* voters of Georgia. In his study of the American system of government, he had from the beginning given careful thought to the responsibility of a representative of the people in a republic to vote as he felt the majority of his constituents wished, not as he himself believed. He had never contrived a way to resolve this question without feeling that he would be going back on his word.

When the Soviet Union launched the first space satellite in fall 1957, the famous *Sputnik*, the specter of a Soviet-dominated space raised its fearsome head, causing alarm nationwide and especially in the chairman of the Senate Armed Services Committee. Russell had been preaching the threat of a communist-dominated world for ten years by this time. In 1955 he had made a visit to the Soviet Union to see for himself how life progressed under the communist regime. He reported that although the people seemed well-fed and clothed, the Soviet Union was not a place he would choose to live, and Americans should not underestimate the economic and military potential of the Soviets. Now, two years later, here was stark evidence that his country was falling behind the Soviet power. When he heard on the radio on his way to work that the defense department was funding a study to determine how and under what circumstances the United States might surrender in case of total war, he was shocked and angry. Without investigating, he went onto the Senate floor and told his colleagues that he could not believe that the defense department would spend money on such an outlandish study. He was sure the Armed Services Committee had not approved a dime of taxpayer money to study plans for surrender. Instead, the committee had concentrated on seeing that America was ready to meet any attack that might come with return destruction so horrific the first attack could not be contemplated. It was later determined that the study was on "strategic surrender" and had nothing to do with the surrender of the United States in a modern war. Nevertheless, Russell introduced and passed an amendment in the Senate that forbade federal expenditure on surrender studies by a vote of 88 to 2.

Dick Russell was sixty years old in 1957, and he had been in the US Senate twenty-five years when the 1958 Congress convened. His colleagues took note of that fact with words of appreciation that genuinely humbled him. His dual devotion to his country and his state spurred him because he understood that his position of power enabled him to accomplish much good, especially in national defense. By now, however, it was clear that the battle for civil rights was being waged by combatants ready to fight long and fiercely and that the South was again in the position of being hopelessly outnumbered. Visions of lost Civil War battles he'd studied since childhood haunted him, as well as horror tales of Reconstruction evils against white Southerners.

It is evidence of the stress this entire situation placed on Dick Russell that he became increasingly anxious about what he called the "miscegenation" or, less frequently, "mongrelization" of America. More immediately, he feared the violence that would erupt if the South were forced to integrate its schools and public spaces, as seemed more and more likely. His usual quiet and reasoned appeal could become overshadowed by the threat of too much federal power raised against Southern states. The picture of a South once more prostrate at the feet of stomping enemies determined to humiliate her possessed his imagination. An irrational fear of mongrelization might have made him vote against statehood for Hawaii and Alaska and to write in one of his notebooks that their entry into the union was a sad day for the country.

It is tragic that a person of Dick Russell's high moral character and consummate ability in governing was so poisoned by the skewed history of his beloved Southland that he could not see that, as Hubert Humphrey had urged, human rights had to take precedence over states' rights. The fact that taking even a modest stand for civil rights would end his Senate career cannot be discounted as a reason for his continued determination to defend the indefensible. He had given his adult life to serving the people of Georgia, and he was now in a position to serve them even better. His work had brought benefits to black and white individuals. What would be the use of giving up a job he loved and at which he excelled for a cause which would take him out of the Senate and deprive all Georgians of his help?

It might seem from today that a leader of Dick Russell's magnitude could have exercised some influence in changing hearts and minds in the South, but his keen political sense told him this was not true. The response of his constituents to the weak 1957 Civil Rights Bill remained an obvious barometer, and another situation in Georgia stalked him. In 1956 Walter George, having served in the Senate from Georgia for thirty five years, was up for reelection. George was chairman of the Senate Foreign Relations Committee, a frequent adviser to the president, and one of the Senate's most respected members. When Herman Talmadge, governor of Georgia from 1948 to 1955, and son of Russell's rival Gene Talmadge, decided to challenge George, the elder statesman was compelled to withdraw from the race. Talmadge had a powerful political machine inherited from his father, and opinion polls showed that Georgians were ready to put the venerable George out to pasture, even though he did not want to go. Dick Russell watched these developments with regret for his longtime colleague and friend and a painful awareness of how fickle voters could be.

It is highly unlikely that Russell ever considered moderating his civil rights stance because that would have required changing his view of the superiority of Anglo-Saxon culture. Through the years he had often been compared, during Senate considerations of civil rights legislation, to General Robert E. Lee. Russell was called the modern equivalent of that great military strategist, one who often had been able to pull victory out of what looked like sure defeat for outnumbered white Southerners. Russell was flattered by these comparisons because Lee had been his hero since childhood. Nevertheless, the duty to fill an age-old hero's shoes became a heavier and heavier burden as the world shifted to a less hierarchical and more humane view of the life of the human family.

In Washington, as his Senate power increased with onrushing world events, Dick Russell led what seemed to outsiders a lonely life. It is true that he lived alone most of his life there in hotel rooms, and even when, in 1962, he finally bought an apartment, he did little to furnish it, to make it a home. Years after the fact, Pat Collins recalled that his hotel rooms, which she said she visited many times, were pleasant and clean but cluttered. In later years his administrative assistant, Charles Campbell, found his apartment a messy marvel of books and papers, more like an office than an abode, except for well-worn reading chairs. When a young student aide, Norman Underwood, helped the senator move from his hotel to the new apartment, he could not believe how little the statesman had. Books were the main thing that filled the boxes they hauled.

In contrast to this hermit-like life, Dick Russell had a large, active family with whom he shared a strong bond of fellowship, particularly those living in the DC area. His sisters had acted as a natural, capable, and loving support group. He valued knowing his nephew Hugh Peterson, Jr., who remembered weekend family gatherings at the Peterson apartment when Jean Stacy played the piano and family songfests rang out. William Don Russell, son of brother Fielding and Virginia, worked for his uncle for seven years and became a trusted and valued aide. When Bill, as he was called, got up the courage to scold his uncle because he was not going to speak to constituents who had waited all afternoon in the senator's office, Dick grumbled that Bill was just like his mother, always reminding him of how he ought to treat people. Then he went out and spoke to the patient callers. Bill took the word and the action as a compliment.

During the 1950s, however, the group was diminishing as the Greens and Ina junior retired and moved back to Georgia. Bill decided to study for the ministry instead of studying law, and when he told his uncle, the senator said, "I understand your decision, but I never thought you'd leave me." Ralph Sharpton died in 1952 and sister Harriette in 1959, leaving only Pat in Washington. During this time Dick Russell stopped attending almost all official parties unless they had something to do with Georgia. He had simply done all socializing he felt obligated to do. As his power increased, so did his Senate work, and he spent his time working.

Offsetting the loss of his sisters nearby, Dick Russell's long friendship with Harriet Orr deepened. Their relationship was kept intensely private, even for those times, and the press and others left them alone. They enjoyed an intimate dinner together on weekends, usually at Harriet's apartment, drives in the country, and occasional movies. They travelled together, most often when on their way to their homes. Harriet had grown up in Charlotte, North Carolina, and her parents had a summer home in Cherry Grove, North Carolina. Dick was welcome in the Orr home and came to know and appreciate the entire family, including Harriet's mother and her brother and sister. He wrote notes to her nieces and took them out with their aunt when they came to Washington. Harriet evidently was willing to adjust her social calendar to times when Dick Russell could let his Senate work go for a few hours or days. Sometimes he called up asking for a short-notice date, and even occasionally missed these times. Harriet sent good-humored notes accepting his apology.

When Harriet's two nieces came to Washington to visit her, Dick Russell invited them to dinner. The nieces wanted to go to a nightclub, and the senator agreed. He asked his nephew Bill Russell to come with them so that there would be two men to escort the three women. Bill was twenty, and he had already made a date for that evening, but he did not consider telling his uncle that he could not go with him. He asked how old the girls were, and when his uncle said, "Thirteen and fourteen," Bill said, "I get the fourteen-year-old."

At the club, they had dinner and then began to dance. First the senator danced with the young girls, then with Harriet. As he and Harriet were dancing, a black couple came onto the dance floor. Bill watched his uncle leave the floor and come quickly back to the table, calling his nephew to the side.

"I can't afford to risk being photographed dancing in an integrated situation. You'll have to bring the girls home," he said.

With that he disappeared, leaving Bill with the girls and the check. Neither Harriet nor the girls seemed to hold this exodus against the senator. He received an enthusiastic thank-you note for the evening at the nightclub from the nieces, and Harriet continued to be glad to see him when they could get together.

Dick Russell also continued to accept invitations to quiet personal dinners with Senate friends, such as the Johnsons and the Fulbrights. Almost from his earliest days in the Senate he had enjoyed going out to visit Harry Byrd (D-VA) and his family. The Byrds, although a First Family of Virginia, came from the kind of genteel poverty that Dick Russell had grown up in, and the two Southerners, each as much a gentleman as the other, understood how long the road back to prosperity had been for the South.

Two men who became his closest friends in the Senate were John Stennis (D-MS) and Milton Young (R-ND). Although an alliance with a Mississippi senator would seem obvious, Stennis and Russell worked as much together on defense as on civil rights. Young and Russell were formidable collaborators on farm legislation, and Young endorsed Russell during his bid for the Democratic presidential nomination in 1952. Certainly a single person, man or woman, has times of being lonelier than happily married couples, but it is possible that Dick Russell, an intensely private man in a highly public position, had all the company he wished, when he wished it. He was exceptionally good company, and friends would make the effort to spend time with him. In addition, he enjoyed being alone after a day in the Senate, preferring to relax with a good book than to buzz about town, drinking too much at noisy parties.

A lifelong pleasure that he never abandoned, baseball gave Dick Russell a way to relax. He enjoyed going to the Washington Senators' games and might be asked to give the opening pitch. Lowell B. Mason, a wealthy businessman who sponsored something he called the "Baseball, Marching, and Luncheon Club" among senators, congressman, and Supreme Court justices, had long been impressed with Russell's baseball knowledge. Along with other congressional club members, Russell usually sat in Mason's box at games, and in April 1956 the senator was called on to pinch-hit during a game against the New York Yankees. This was not a chance Dick Russell would miss, and he gladly signed the "contract" that allowed him to bat. His performance, a weak dribble along the first-base line, did not put him on base, but it drove home the winning run. Mason published this amazing feat in a hardcover book with a print run of ten. Dick Russell sent his copy home to his sister Ina.

In 1958 Dick began to experience chronic health problems. The boyhood pneumonia that had nearly killed him in 1915 had weakened his lungs, and continued heavy smoking had increased his tendency to respiratory problems. He struggled with annual bouts of flu and in 1956 had again suffered an attack of pneumonia. In the age of modern drugs, it was not as serious as the attack in 1915, but by 1958 he had had to fight respiratory battles to such an extent that he checked into the Walter Reed Army Medical Center for a complete check-up. It was far from good news to learn that he had emphysema. Following this diagnosis, Dick Russell was finally able to give up smoking, but the damage to his lungs was irreversible. Bill Russell, who had become a trusted aide-de-camp for his uncle by this time, saw a man powerful in his work, one who was able to influence weighty questions of national government, struggle to surmount the depression that came with the diagnosis of emphysema. A rough road of disappearing health and vigor lay dark ahead.

The 1958 November elections returned the Democrats to Congress with an even larger majority than they had won in 1956, but that did not translate into easier work for Johnson and Russell. Although a basic difference was not obvious at first, the new senators came in with modern ideas about what constituted senatorial behavior. They liked the idea of being team players, but they were more interested in their own images than in party unity. Now television and other media governed how a man responded to any question. A comfortable majority for the Democrats meant that all senators had more independence. The new kids were not going to be eager to get on Johnson's bandwagon.

Although Dick Russell had never thought it part of his job to promote his own image—he thought paying a press secretary an unethical waste of taxpayers' money—Herman Talmadge came into the Senate wielding such a powerful publicity machine that Russell joked that soon Georgians would be asking the name of their other senator. He predicted sardonically that he might be required to hire someone to "magnify my activities and minimize my failings." The senior Georgia senator did not approve of these changes in Senate attitude, but he was finally persuaded to hire a press secretary in 1959.

Dick Russell did everything he could to make Herman Talmadge's transition into the Senate a pleasant one, and from the beginning of their work together, the younger Talmadge acknowledged a heavy debt to Russell as mentor and friend.

Another major change in how the Senate operated under Johnson's direction of the Democrats in power occurred when William F. Knowland, Republican minority leader from 1955 to 1959, left the Senate to run for the governor's office in California. Knowland was a man whom Johnson understood how to manipulate, and the Texas senator had done so easily. When Everett Dirksen of Illinois became the Republican leader in 1959, the scene changed. Dirksen was a giant of the Senate, known for his oratory and, like Russell and Johnson, his keen perception of how the Senate operated. He would not be manipulated even by a master manipulator like Johnson.

The Senate atmosphere was charged with a different current in 1959/1960, with several senators already maneuvering to win the presidential nomination and run against Vice President Richard Nixon, whom experts predicted would be the Republican nominee. Hubert Humphrey, Stuart Symington, Lyndon Johnson, and John F. Kennedy were all prominent in stories of the upcoming race.

With an essentially lame-duck president, Johnson decided not to wait for Eisenhower to initiate legislation and then try to change it to be acceptable to Democrats. Johnson would, instead, take the initiative and introduce many bills himself. If he could stop Russell and Dirksen from joining conservative forces, he could pass nearly anything he wanted.

This new tactic did not sit well with Russell's philosophy of government. He was a minimalist, believing that no bill was better than a bad bill, and he did not base his assessment of how effective a Congress had been by the number of bills it had passed. Eisenhower, alarmed at the scope of Johnson's 1959 legislative agenda and the speed at which he went after realizing it, refused to go along and was not shy about using his veto power. He brought a housing bill to a halt, and, using the threat of veto, got the Senate to water down an airport construction bill. For the first time, Lyndon Johnson was stymied in the Senate.

With such a large majority of Democrats, another Civil Rights Bill was inevitable, and it came on the Senate floor early in 1960. The Southern Bloc, under Russell's leadership, mounted a full-fledged filibuster, and once again it was successful enough to have the bill generally emasculated before it passed in May 1960. Yet pass it did. The handwriting on the white walls of the South scrawled larger, darker.

The national party conventions in the summer were a matter of keen interest as the Democrats struggled to come up with a candidate to beat Richard Nixon. Lyndon Johnson was considered a principal contender prior to the primaries, and Russell backed him from the start. However, the Georgia senator did not think an active participation on his part, with his reputation for Southern preferences, would benefit his friend. Johnson made a weak showing against John Kennedy, the man of the hour, but in the end Johnson was offered the vice presidential slot and, to the surprise of many, including Dick Russell, the Texan accepted. This Democratic ticket was a strange combination, but the Kennedy camp saw that it could not possibly win the election without Johnson. He was a candidate acceptable to both liberals and conservatives, and in the final analyses of that historically close election, it is judged that Johnson did, indeed, put the Democrats over the top. All of the South had gone against Kennedy just after the convention, but in the election, Johnson won back at least part of that region.

Russell was appalled that Johnson would give up his powerful seat in the Senate for the do-nothing job of vice president, and he said as much. When it looked as though Johnson would accept, Russell phoned his nephew Bobby Russell at the convention and sent him to try to persuade Johnson against accepting the offer, but to no avail. Disappointed, Russell made it known that he supported the party ticket, but he was loathe to do any active campaigning. As he was wont to do at election time, he left on a working trip to Europe, inspecting military bases. When Johnson's whistle-stop train through the South paused in Macon, Georgia, at Mercer University, however, there was a Russell letter left to be read aloud that praised Johnson as an able leader. In addition, Dick Russell's nephew Bobby was one of the most visible Georgia politicians to board the "LBJ Special." Everyone in politics knew that Dick Russell had high hopes for his nephew, so Bobby's presence was a strong endorsement of Lyndon Johnson.

As the election progressed toward November, the outlook grew less and less predictable. Tensions ran high. When a crowd of upscale Republicans saw Lyndon and Lady Bird in a Dallas hotel lobby, they became abusive, and it took Johnson nearly thirty minutes to shepherd Lady Bird protectively through the shouting, swearing mob. When Bobby Russell, a complete devotee of LBJ, heard about this incident, he phoned his uncle Dick in Europe and urged him to come home and get on the bandwagon. It was unthinkable that anyone would subject Lady Bird to such indignities as being spat upon. Although Russell would not have come for Johnson alone, he could not bear to think of Lady Bird's being endangered by a mob of "unruly, rich and profane" Republicans. He cut short his trip and came home to join the campaign, traveling on Johnson's chartered plane in the final days. He spoke actively for the Kennedy-Johnson ticket, and his campaigning was another small event that took on a larger significance when analysts began looking at the narrow Kennedy-Johnson victory, for Russell's support likely swung Texas, Georgia, and South Carolina into Kennedy's column.[14]

Dick Russell himself was up for reelection in the 1960 race, but he had no opposition. His entire campaign expense was the $1,500 filing fee. A few people had sent contributions, but when he did not need them, he returned them, as was his usual method.

Mindful of the debt he owed the South, John Kennedy or his associates consulted often with Dick Russell as they filled cabinet positions and other administrative posts. Dean Rusk, as secretary of state, was one of the questions. Russell first wondered if his fellow Georgian would be tough enough, then worried that he would get the country into a war. Although these assessments might seem contradictory, they represent a concise summary of the razor's edge that any secretary of state must tread.

By the end of 1960 the Senate was changing, Russell's health was deteriorating, and he could find no way to adapt some of his own views to the new world dawning. When he was a fourth grader, he had

---

[14] Popular vote: 34,220,984 for Kennedy vs. 34,108,157 for Nixon; electoral vote: Kennedy: 303, Nixon: 219.

inscribed in his notebook the sentiments of an imaginary star: "I cannot do much," said the little star, "to make the dark world bright. My silver beams cannot pierce far into the gloom of night. Yet I am part of God's plan and I shall do the best I can." This modest statement about using one's gifts to the best of one's ability had stayed with him through more than twenty-five years of ascending power. He had shared this vision and its source with his good friend in the Senate, Milton Young. Now that metaphorical star, having risen far and bright, would begin to wane. Yet because of his dedication, integrity, and desire to serve, Russell's light would remain one of worth and strength to three more presidents, to the unique legislative body that he venerated, and to the country he loved.

JOHN FITZGERALD KENNEDY: 20 JANUARY 1961–22 NOVEMBER 1963

"He was a man of tolerance and understanding. He fought hard for those things in which he believed, but he well knew that all men would not see the same issue in the same light.... The world is a much better place because he lived and passed this way."
—Memorial Address of Hon. Richard B. Russell to John Fitzgerald Kennedy in the United States Senate

With the Kennedy administration, Dick Russell faced a difficult dichotomy. Obviously, he had not supported the liberal Democratic platform that promised the civil rights legislation the Georgian had fought against since arriving in Washington, and his hope was that Johnson would be effective in moderating the sweeping changes. While Russell had an old-fashioned and idealistic view of life in the South, one based on relationships rather than law, by this time he understood changes had to come. He feared, however, that rapid change would create unnecessary violence and bitterness. He was the champion of the unpopular cause now, caught on the wrong side of social history. Nevertheless, he was not a man to change for the sake of popularity. However he might disagree with John Kennedy on this particular issue, the veteran and undisputed lion of the Senate stood ready to serve his chief executive with all his skill. For Dick Russell, that would always mean offering opposing views when he felt they were needed.

Before Kennedy could be inaugurated on 20 January 1961, Russell saw a civil rights crisis develop in Georgia that was something of a family affair. Georgia's governor was Ernest Vandiver, who was married to Betty Russell, daughter of Richard B. Russell's brother Robert Lee Russell, Sr. Although Dick Russell loved all his nieces and nephews, it was natural for him to feel especially close to the children of his nearest brother, with whom he had shared so much of his early career, a brother who had crossed the Great Divide six years before. Ernest Vandiver had been elected governor of Georgia in 1958, and one of his campaign slogans had been "No, not one," signifying that he would not allow Georgia schools to be integrated. The slogan might have come from his brother-in-law, Robert Lee Russell, Jr. On 9 January 1961, two black students, Charlayne Hunter and Hamilton Holmes, sought to be enrolled at the University of Georgia. Governor Vandiver had to decide whether to close the university in order to prevent their being admitted or to leave it open and admit that segregation was finished.

What happened over the next few days showed Dick Russell that life in his beloved Georgia would adapt to a new order of things. That Georgia conducted this first attempt at integration with more dignity and calm than almost anywhere else in the South has to have made him proud.

After several days of trying to come up with a legal reason to close the university, Governor Vandiver decided that the most important thing was to keep the university open and that this goal could best be achieved by a peaceful integration process. Accordingly, in spite of his pledge, Vandiver announced that he would not close the university and that integration of the student body would occur in a lawful manner. His compliance with the federal authorities resulted in a relatively peaceful event. Although there was one evening of media-hyped "rioting" outside Center Meyers Dormitory where Charlayne Hunter was housed, the two black students began their studies without further serious problems.[15]

---

[15] I was a freshman at the University of Georgia that year and lived in Center Meyers. The night reported as one of rioting was not disturbing to any real degree.

One of Vandiver's most trusted advisers was his brother-in-law, Robert Lee Russell, Jr. Seeing these two younger men choose a path toward ending the segregated South did not disturb Dick Russell. It might even have made him feel a little envious, because this was a choice he did not feel he had the right to make. His constituents expected him to be the champion of the white South as always. The younger men never discussed this situation with their powerful and conservative uncle, but the force of the white opinion that Russell avoided confronting was such that, even as times became more progressive, Ernest Vandiver was never elected to another public office in Georgia. He believed that his stand on civil rights cost him his political career.

A few days after this drama, Governor and Mrs. Vandiver travelled to a snowy Washington to attend the inauguration of John Fitzgerald Kennedy. The governor and his wife were seated in a special section for dignitaries, and their children, Chip, Beth, and Jane, ages twelve to seven years old, sat on benches below the platform, close enough to see the poet Robert Frost lose his copy of his poem to the wintry winds. President Kennedy's bright auburn hair impressed seven-year-old Jane. After the ceremony, the children were taken to Uncle Dick's office to dry out shoes, socks, and gloves. When the senator arrived, he found children's clothes draped all over the radiators, a sight that made him smile. To have family close to him, joining his life in Washington, was a genuine treat.

As the civil rights movement gained momentum, Dick Russell continued to lead the opposition to it, and the veteran senator questioned other liberal aspects of the Kennedy administration as well. Russell was not willing to blindly extend the responsibility of the federal government deeper into people's lives through more aid to education, help for cities, medical care for the aged, and similar programs of social

---

The radio reports were of a thousand students assembled outside Meyers. My memory is of perhaps half that. I believe one rock was thrown that broke a window, which happened to be a window in my room. But all the girls were downstairs, huddled around a small black-and-white television set, waiting to hear what Governor Vandiver would say about closing the school. When he announced that it would remain open, the large majority of students were relieved and wanted to get on with their studies.

and economic reform. Russell has been called a nineteenth-century man stuck in the twentieth century, and as the 1960s progressed, it became clear to him that he was more and more out of step with the times. He grew weary of the burden of inspiring his Southern senate colleagues during civil rights fights, not because his views had changed, but because he understood that the mood of the rest of the country had changed. In Georgia his old friend Ralph McGill, editor of the *Atlanta Journal-Constitution,* and others were coming out strongly for leaders with different outlooks, leaders who could transcend the issues of segregated schools and public transportation. The old Southern way of life that Russell cherished was doomed, and he was powerless to change that. Yet his main constituency had not changed, and he was expected, if he wanted to remain in the Senate, to lead the losing fight.

That Dick Russell wanted more than anything to remain in the Senate cannot be doubted. He had come to Washington at the age of thirty-five. In 1961, he began his twenty-eighth year in the Senate. Coming from long-lived people, he could envision at least two more terms as United States senator from Georgia. Time only strengthened his respect for the Senate and its traditions as he understood its unique function in the American system of government. It was to this ideal of government that he had given his considerable talents, energy, and love.

Becoming a master of the Senate legislative body must have astonished the Georgia senator, because he had set out to serve, not to master. Yet now he knew that his position made it possible for him to serve his state and nation as no other Georgian could at that time. Dick Russell knew Georgia could produce Gene Talmadges and Marvin Griffins, the kind of Southern politicians who gave the South a bad name for their devotion to demagoguery. That his growth into statesmanship balanced that opposite view was reason to feel pleased and to stay the course. Even as public opinion changed, and even if his own convictions had moderated, Russell would not have contemplated any stand that might take him out of the Senate. Such a move would have cost Georgia her powerful place in national government. Knowing the workings of this world as he did, Dick Russell would have seen no advantage whatsoever to his state or his nation in surrendering his seat.

The Kennedy years provided many opportunities for Russell, as chairman of the Senate Armed Services Committee, to guard his country zealously so that it remained strong in the Cold War. Russell's conviction that the United States had more worth protecting than any other nation in the world had not wavered, nor had his belief that the USSR was the most imperialistic nation on earth. As a result, the citizens of the United States had to stand ready to defend their land, even though the price was high. Russell continued to back strong defense bills for conventional forces, development of missiles and other sophisticated weapons, long-range bombers, and the space program. He and President Kennedy generally agreed on these issues.

When the Berlin crisis in early 1961 led to a build-up of American forces in Europe, Russell was a strong supporter as Kennedy responded to Russian threats to seal off Berlin and East Germany. This move had become necessary in the Russian view because of the increasing general exodus of skilled labor from East Germany into West Germany, where work opportunities were so much greater than in the Russian-dominated sector. The Berlin Wall was built to halt the exodus, and the world watched fearfully as France, Great Britain, and the United States faced down their old ally and refused to leave Berlin. Events such as these confirmed Russell's view that the Russians were constantly seeking ways to exploit weaknesses in the Western alliance. There must be no failure to show a united front and to continue building defenses.

Another confrontation with the Russians that likely embarrassed Russell was the infamous Bay of Pigs incident of April 1961.[16] Richard Russell had been one of the first to insist on the forming of a Central Intelligence Agency in 1947, and as the agency developed, he became its champion. He worried that one of the places that America was weakest in defense was in keeping military secrets. In spite of his belief in America and the ideals of an open society, Russell was pragmatic enough to realize that the country would not be served by displaying for the public our true capabilities in war. It was his belief that as long as the Russians feared what the United States could do in retaliation, there would be no war. Consequently, Russell gave the CIA a loose rein,

---

[16] The Bay of Pigs Invasion was a botched attempt to invade Cuba, supposedly by counter-revolutionary forces without direct American involvement, but actually with heavy support from the CIA. It left the communist-fighting American government red-faced.

although it was meant to be under the supervision of an Armed Services "watchdog" subcommittee. During the 1950s, the powerful senator let it be known that he trusted CIA operations and preferred not to know about some of its activities. Not surprisingly, it had become a nearly independent branch of the government.

President Kennedy was upset by the Bay of Pigs incident because the CIA had acted independently and with poor judgment. Russell had opposed the plan because he did not think the 1,300 refugees seeking to overthrow Fidel Castro had enough force to succeed, and he was right. When the invasion went ahead anyway, thanks to the CIA, Russell did not comment to avoid giving away CIA involvement. Kennedy, however, relieved Allan Dulles as director of the CIA and ordered a review of the agency's operations.

In 1962, when it was discovered that Russian missiles were being shipped into Cuba, Russell and Kennedy again collaborated on what to do about the communist threat in American territory. Along with the Berlin crisis, this event would go down as one of the most frightening confrontations between the two superpowers during the Cold War. Whereas Russell advocated slow response to any act that put the United States in the guise of policing the globe, this view applied only to the world outside the North American hemisphere. A staunch believer in the Monroe Doctrine, it was Russell's opinion that when the missiles were discovered, the United States should have invaded Cuba and destroyed these weapons as well as Fidel Castro's avowed communist regime.

Russell held secret meetings of the Senate Armed Services and Foreign Relations committees to determine the extent of the Soviet threat. As the crisis deepened in September 1962, he was often in touch with President Kennedy and other White House staff. More military than the military, according to Secretary of State Dean Rusk, Russell spoke passionately for the use of American air power and for a determined effort to wipe out the Russian planes and missiles in Cuba. Kennedy and Rusk disagreed with this policy, and others, as well as Russell himself, reported that he became a nuisance in the meetings as he put his opinions forth. This was the perfect time, he said, according to the age-old Monroe Doctrine, to stop interference in our hemisphere. Russell was joined by Bill Fulbright and other congressmen and senators in urging the president to take vigorous action, but Kennedy went for a softer approach. By mid-October the president had reached an agreement with USSR leader Nikita Khrushev, and the missiles were withdrawn.

Richard Russell continued to distrust the Russians, and a year later in 1963 he made an agonizing decision: While recognizing the need to stop nuclear arms proliferation, he decided to vote against the Nuclear Test Ban Treaty. He did not believe the Russians would abide by the treaty, and therefore this treaty would put the United States in a dangerous position that he was not willing to risk. He was overwhelmingly outvoted on this issue when the treaty was ratified on 24 September 1963 by a vote of 80 to 19.

During the Kennedy years, Russell continued to get defense contracts for Georgia, and his role in defending America remained primary. Although a genuinely modest man, never a seeker of headlines, he was pleased when Kennedy asked him, as chairman of the Senate Armed Services Committee, to take Kennedy's place on Memorial Day and lay a wreath on the tomb of the Unknown Soldier. When the president invited the Georgia senator to accompany him on Air Force One to the United States Air Force Academy for graduation exercises on 5 June 1963, Russell was again delighted. Although he had handled the legislation to establish the academy and the appropriations to build it in 1954, Russell had never visited Colorado Springs. To be thus included on a presidential visit pleased the warrior's advocate.

Although Russell and Kennedy enjoyed warm personal relations, beginning when John Kennedy joined the Senate in 1953[17], their friendship pales compared to Russell's and Johnson's. During the Kennedy years, as Russell had warned his friend would happen, Johnson was sidelined and seldom consulted by the New Frontier people. Yet Russell and Johnson continued to get together and to consult with one another on various problems. Russell retained great faith in Johnson's consummate ability as a politician, though he might have been surprised that Johnson pushed for more civil rights legislation than did Kennedy. This issue became one that the two friends did not discuss, each respecting the other's right to his own view.

---

[17] One of Russell's aides recalls a letter Senator Kennedy sent around to other senators asking for contributions to a fund to help Senator Russell afford to wash his car. This good-natured joking about Russell's frugality pleased the Georgia senator.

As John Kennedy was having a Civil Rights Bill drawn up, he conferred with Dick Russell about its contents, inviting the Southern senator to the Oval Office to discuss the potential bill. In the kind of working of the American system that Russell revered, the two men talked over the proposals from the viewpoints of various factions. Finally, the president asked, "Do you think this will be enough, Senator Russell?"

With characteristic honesty and a double-barreled wisdom, Russell answered, "It will never be enough, Mr. President."

Dick Russell was in the Marble Room behind the Senate Chamber reading the Associated Press and United Press International news ticker tapes on 22 November 1963 when word came of the president's assassination in Dallas. Stunned, shocked, disbelieving, with tears streaming down his cheeks, Russell's first thought was of his duty to the defense of the nation. He went quickly to a telephone and called Secretary of Defense Robert McNamara to learn if the nation's defenses were ready for anything. When McNamara assured him they were, the Georgia senator sat with his friend and colleague Mike Mansfield of Montana in the radio-TV gallery and wept. When media commentators questioned him, he could hardly answer their questions.

Dick Russell knew that his friend Lyndon Johnson was facing the most serious crisis of his life, and the Georgian stood ready to support the new president as a friend and as a senator. Nevertheless, Russell decided not to go to Andrews Air Force base in the darkness to meet Air Force One returning tragically with two presidents. It was not his style to be where the cameras were clicking, especially not during a time of mourning. Johnson looked for Dick Russell in the throng and was disappointed not to find him, but both men knew their friendship had entered a new phase. After leaving Air Force One and making the short trip to the White House via a Marine helicopter, Johnson called Russell and asked him to come to the White House the following morning. Lyndon Johnson relied heavily on his mentor in the ensuing days, as the new president sought to reassure the nation of continuity and responsibility in the United States government. Russell abided completely by tradition in the changed relationship. He no longer called his friend Lyndon. It was now, unfailingly, "Mr. President." That

Lyndon asked him to call him by his Christian name as before made no difference. Such was Dick Russell's adherence to tradition and his abiding respect for the office of the president.

Throughout his youth Dick Russell had seen his own mother accept again and again the disappointing consequences of her husband's political involvement. His failed love affairs also bore witness to how women, no matter how innocent, become victims of politics. Knowing well how stern the stuff of ambition must be for any woman tied to a politician, this bachelor watched Jacqueline Kennedy conduct herself with consummate dignity during this national tragedy, which had required of her the life of her husband and the father of her children. Television had come of age in its live broadcasting of the historic event, and Russell was aware that Mrs. Kennedy's behavior had been exemplary and inspiring to the entire nation. His admiration took precedence over other considerations. Although he feared being thought presumptuous, he had to write her to express his unbounded admiration of her demeanor and every act during the four tragic days since 22 November. On 26 November, he wrote:

> No queen, born of the purple, could have acquitted herself more admirably. Your calm dignity vanished the hysteria which threatened millions of your fellow Americans who followed your every movement on the television screen.
>
> I am so old-fashioned as to believe that those who have departed this earth still know what transpires here, and I therefore believe that President Kennedy was prouder of you then than he has ever been in this life. Only a great lady in the finest traditions of the old school could have displayed such magnificent courage....

In spite of the harsh realities of his political life, Dick Russell could still nurture the romantic ideal of heroines as well as heroes.

LYNDON BAINES JOHNSON: 1963–1968

"You tell Lyndon that I've been expecting the rod for a long time, and I'm sorry that it's from his hand the rod must be wielded; but I'd rather it be his hand than anybody else's I know. Tell him to cry a little when he uses it."[18]
—Richard B. Russell, Jr.

As an old friend and as a senior senator, Richard Russell was a member of the Senate-House group named to escort the new president into the House chamber for the joint session of Congress shortly after noon on 27 November 1963. In the House gallery, seated with Lady Bird Johnson among other guests of the president, was Carl Sanders, governor of Georgia, who was gaining a reputation as the epitome of the New South. Johnson was well aware that the stand he was about to take on civil rights would not go down well with the Old Guard, and he understood why they could not side with him. Consummate politician that he was, he would cover all the bases.

Dick Russell could not have been surprised at what Johnson proposed in this short, passionate, and beautifully presented speech to the country and to the world following an event as tragic as the assassination of a young and beloved president. Johnson called for the earliest possible passage of Kennedy's Civil Rights Bill as the most fitting memorial to honor the fallen president. The new president reminded everyone that it was he who helped pass the 1957 Civil Rights Bill and that he had tried again in 1960. As an advocate of civil rights, he was no novice. Now was the time to eliminate from the nation every trace of discrimination based on race and color.

Whatever Dick Russell thought about timing, he would not have the luxury of changing his stance on this issue. He would not turn against the traditions of his cherished Southern ideal simply because the events of history had dealt him a losing hand. He would use every legal means at his disposal in the fight, every Senate rule, as he always had, standing on constitutional rights, but he knew that it was a lost battle now. Nevertheless, his assessment of Kennedy was that he would not have

---

[18] Richard Russell's message via White House aide Bill Moyers to Lyndon Johnson regarding impending Civil Rights legislation in 1964.

wanted anyone to stultify his own conviction merely to conform to a fallen hero's opinion, and the Georgian calculated that it was within his power to make it a long and arduous fight.

President Johnson dealt him further complication in this fight. Determined to put to rest rumors of conspiracy and intrigue surrounding Kennedy's death, Johnson formulated plans for an investigation to issue an irrefutable report on the tragedy. The president wanted the best people in government on this commission, and to make sure that no one declined to serve, Johnson called each man personally. Chief Justice Earl Warren was his choice to head the investigation, and Warren objected strongly at first until Johnson insisted this was his patriotic duty.

Dick Russell was his second call, and Russell, too, objected. He did not have to explain to his friend that he would be totally consumed with fighting the Civil Rights Bill. He merely said his current schedule of legislative duties was nearly impossible. He could not add such a time-consuming duty. In addition, Russell had no affection for Earl Warren, feeling, as he did, that the Warren court had brought about too much judicial law. Laws should be written by Congress, in Russell's view, yet the Supreme Court had undertaken to change basic laws without debate and had succeeded. Here was a man with whom Russell had deeply fundamental differences. In spite of a long telephone conversation with the president at his most persuasive, Russell resolutely refused to serve on the commission. Johnson made his other calls, and when the commission composition was about to be announced, he called Dick Russell again and said that Russell's name was on the list and the senator would just have to deal with it. Russell later said he was conscripted on the commission. There was no suggestion that Johnson put Russell on the commission to weaken his ability to fight the civil rights legislation. It was clearly Johnson's desire to have the best men available to do an extremely difficult job. Knowing Russell's integrity, his keen mind, and his unswerving patriotism, Johnson insisted on having him for this work.

As Russell feared, he did not have enough time to attend all the commission meetings and lead the civil rights fight that would result in the longest filibuster in the nation's history. In addition, he was, as chairman of the Senate Armed Services Committee, trying to keep up with ominous events developing in Laos and Vietnam. True to his work ethic, he kept up with the commission's hearings by reading every line of testimony when he could not attend, preparing appropriate questions for meetings he could attend. As the year unfolded, there were some days he never left the Senate complex, eating every meal in the Senate restaurant and sleeping in his office.

By February Russell had become so frustrated that he threatened to resign from the Warren Commission, which he pointedly called the Assassination Commission. He did, in fact, write the president a long letter explaining his difficulties and asking him to accept his resignation. Johnson ignored the letter, and by 1 March, Russell was able to announce on the television program "Face the Nation" that he would not resign and would do his best to get all of the facts about the Dallas tragedy to the American people.

By this time it is certain that Russell understood that the next Civil Rights Bill was going to pass. He knew Johnson's determination and his skills, and he had been warned, early in the fight, at one of his frequent visits to the White House. "Dick," Johnson had told him outright, "I love you. I owe you. But I am going to run over you if you challenge me or get in my way. I aim to pass the Civil Rights Bill, only this time, Dick, there will be no caviling, no compromise, no falling back. This bill is going to pass."

The composition of the Senate and the mood of the country had changed to such an extent that Dick Russell knew the days of the segregated South were numbered, even without Johnson. Nevertheless, he would not be accused of capitulation. Perhaps something they could do would moderate the sweeping effects of the bill. Whereas Southerners believed Kennedy had put items in the original bill on which he was willing to compromise, following his death, there was no mood for compromise. Indeed, some of the measures had been strengthened and omissions corrected. There would be no stopping this steamroller. Dick Russell knew that a dam was going to burst that would destroy the South as he had known it. Beyond that, he understood that repairing ancient wrongs of this magnitude was impossible. Of an intensely practical nature, he could not see the sense in expecting legislative action to become a panacea for centuries of social wrongs.

During this time, Russell suffered when people accused him of racism, of hard-heartedness, of blindness. His views are best summed up in his own words. In a letter to a Georgia clergyman who had written exhorting him to see the truth and act on it, he responded that he had a brother and a brother-in-law and two nephews who were men of the cloth and that one of these was a strong supporter of the bill. Russell wanted it understood that he was as honest in his position as supporters were in theirs.

"I wish I were as sure of what the 'truth' is as you are," he wrote to the pastor. "As an humble layman and confessed sinner, I can only follow my judgment and conscience, and my judgment tells me that we will not reverse history in the United States." He was ever concerned that a mixed race would not be able to maintain a great civilization. That these convictions were misguided might be asserted, but that they were honest and sincere, based on his half-century of reading history, is certain. It pained him to see that the views of the world were changing, making his own views seem cruel and heartless. In commenting on his Senate career in 1969, he expressed his chagrin: "I have known [in the past 35 years] the exaltation of success in measures that I felt to be of great benefit to my country and my people...and others when I have had forced upon me the bitter wine of disappointment and defeat. Indeed, I often feel that I have had perhaps more than my share of disappointments as I have followed the dictates of conscience and convictions."

CBS-TV congressional correspondent Roger Mudd knew Russell for more than a decade, and although disagreeing with the Georgian's civil rights stand, Mudd saw no animus toward black individuals in the senator and did not define him as racist. Rather, he pointed out that Richard Russell was protecting and defending a way of life in which he had been reared and in which the majority of his people had been reared, the majority of his constituents. "[A]nd that's what a man is sent here [to the Senate] for—to defend the way of life that most people who sent him enjoy." Mudd felt that in his own quiet way, Russell made adjustments to the changing times.

In a graduation address at Mercer University in Macon, Georgia, Russell expressed his pain at being thought cruel for his conservative constitutional defense of states' rights. He pointed out that he had backed liberal legislation during the Great Depression and urged sacrifices that were difficult during the war. His record showed, he said, that he was not opposed to change. He did not, however, believe that cherished freedoms should be lightly discarded, nor did he believe that the best road to individual security was in an all-powerful state that sapped and absorbed local governments. He would fight that theory to the bitter end.

Russell went on: "We hear much these days about the 'brotherhood of man' and the need for sympathy, tolerance, and understanding. I believe in the qualities of sympathy, tolerance, and understanding. They are among the finest qualities of human character. I also believe that *nothing can disrupt them quite so quickly as an effort to impose them by legislative fiat."* [19]

To build a true brotherhood of man, Russell believed we must voluntarily learn to respect each other and accept our fellow mortals on the basis of their strengths *and* their weaknesses. We were in danger when we tried to make everyone the same, when we were willing to ignore differences. For him, the injunction of the prophet Micah simplified the question of brotherhood: "What does the Lord require of thee, but to do justly, love mercy, and walk humbly with thy God?"

Significant in Russell's belief in the superiority of Anglo-Saxon culture was his concurrent belief in the responsibility of the ruling class to care for those beneath them in the hierarchy. He often spoke about "noblesse oblige" to younger members of his family. He would define the term to be sure they understood that "to whom much is given much is required." He was pleased when his efforts, such as the school lunch program and rural electrification programs, benefitted all levels of society, without regard to race, and he supported legislative efforts to improve black schools and housing.

In his personal contacts with black individuals, Russell was supportive and friendly. When he knew the circumstances of anyone, he would sympathize and wanted to help. There are stories of his bringing black soldiers home to see dying kin or for other emergencies. The black waitresses in the Senate dining room, where he had breakfast every day, testified to his help on various occasions, for work or for education of

---

[19] Italics mine.

their children. They appreciated that he never failed to introduce them to his family members who came to dine with him, crediting them with good care, an attitude of recognition they said was not common among other senators. He was rumored to have "stock" in a DC cab, having contributed to its purchase in order to help a disabled veteran.

As the civil rights fight of 1964 heated up, the president sent Hubert Humphrey to court and win over Republican giant Everett Dirksen. Although the Southern Bloc mounted a formidable filibuster campaign, Humphrey took pages from Russell's book and kept his people on hand with schedules that allowed everyone some rest time. First there had to be debate over whether to take up the bill or not, and this lasted from 9 March until 26 March. The official filibuster began after the motion to take up the Civil Rights Bill finally came to a vote with only 17 against. Including the debate on the motion and the bill itself, this became the longest filibuster in the history of the Senate, lasting seventy-four working days.

On 10 June 1964, the Senate voted by 71 to 29 (at least 67 ayes were required) to close off debate. During Dick Russell's earlier career, filibusters had successfully blocked eleven previous civil rights bills and two attempts to amend the anti-filibuster rule. Clearly the Senate had changed, and now Russell could not stop the resulting stampede of amendments. Russell complained that "a lynch mob" had taken over. As a last resort, he proposed that certain provisions of the bill be submitted to a national referendum. That proposal was swept aside on 12 June, and on 19 June, the bill passed the US Senate by a vote of 73 to 27.

While this drama played out on the national stage, another drama was unfolding in Dick Russell's personal life. After his mother's death in 1953, as the family patriarch, he became determined to keep the numerous and diverse family members aware of each other and their extraordinary parents/grandparents. By this time there were a number of great-grandchildren of Richard and Ina Dillard Russell, particularly in the families of the older children, Billie, Margo, Rob, Walter, and Fielding. Dick Russell, Jr. kept up close relationships with many of these, especially the grandchildren of his brother Rob. As his mother had encouraged, even begged for in her last years, Dick Russell sponsored the family reunion in June at the homeplace in Winder, on the weekend closest to his parents' wedding anniversary of 24 June. In 1964 the main event of the weekend, a memorial service at the family cemetery, was scheduled for 20 June. It would be followed by Southern barbecue, Brunswick stew, sliced tomatoes, watermelon—there was always a birthday cake, preferably caramel, for Walter and Ina junior, who were born on 18 June and 22 June, respectively—under the pecan trees in the side yard.

This was to be the eleventh consecutive reunion since Ina Dillard Russell's death, and each year the family gathering became more and more of a command performance. Although Dick Russell never tried to force anyone to do anything, the strength of his character and the importance he placed on the event meant that family members made every effort to attend. It was not unusual for 60 to 75 people to turn up, beginning with a hamburger supper on Friday night. All were guests of their uncle or brother Dick, but the details of the weekend were coordinated by family members living in Winder or Barrow County. Those who lived away were called Outlanders and the others Inlanders. At this date, Inlanders were still able to house Outlanders.

Able help was also provided by Modine Thomas, and sometimes Modine found other women willing to work these special occasions. The Russells, however, never had servants to do most of their work. From the earliest days of Ina and Richard's family, it was difficult to find household help because the family was so numerous that servants could and did find easier places to work. Although there was almost always some outside help, the family also had to do much of the cooking and cleaning themselves, and they did this as a matter of course under their mother's tutelage and example. For the reunions, whether before or following Ina Dillard Russell's death, black and white individuals worked together, pitching in to get things ready beforehand, making beds, cleaning, doing kitchen chores, or cooking the pork all night in a pit near the pecan orchard.

A crowd of Russells had gathered at the homeplace on the afternoon of 19 June 1964. News from every television station all day had heralded the civil rights vote taking place in the Senate, and jokes went 'round that perhaps the senator would miss his own reunion. There was some tension because the family was divided, generally speaking, among the old and the young, in hopes for the outcome of the vote. Almost all the senator's younger nieces and nephews wanted the civil rights legislation to pass, and though we respected our uncle for the remarkable mind and spirit that he was and loved him as a pleasant family duty, we were quietly hoping that this battle would be decided on the side of a changed South. For whatever reason, it was easier for those of us in the generation born after the Great Depression to see the idea of integration as entirely reasonable.

Conversation on the subject with other aunts and uncles would have been tentative at best, but another development made it even more delicate. Bill Russell, who had worked for his uncle Dick in Washington for seven years while studying at George Washington University, was a brand-new graduate of Columbia Theological Seminary in Decatur, a Presbyterian institution. Bill loved and respected his uncle and might have known him better than any of us. A week or so earlier, Bill had been asked to sign a petition by Georgians for the Civil Rights Bill, and, believing in the bill, he had signed. An Atlanta reporter sniffed out the Russell name and phoned Bill to learn why a nephew of Senator Russell's was for the bill. This news became state headlines, much to Bill's chagrin, because he had never dreamed his signature would result in publicity that might embarrass his beloved uncle.

Worse, after the story made the papers, Bill and his wife Barbara began to receive anonymous phone calls threatening their home and child. Bill's older brother Fielding, already a Presbyterian minister serving a small church in rural central Alabama, also received threatening calls and even a nighttime visit to his home by men in pick-up trucks demanding to know if it had been he who had signed the petition. Bill arrived at the family reunion wondering if his uncle Dick or any of the others affectionately called the Old Guard were going to speak to him. Not one of the older generation mentioned the petition to the young minister, although he thought he felt a distinct reticence from some of them, a dreaded chill.

The afternoon waned, we learned quietly that the vote was finished and the bill passed, and then word came that Uncle Dick would arrive in an Air Force jet at the Winder airport about eight o'clock. Hamburgers and hot dogs had already been served to most of the gathered family as twilight descended. The boisterous youngsters had drunk a prodigious quantity of soft drinks from a generous supply iced down in large washtubs. Uncle Dick always said they could have all the drinks they

wanted, and his word trumped their parents' directives at the Russell
Reunion. The children were sugared up for the requisite game of
Capture the Flag played late into the night around the old house, with
"flags" on both porches. The adults were sitting at tables in the pecan
orchard beside the house, talking and telling jokes and nibbling Aunt
Pat's tea cakes. There was tension because of the civil rights question,
divisions we dared not discuss, and due to our sympathetic feeling for
the leader of our clan, who had just suffered what was to him his
Waterloo, or perhaps more fittingly, his Appomattox Court House.

Usually two or three younger nephews, college boys, would be
dispatched to pick up the senator. That evening, when the hour was
judged near enough to drive the two miles to the airport to wait for the
plane, someone asked, "Who's going to pick up Uncle Dick?" There was
a brief silence, and then most people got up and simply went to their
cars, and we caravanned to the Winder Airport, perhaps two dozen in
number. We stood waiting on the runway, no one saying much. Bill
Russell made a little joke: "I guess we know how Uncle Dick really
stands on civil rights. He let 'em pass that bill so he could come to this
reunion."

It was almost the longest day of the year, and it was not yet entirely
dark when the fighter jet eased down on the tarmac and taxied to where
we were standing. Behind the pilot, we could see our uncle getting up to
climb onto the wing. He looked as tired as if he had been in a battle, but
a flickering smile came to his lips as he stepped onto the wing and saw
his large family waiting for him. He spoke a word of thanks to the pilot
and shook his hand. Then he turned back to us, and spontaneously we
broke into a rousing chorus of "For He's a Jolly Good Fellow." It was not
easy to make it rousing when most of us were weeping, both for joy in
the changes that would now come and for sympathy with this good man
who had fought an honorable fight on what was judged the wrong side,
a man whom we wanted to know, above all, how we loved and honored
him.

After the barbecue the next afternoon, Bill Russell determined to
find a moment to speak with his uncle, to try to tell him that he had not
meant to embarrass him by the publicity that came from his signing the
petition. He found the patriarch sitting on the front porch in one of the
old oak rockers, miraculously alone. Working for his uncle in

Washington, Bill had learned to speak up about what mattered to him. He sat down in a chair beside the senator and said he had been upset about the publicity and needed his uncle to know that he would never have done something like that, whatever his beliefs, if he had known it would cause trouble for the senator.

His uncle looked him straight in the eye and asked, "Bill, is that really what you believe, that the Civil Rights Bill is best for the country?"

Bill looked straight back at him, feeling only an overwhelming sense of acceptance, and answered, "Yes, sir, it is."

"Then you did the right thing to sign that petition. I was only worried that somehow the press had twisted the report some way that you did not intend. You know I don't trust the press."

Bill smiled, knowing from his many years in Washington that this analysis was true. Telling the story years later, Bill Russell still gets a little choked up as he recalls how his uncle was completely gracious to him, so much so that he was emboldened to say, "Uncle Dick, that is what I believe, and I want you to believe it, too."

"Well, Bill," his uncle replied, "I don't believe it, and what's more, I don't think the majority of my constituents believe it, and it's my responsibility to represent them."

On 15 July, at a meeting of the Coosa Valley Area Planning and Development Commission in Rome, Georgia, Dick Russell made an historic speech.[20] He was without doubt the most respected statesman in the Senate, and as a Southerner, his comments on the Civil Rights Bill's passage would be repeated. While he deplored the passage of the new civil rights law, which he called the Federal Force Bill, and pledged to continue the legal fight against intrusions into the traditional Southern way of life, he made it clear that there was no question of not obeying the law. It was on the books now, having been signed into law by President Johnson on 2 July. As Russell stated,

> It is the understatement of the year to say that I do not like these statutes. There are hundreds of thousands of people in this country who feel as I do about them. However, they are now on

---

[20] Over a thousand people had gathered for the meeting of this organization, credited with contributing to the rapid growth and development of industry in northwest Georgia.

the books and it becomes our duty as good citizens to learn to live with them for as long as they are there.... [A]ll good citizens will learn to live with the statute and abide by its final adjudication, even though we reserve the right to advocate by legal means its repeal or modification.

Deploring the campaign for civil disobedience waged during the agonizing legislative struggle, the Georgia statesman went on: "This strange doctrine that a citizen may pick and choose the laws he will obey and ignore those he does not like is, to me, totally reprehensible. It is a form of anarchy.... It is therefore our duty as good and patriotic citizens, in a period that will undoubtedly be marked by tension and unrest as this statute is implemented, to avoid all violence."

Dick Russell was the only major government official in the Deep South to make such a statement advocating obedience to the law. Yet this stance is entirely in keeping with his character. He had protested the law always on Constitutional grounds. While longing to preserve the old Southern ways, he yet maintained that it was up to the states to make changes they perceived as necessary. When the system of government had enough supporters to challenge his view and pass a different law, he stood ready to obey it while continuing legal protest. This was, to Dick Russell, the American Way.

A letter from Lyndon Johnson on 23 July noted the importance of this public stand:

Dear Dick,

The statement you made in Georgia last week on the need to comply with the law was as significant as any I have heard made by a public official in this country. As the acknowledged leader of the opposition to the Civil Rights Bill, your reputation and your standing could not be higher in those areas where the adjustment to the Bill will be most difficult. Your call for compliance with the law of the land is, of course, in keeping with your personal code and I am confident it will have a great impact.

It was the right and courageous thing to do, and I am as proud and pleased as I can be.

Such praise from an old friend who was now president might have pleased Russell, but it is doubtful that he gave much thought to what others would think of this stand. It was simply, as the president said, in keeping with his personal code, and he would not have considered a different reaction. This was the kind of integrity he had continually demonstrated and which won the admiration of his Senate colleagues throughout his long years of service. What he believed was known, and it was known, too, that he lived by these beliefs. His character could be trusted. Ironically, it was this admired integrity that made him such a formidable enemy in this particular battle, because it was hard for many to doubt his wisdom in this matter when his patriotism, his humanity, and his compassion were unquestioned in other areas. That he truly believed his stand was what was best for the country and that the majority of Georgians wished him to speak for them in this way were his motivation, not thoughtless racism. His racism was, in fact, a deeply considered belief that was not founded on hatred. Rather, he took entirely seriously his responsibility to care for those beneath him in the hierarchy in which he believed. Such a conviction is a far cry from a belief in one's right to abuse or at least ignore those judged "beneath one."

Another important tenet in this speech reveals what Dick Russell felt as the senator from Georgia and underscores why he was not willing to do anything that would be risky to his chance to remain the senator from Georgia. All Georgia politicians had to tread a razor's edge when it came to the race question, for if they were suspected of being soft on segregation, they were quickly out of a job. That Russell chose to present his views in a reasoned and law-abiding way is significant. He had always refused to "cry nigger," the accepted and easy way in the state to gain votes. In Washington, he had been determined to present a new and more respectable national image of the Southern politician. It was in this way that he paved the way for so many projects beneficial to his beloved Georgia. Understanding the way the national government works, he knew that by 1964 he had been in the powerful position of Senate leader long enough to have made a great difference to his state. He wanted to remain there, able to guide funds into Georgia. In this same speech in which he commented on the civil rights changes, he also pointed out Georgia's strong economic stance, citing figures proving that Georgia was "helping lead the way in the economic renaissance of the Southland." Georgia industrial and economic growth in the past decade was reason for rejoicing, but "we must not be satisfied to rest on past accomplishments. We must keep our eye on the future and remain dedicated to the task of keeping Georgia forging ahead." It was Dick Russell's lifelong ambition to keep Georgia forging ahead.

Although the civil rights fight, with its fatiguing days and sleepless nights, had ended, Dick Russell had no chance to rest. The work of the Warren Commission went on through the summer, and ominous events occurred in Vietnam, requiring meetings with the president, the secretary of defense, and military leaders. In addition, 1964 was an election year, and when Hubert Humphrey was chosen as Johnson's running mate, this liberal ticket caused Dick Russell once again to keep as much distance as he could from the national campaign. Another European trip touring military bases and taking some much needed rest was in order. Nevertheless, he felt regret that he could not support his friend and, more especially, Lady Bird, who contacted him several times to ask him to ride her train touring the South. Even this admired and loved lady's pleas did not persuade him.

Although Johnson and Humphrey won by a landslide, Georgia was one of the six states that went for Barry Goldwater, prompting many Georgians to criticize their senior senator for his lack of support. This high feeling against Johnson surprised Russell as much as it did others. Another faction felt Russell should do as Strom Thurmond of South Carolina had done and switch to the Republican camp. Russell's love of Georgia would never have permitted him to make this change. Furthermore, he still had faith in his party, which was not one that forced its members to follow every party line, whereas he felt the Republican Party allowed much less independence. More important and practical was the fact that he could best serve Georgia as a Democrat with his long seniority. He had worked too long and hard for valuable public projects and military installations that were now vital to the economy of Georgia. It was unthinkable that he would, by changing parties, sign Georgia's strength away with one stroke of the pen.

In September Russell headed an informal subcommittee of the Warren Commission that travelled to Dallas to interrogate Marina

Oswald again. In the thick of the civil rights filibuster he had missed her testimony on 11 June, and he wanted to try to learn if there were any indications of a conspiracy between Oswald, Jack Ruby, and other unknown participants. In addition to questioning Marina Oswald, Russell traced the route of the Kennedy motorcade, and with Representative Hale Boggs (D-LA), went to the sixth floor of the Texas School Book Depository Building from which the fatal shot had been fired. Taking a rifle, Russell leaned out of the window and tried to aim at the spot the Kennedy car would have been. An experienced marksman since boyhood, he concluded that Oswald must have been an expert shot. A photo of the venerable senator leaning out the window of the depository building, rifle aimed, often accompanied the many stories that appeared in newspapers reporting this Dallas trip.[21] Russell refused to discuss Marina's testimony in any detail, saying only that they had learned nothing new or shocking.

Johnson was anxious to lay to rest fears of conspiracy, as were many others. Russell would have been happier if the investigation had gone on a bit longer, but there was pressure to issue the final report by the end of September. An early draft stated categorically that the evidence indicated that Oswald acted alone. Russell refused to agree to this statement, insisting that it be changed to "the Commission has found no evidence" any conspiracy existed. Having been the principal person in the Senate with oversight of the CIA since 1947, Russell knew that the commission had not had access to all information. Whether he knew anything not available to the Commission has never been determined, but he clearly wanted the question left open. Commission member Gerald Ford would recall more than ten years later Dick Russell's command of that situation.

Because Russell was not entirely ready to sign off on the final report, Chairman Earl Warren had to insist so that the report could be submitted to President Johnson on 27 September 1964. Russell gave a

---

[21] It was important to Dick Russell to feel certain that Oswald could have fired three shots and hit his target with two of them. He had a copy of the Warren Report sent to his sister Ina Stacy in Winder, and a note inside directed her to page 19, where he had marked a passage that stated that the shots that killed Kennedy and wounded Connoly were all fired by Lee Harvey Oswald.

lengthy interview that same day to let it be known that there were still many unanswered questions. While he felt the report was the "very best we could have submitted," he frankly admitted that speculation and debate over the assassination would likely go on for a hundred years.

During the summer and fall 1964, the family received a bludgeoning blow when Robert Lee Russell, Jr. was diagnosed with terminal cancer. When Lady Bird Johnson heard this news, she said to her husband that she wanted to invite the family to spend a few days with them at the White House. Lyndon readily agreed, and Bobby and Betty Ann Russell and their five children came for a visit. While they were there, Uncle Dick was included in family meals, and he tried to take heart on hearing that Bobby would be given experimental chemotherapy treatments that might change his diagnosis.

Dick Russell had reservations about many of the programs Lyndon Johnson proposed under his Great Society umbrella. Russell was not against antipoverty initiatives, but he believed that Congress was passing more legislation than necessary and certainly more than could be administered properly, thus resulting in huge amounts of waste. He counseled caution and practicality and saw clearly that there were too many agencies with overlapping services. He did not like to see more and more power gravitating toward the executive branch with these agencies instead of toward Congress. Like Thomas Jefferson, Russell was a believer in a government of law as opposed to a government of men, and to him the executive was too much 'man.' He understood that the system of checks and balances created by the Founding Fathers would not work if Congress did not do its job; therefore, he was vigilant.

Vigilance caused him to express reservations even about programs for education, which he usually supported, and about Medicare, which he had favored for several years. On the other hand, when the Appalachian Regional Development Act was considered in 1964, he understood that the act would affect deep pockets of poverty in an eleven-state region of the southeastern United States, which would benefit Georgia. How could he vote against that?

In late November 1964, Russell was once again invited to a hunting party on the LBJ ranch in Texas. This was about the fifteenth year that Russell and Johnson had shared such a hunting trip. This year, however,

Georgia's young governor, Carl Sanders, was also invited. Sanders had headed up the Johnson-Humphrey campaign in Georgia that had ended with the state's going for Goldwater, and the young governor was evidently a favorite of the president. This was a delicate situation for all concerned because it had been rumored ever since the summer that Sanders was considering running against Dick Russell in 1966. Some long-term Russell supporters had already sent checks for a reelection campaign, but Russell did not believe this threat was serious and returned the checks.

Dick Russell had been a heavy smoker since his youth. Although he had often tried to give up smoking, even the loss of his brother Rob to lung cancer, a man he loved as much as he thought a man could love another, had not been able to make him put away cigarettes for good. By 1964, he had been successful in giving up "the weed," but it looked as though this move had come too late.

In February 1965, an illness struck Dick Russell that made opposition in his 1966 reelection highly likely. His arduous year's work in 1964 would have threatened a younger and healthier man, and it soon showed what a toll it had taken on sixty-seven-year-old Dick Russell. As the winter progressed, Russell had to fight chronic bronchitis, which he began to suspect might be his old nemesis, pneumonia. He went to work each day, as was his wont, and on 1 February, although quite ill, he arrived in the office at the usual early hour. He wanted to be on hand for the vote on the Appalachian Regional Development Act that he felt would benefit Georgia so much. On 2 February, however, he was taken to Walter Reed Hospital at about ten in the morning suffering from a severe case of "pulmonary edema," a condition in which the lungs fill with fluid. If unchecked, the malady amounts to drowning in one's own fluids. In the hospital, the senator's condition worsened. His sister Ina in Winder was notified and hurried to Washington. The president, hearing of the crisis, asked for periodic reports on his friend's condition.

Within two days, doctors at Walter Reed were forced to perform a tracheotomy to ease Russell's breathing. By 5 February, they had advised the president that his friend and colleague was improving but was still a very sick man. A few days later the president wrote saying that "not a day goes by that my thoughts and those of the girls are not with you."

"The girls" included Lady Bird, who also sent word that she would be glad to accommodate any visiting Russell family at the White House. Several other family members had joined Ina for the bedside vigil.

Soon after the tracheotomy ended fears of immediate demise, Dick Russell asked his young aide Proctor Jones to call someone else. At the senator's instruction, Proctor phoned Harriet Orr, who had only seen a brief article in the paper mentioning the hospitalization and had no idea that her cherished friend's illness was so serious. Within the hour, a bouquet of a dozen red roses was delivered to his hospital room from Harriet. Although Dick Russell was routinely believed to be a lonely old bachelor, his relationship with Harriet was steady and nourishing. They were together often on the weekends, at Harriet's apartment, where they shared a steak Russell brought in. Ina Stacy had dined with them there and felt they were like a long-married couple, comfortable with each other and with their life. They travelled together, especially when going South, in Dick's Chrysler. They would stay at Harriet's home in North Carolina before Dick travelled on alone to Georgia. Harriet also visited Dick a few times in Georgia. Modine, his incorrigible housekeeper and cook, admired Harriet's luxurious hair that hung to her waist as she brushed it. In typical Modine style, the black woman brusquely asked the visitor how long it took to put such hair up each morning. Although the family knew and approved of this friendship, Harriet and Dick kept it private in the extreme.

By 20 February, the ailing senator was up for short walks in the hospital, but doctors were adamant that his convalescence would be long. He would need to go somewhere warm to rest and soak up sun and try to regain his strength. His lung capacity was certain to be reduced for a long time, likely for life. President Johnson, while missing his trusted and able adviser, urged him to follow doctor's orders and get away. His nephew Bobby sent word that he was responding well to his own treatment and that doctors were more optimistic about his future.[22] On 9 March, Russell was discharged from Walter Reed after a five-week stay. He then spent several weeks in Puerto Rico and Florida before returning to Winder in April for more rest and recovery.

---

[22] This was, in fact, not true, but Bobby was so concerned about his uncle's health that he did not want him worrying about his nephew.

Meanwhile, in Georgia and in Washington, rumors flew about whether Dick Russell would be able to serve out his term, and if he did manage that, would he be able to seek reelection? Those who thought or hoped he was finished underestimated the old veteran of political wars. In late April he announced that he would be back at his desk in Washington before the end of the current session, and on 23 May, a few days before he returned to work, he held a press conference and announced that he had no plans to retire and would seek his sixth full term. Looking tanned, trim, and rested, he said he wanted people to see how well he felt. He expressed the hope that he would not have opposition in 1966 and said he knew of no one likely to oppose him. In later years he would comment wryly that he had run with opposition and without, and he could say beyond a shadow of a doubt that a race without opposition was to be preferred.

When Dick Russell returned to the United States Senate on 24 May, after a four-month absence, he was greeted with lavish tributes and expressions of pleasure at his return. He did not downplay the seriousness of his illness, but now that he was back, he said, he would strive to live up to these tributes, which he would always treasure as priceless jewels. His colleagues rose and applauded. Dick Russell was still the lion of the Senate.

Less than a month later, Dick had to face another deep grief when Robert Lee Russell, Jr. died on 14 June 1965, son and namesake of his brother Robert Lee, his best friend and companion until cancer took him in 1955. The elder brother and venerable uncle was never able to understand how he had escaped death when two much younger and, he thought, better men had not. He told the family reunion gathering the next year that the only explanation he could come up with was that Providence called the youngest and best in order to spare them some of life's grief.

Lyndon Johnson, who had also become deeply fond of the charismatic Bobby Russell, Jr., once more overcame his aversion to funerals and came to Winder to attend the service. He walked with others in the family to the burial site on the hill behind the old homeplace. The streets of Winder were lined with people who wanted to catch a glimpse of the president and pay their last respects to one of their own.

Georgia's senior senator was well aware that Carl Sanders was showing strong interest in running for Russell's seat in 1966. Counting on Georgians to appreciate his service and the power that his seniority gave him to direct funds into the state, Russell felt he could wage a successful campaign against the younger man. A safe strategy, and a less demanding one physically, however, was to discourage Sanders from running at all. During summer 1965 Russell became highly visible in Georgia, assuring voters that he was not about to fall to pieces physically and that he was in a better position than ever to serve Georgia well in Washington. To answer the criticism that he was out of touch, Russell visited college campuses and even appealed to conservative black voters who knew, he was sure, that he had helped bring the jobs they held at places like Lockheed and Warner Robins. "The pocketbook is still the most sensitive nerve in the human animal," he said, and that was a nerve he knew his work had eased for all Georgians.[23]

Not having run against opposition in nearly thirty years, the senator was surprised at how much money was needed for a full-fledged campaign. He had been opposed to politicians raising large sums of money through contributions from special interest groups, but he had not required large sums. It was gratifying to find that many people both in Georgia and elsewhere were willingly sending in contributions for a "Reelect Russell" campaign.

Dick Russell appeared confident when questioned about his reelection, and political polls revealed that in a race against Sanders, the veteran senator would get 59 percent of the vote and the governor 25 percent, with the rest undecided. Nevertheless, Dick Russell feared the handsome young rival. At home in Winder near Christmas in 1965, a college-aged niece was watching with her uncle Dick a news broadcast reporting the Georgia governor's activities for that day. At the end of the broadcast, the senator commented, "Seeing Governor Sanders like that just scares me to death."

---

[23] Nearly twenty years later Dick Russell's nephew Walter Brown Russell, Jr. ran for chairman of the Dekalb County Commission. While campaigning, he found that many Atlanta-area black voters were backing him, they said, because he was Dick Russell's nephew.

Having never known anything but adulation from people regarding Senator Russell, the young woman was shocked. "Why on earth should you be afraid of Governor Sanders?" she asked.

"Well," her uncle answered, "he has so much hair." From one who had once been the young, handsome governor of Georgia, this might have expressed the crux of the matter, but it was more likely Dick Russell's wry amusement at his niece's naiveté.

On 30 March 1966, Carl Sanders announced that he would not be a candidate for the Senate, explaining that his original interest had been only because of the senator's illness. Now, the governor said, the senator should be sent back to Washington to continue his long and able service. Dick Russell, naturally, was pleased. After precampaign expenses had been paid, he returned the balance to contributors, referring to these checks as rebates or dividends to those who had been so generous.

During Russell's absence from Washington, President Johnson missed acutely the Georgia senator's expertise in matters of defense. The Vietnam conflict had heated up in late 1964, and in January 1965 Russell insisted that Mike Mansfield, head of the Senate Democratic Policy Committee, go on a private mission to advise the president of the committee's conviction that the United States should find a way to withdraw from Vietnam. Russell was more and more concerned about the consequences of an increased United States commitment there. He felt there was perhaps only one other place where involvement might prove worse: Afghanistan.

In February, following a Viet Cong attack on US Air Force barracks that killed eight American soldiers and destroyed ten US planes, pressure intensified in Washington and Saigon for retaliatory action. Russell had been too ill to be consulted at this time, but later Johnson visited him at Walter Reed and heard again that we should not become further involved in Vietnam. It seems likely, however, that major decisions had already been made to take more aggressive action, and the conflict escalated. Johnson soon found himself embroiled in a nightmare from which he could not awaken. Many people, from congressmen to the average citizen, protested the war totally. Others wanted him to wage war even more aggressively than he was doing.

In addition, the president found civil rights advocates stirring up more trouble. The now-famous march for voting rights in Selma, Alabama, on 7 March 1965 galvanized the country's attitude toward sweeping change to allow black individuals to register to vote. When Alabama's governor George Wallace refused to protect the marchers, Johnson sent US marshals, FBI agents, regular troops, and federalized Alabama national guardsmen to ensure their safety. On 15 March, during prime television time, Johnson addressed a joint session of Congress to ask for quick approval of a new Civil Rights Bill designed, at long last, to assure all Americans the right to vote without poll tax or literacy tests.

Dick Russell was convalescing at his home in Winder and watched the speech on television. When Johnson returned to the White House, he took a call from the Georgia senator. Russell said he could not support the bill, but he wanted Johnson to know that his speech was the best he'd ever heard any president give. Johnson could have hoped for no more lavish praise than this from anyone. Coming from his respected friend and colleague, who disagreed with him on the issue, it was a lifeline to the beleaguered president. The act showed that Dick Russell practiced the deep meaning of friendship and magnanimity.

When Russell returned to Washington a few weeks later, President Johnson asked him to the White House one evening for a family meal. Teen-aged Luci Johnson listened as her father began to talk about the Voting Rights Bill, urging his friend to come over to his side. The girl heard her father turn on his most persuasive tone—a powerful weapon—but saw that "Uncle Dick" was not responding to it. The majority of his constituents were not in favor of the bill, the senator said. The two men paced while the discussion heated up, but neither would budge. The discussion ended when each realized there was not going to be any change in the other. For a moment they faced each other, their noses almost touching, tears streaming down their cheeks. Luci felt she was seeing two dear friends saying their final good-byes.

Russell was not on hand to lead Southerners in their opposition to Civil Rights Bills after 1964. Senator Allen J. Ellender, Democrat of Louisiana, performed quarterback duties using many of the Georgian's tactics, but fire had gone out of the fight. Discouraged by the growing power of liberals in the Senate who believed that everything should be directed by Washington bureaucrats, Russell realized the days when a Southern bloc could slow radical change were over. With regret he saw what he called "ancient landmarks" destroyed and did not believe that the American people recognized the enormity of the changes in the old system, changes brought about by executive order, not legislative process.

The Supreme Court also usurped power, according to Russell, especially when it required legislative reapportionment and affirmed the one-man, one-vote principle. Legislative apportionment of state houses was a constitutional right of the states, the Georgia senator pointed out. A die-hard Jeffersonian, he objected to putting greater political power in the hands of urbanites, which is what reapportionment achieved. Johnson and others had said that Dick Russell was a nineteenth century man trapped in the twentieth century. Perhaps nothing illustrated this fact more than his faith in rural people and the wisdom of local government, the government he saw as truly belonging to the people. The era of the 1960s, however, was not a time in which this belief received appreciable support.

Russell's closest personal aide in his final years, Proctor Jones, recalled that the senator was careful to listen to news broadcasts reporting the activities of Martin Luther King, Jr. and would shush anyone else in the room so that he could be attentive. According to Jones, while he considered King a troublemaker, Russell did not speak derogatorily of him. During the height of civil rights activities in the 1960s, the senator was receiving frequent detailed reports from the FBI about King's activities, particularly some of the less savory ones relating to King's sexual activities, as well as those seemingly pointing to communist plots. Russell, according to Jones, took these with a grain of salt and did not seem overly impressed or worried about them. Russell told his friend Luke Austin that some of the information garnered on King was done by illegal means and was, as a result, meaningless. It is likely that the Georgian recognized King might indeed be the charismatic black leader long-awaited to lead his people out of bondage. Russell did not approve of unlawful activities such as sit-ins, but he had to appreciate the nonviolent approach that King preached.

In spite of his stance, some black civil rights leaders came to see Russell. After a visit in the late 1950s with Roy Wilkins, the distinguished leader of the National Association for the Advancement of Colored People, Russell told his nephew Bill Russell that Wilkins was one of the most intelligent people he'd ever met. He could not resist adding, however, that "he has a lot of white blood in him." At the senator's death, Wilkins had words of praise for Russell's contributions in fields other than civil rights. These two great men, far apart on a critical question of their day, showed their mettle in their ability to appreciate each other.

After 1964 Richard Russell was willing to let the civil rights question unfold as it would in the hands of a determined majority. That was the democratic way. Whatever his opinions, he recognized that this was a new era. Once he felt there was no chance to stop developments within the legislative system, he turned his attention to matters of national defense, agricultural research, medical research, conservation, and education. Russell's biographer Gilbert Fite points out repeatedly that Russell spent more time on civil rights legislation than on any other domestic issue in the 1940s and 1950s. Nevertheless, the Georgia senator was multitalented in dealing with issues. His work ethic did not allow him to neglect other fields, and the legacy he left in these areas proves that he spent highly productive time in attention to them.

Although the characterization of Russell as a nineteenth-century man trapped in the twentieth century is a fair one, the old-fashioned man never lost sight of his duty to work for the future good of his people. His personal library shows that he read widely about water conservation, space travel, nuclear power, the environment, and education.[24] A speech made in 1963 at Georgia State University indicates that he reflected deeply on progress as well as on history. He predicted that although our progress in science and technology had been admirable up to that point, "tomorrow's feats...will make today's look like high school physics experiments." Taking his figures from an article in the *Atlanta Constitution*, he noted that population growth was bound to produce major changes. By 1970, he noted, "our population will move past the 200 million mark, and by the year 2000, it may climb to 350

---

[24] Dick Russell also read modern books on sexuality, but in keeping with his nineteenth-century character, he turned the covers wrong-side out so that the subject of his perusal was not evident.

million." This population growth meant the country would need more roads, more schools, and more medical services. His legislative record shows he followed through on these insights.

As graduation speakers must do, Russell spoke of the need for the youth of the nation to take up these challenges, and he was optimistic about their ability to do so. The one thing that Dick Russell worried about regarding the future of his country was that too much consumerism and too much prosperity would soften the sturdy warp of her people. When he said in a national interview that he did not like to see a man make too much money, the interviewer asked why not? "Because it saps his character," the senator said. That idea of too much wealth being dangerous to character might have been part of his nineteenth-century make-up, but it has not been proved an invalid one.

Lyndon Johnson and Dick Russell were appalled by the riots and lawlessness that resulted in America's cities following the passage of civil rights laws. Contrary to expectations, it was not in the rural South, nor even in the South in general, that the worst violence erupted. Rather, it was in Los Angeles in 1965 and in Chicago in 1966. Neither of these veteran lawmakers could understand the bitterness and wreckage that came following increased rights. Even Martin Luther King, whose nonviolent approach had succeeded until then, had not anticipated the vast differences between the church-oriented South and the despair-ridden ghettos of the North. It was a lamentable irony that these race riots shifted white opinion against black demands. They also alienated Johnson from many black leaders, including Dr. King, whom the president had sought to support.

Following the assassination of Dr. King on 4 April 1968, riots, looting, and burning broke out in the streets of Washington, DC, in the inner-city core, not far from the Capitol grounds. Dick Russell was appalled, shocked, and aggrieved. Ever a law-and-order man, he could not understand why anyone would use such a tragedy to commit lawless acts that only compounded the problem. Russell sent his female staffers home early as the rioting increased. He phoned his sister Ina in Winder and told her, his voice almost breaking, that he was watching Washington burn from his office window. When staff members Charles Campbell and Proctor Jones sought to protect him by taking him home—

his route lay through the hardest-hit districts—he refused to let them get in the car. The two young men were concerned because of his Georgia tag and the fact that they had seen him take a pistol from his desk before going to the car. They followed him to ensure his safe arrival at his Foggy Bottom apartment.

The next morning he was summoned by a call from Johnson to be at the White House by 8:00 A.M., and although Russell was a frequent visitor, recognized by security staff, he was stopped that morning and asked if he minded if his car was searched. Infuriated, the veteran senator returned that indeed he did mind. He'd been living in Washington for thirty-three years, he said, was a close friend of the president, and was here only at his bidding. He had to come if the president called, and yes, he did mind his car's being searched. The Chrysler was waved on, and his pistol, still in the glove compartment, was not confiscated.

As an armed services advocate, Russell was also infuriated when he learned as he entered the Capitol grounds that the Marine Corps guards stationed around the Capitol had no live ammunition. He had his staff check other sites, and when he found that none of the armed guards had live ammunition, he called the president and protested furiously. Johnson might be reluctant to use force against those rioters laying waste to private property in DC streets, but the Capitol building belonged to all Americans, and it was the duty of government to protect it. Trying to calm his friend, Johnson put General Earle "Buzz" Wheeler on the phone. Wheeler, chairman of the Joint Chiefs of Staff, had attended the morning meeting with Russell and was still at the White House. General Wheeler said he would look into the matter immediately. A short while later a military staff car screeched up to the Capitol building, where Proctor Jones from the Russell office had also been dispatched. It was soon revealed that there was live ammunition nearby in a truck, and a delegation of military officers was sent to Russell's office to explain. The chairman of the Senate Armed Services committee was somewhat mollified.

In the 1960s, Dick Russell's position as the congressional leader in matters of national defense remained indisputable. He let go of the dream of an unchanged South with a modicum of optimism, but he did not relinquish his fight for a strongly defended homeland. In spite of the many hours he had spent on his Armed Services Committee duties, he now put in more and more time trying to solve the unsolvable problem of Vietnam.

Because Russell had served four other presidents ably in matters of national security, and because Johnson was such a close friend and one-time protégé, the continued escalation yet continued failure of the war in Vietnam became perhaps the most frustrating problem in the senator's long career. President Johnson called upon his friend and colleague relentlessly as both men sought to find a way to get out of a situation they had early counseled against entering when both were in the Senate.

Russell was in a grinding dilemma. He had seen nothing to be gained from involvement in Southeast Asia, but now that the flag was committed, he felt it his duty to support the president as commander-in-chief and to support the troops on the ground with the best weapons the country could afford. No one, either in the president's office, the State Department, or in Congress, ever came up with an honorable way to leave Vietnam. In Congress there was a clear division between hawks, who wanted to fight, and doves, who were ready to get out at once, and the matter was often debated. Russell had early predicted that after the initial chance to wage an aggressive fight was not chosen, there would be no successful way of leaving. Now it seemed ridiculous to continue the limited fight, knowing the only result could be ignominious withdrawal followed by the defeat of South Vietnam. Yet he could not bring himself to criticize his commander-in-chief nor refuse to get him the appropriations for defense that he needed to continue the war.

Russell had always cared deeply about the welfare of the fighting man, and in spite of his judgment that it was wrong to be in Vietnam, he would not forget the common soldier. As chairman of the Senate Armed Services Committee, it was his job to see that the man on the ground had what he needed. No wonder he felt frustrated, as he tried to find a way to bring the soldiers home yet had to be sure they were supplied to fight. His press secretary, Powell Moore, watched him struggle with this situation, in which the official attitude of a contained war seemed to him a confession of moral weakness, a willingness to sacrifice our young men yet protect our own wealth and security. He had, however, no patience with draft dodgers and flag-burners. They seemed ungrateful to him of their citizenship in the best country in the world, which all enjoyed simply by accident of birth. In Dick Russell's patriotism, you had the right to protest, but only within the limits of the law.

A painful personal note tolled in this frustrating scenario. Dick's nephew, Walter Brown Russell, Jr., a West Point graduate who had served in Korea and received a Purple Heart there, was, by this time, a lieutenant colonel in the First Air Cavalry Division. Helicopters being a main instrument in the war, Walt was ordered to Vietnam in 1965. Not long after his arrival, his wife, Nancy, received dreaded news. Lieutenant Colonel Russell had been wounded in action. A serious head wound, which might well have killed him, left Walt partially paralyzed on one side and ended his military career. Dick Russell was at Walter Reed Hospital to meet the plane that brought the soldier back to the United States, he kept up with Walt's progress, and he was on hand when Walt, still in his wheelchair, received a service award. During the conflict, Russell had several other nephews or nephews-in-law serving in the armed forces.

President Johnson began to bank his hopes for resolution on negotiation, and Russell supported him wholeheartedly if not optimistically in this approach. Russell, like almost everyone else, was genuinely shocked when Johnson announced in a speech to Congress on 31 March 1968 that he "would not seek nor would he accept" the 1968 Democratic nomination for president. Johnson, devastated by how the war was ruining his dreams of a Great Society and writing his presidency a disastrous report card, made this decision in the belief that if he were not seeking reelection, the North Vietnamese would be more likely to come to the negotiation table. Russell, who had learned from the White House only fifteen minutes before the speech that Johnson would not run again, felt that this was a noble but useless personal sacrifice. If the North Vietnamese had not come to negotiate before now, such a development was not likely to encourage them, he felt. Subsequent events proved him right.

Russell was not pleased with the nomination of Hubert Humphrey as the Democrats' presidential candidate in 1968 because it signaled a continued shift to the liberal side. Nevertheless, Russell and Humphrey had come to respect each other tremendously in the twenty years they had worked together in the Senate, in spite of serious disagreements on most questions. Russell's ability to work well with men like Humphrey served as an example to all the Senate that men of principle, regardless of how different their origins, can disagree within the traditions of our pluralistic and democratic nation. Senator Edmund Muskie (D-ME) felt that Russell's example reminded all senators that the confrontation of ideas need not fuel ill-will. To Muskie, Russell demonstrated that honorable men can hold honest disagreement without questioning the motives and integrity of another, and thus the Georgian illustrated qualities necessary for cooperation and progress in a free society.

A rumor that Russell secretly supported Richard Nixon rather than Hubert Humphrey surfaced from various conservative corners. There is no question but that Russell was out of step with the majority of Democrats by this time. However, when questioned about whether he supported Nixon, Russell said the idea was too outrageous to discuss.

Divided by the war dissidents, the Democrats lost the White House, and Dick Russell might have felt some relief. Although he and Richard Nixon had never been friends while Nixon was in the Senate, their conservative philosophies were closer to each other than to Humphrey's liberalism. That Dick Russell would be called on to serve this president in national security as he had the others was immediately evident. Only a few days after the election, Nixon telephoned the Georgia senator and was gratified to hear that he would support the commander-in-chief wholeheartedly in the field of national defense.

The Russell-Johnson friendship had cooled sadly during 1968 following a disagreement about the appointment of a federal judge from Georgia. Russell felt betrayed by his friend in the circumstance and would never trust him completely again. When Johnson left Washington and returned to his Texas ranch, the two continued to write occasionally for various reasons, but the old intimacy and regard had disappeared. Johnson kept a low profile as an ex-president, and Russell's health continued to deteriorate so that the two were not to have many opportunities to see each other again. Russell was pleased to be among the dignitaries who helped escort Lady Bird, Lynda, Luci, and Lynn (the president's grandson) to a final reception at the Capitol. It remained a joy to him that the Johnson daughters called him "Uncle Dick," and his familial feelings for them and Lady Bird never waned.

Most of Russell's kin had left Washington in the preceding ten years as brothers-in-law or sisters retired and returned to Georgia. The loss of the friendship with Lyndon and the departure of the Johnson family from the capital emptied his Washington social life further. Pat Collins Andretta, out with a group of friends one evening at a restaurant hotel during this period, saw Dick Russell sitting alone at a table, eating his dinner and reading. She was so shocked to see him looking so lonely that she could not go over and speak to him, as she might have done in other times.

RICHARD MILHOUS NIXON: 1969–1971

"When the security of the United States was at stake, six presidents leaned on this great patriot. He never failed them."[25]
—Richard Nixon on Richard B. Russell, Jr.

When Congress convened in January 1969, Dick Russell's responsibilities there changed. As the longest-serving senator, having completed thirty-six years of service, the Georgian was elected president pro tem, making him third in line for the presidency, after the speaker of the House. The president pro tem presides over the Senate in the absence of the vice president. When asked if he felt more powerful as president pro tem, Russell answered with typical dry humor, "Well, I get that big automobile now." One of the perks of the office was a Lincoln Continental limousine with chauffeur. The senator, in failing health, enjoyed his "big automobile" without apology. He also at this time formally gave up his leadership of the Southern Bloc which, weakened by deaths and retirements, no longer greatly influenced Senate decisions. For the aging statesman, aware that this Southern battle was lost and perhaps even well lost, it had to be a relief to declare that as presiding officer of the Senate, he must be blind on the issues and rule fairly and impartially without any conflict of interest.

The respect and affection that his colleagues had for him was unabated, for there was no one they considered more admirable for

---

[25] From Richard Nixon's memorial remarks honoring Richard B. Russell at the Georgia Capitol, January 1971.

fairness, integrity, wisdom, help to colleagues on special projects, and devotion to protecting the traditions of the Senate. As his emphysema worsened, Russell had to use a motorized cart to get from his office to the Senate chamber, and for the first time in thirty-six years, he shortened his work day. No one knew better than this longtime leader of the greatest deliberative body in the world that he had passed the zenith of his power. Nevertheless, as new chairman of the Senate Committee on Appropriations, Russell was extremely influential in money matters, including the defense budget.[26] Although he hoped handing over the chair of the Armed Services Committee to his good friend John Stennis (D-MS) would free him of some work, the ailing senator had to husband his energies. In addition, the Senate had shifted so in philosophy that he no longer exercised much influence in determining major Senate actions on other questions. Russell had to relinquish his usual attention to agriculture, although his belief in strong and prosperous farmers had not diminished. His interest in conserving the nation's land, forest, and water resources continued. For agriculture and for conservation, he was, he said, "almost immodestly" proud of the research facilities in these fields that he had brought to Georgia.[27]

During these last years, Russell was frequently honored for his long and distinguished service. Genuinely modest, he nevertheless understood the benefits his work had brought to his state and his country, and he deeply appreciated this recognition. A list of those awards would fill a book. In 1966 he was presented the Great American Award at an elaborate banquet in Atlanta. To think that the people of Georgia understood his patriotism and considered him a great American moved him profoundly. When in 1964 the *Progressive Farmer* gave him one of its outstanding service awards for his work on behalf of agriculture and conservation, Russell maintained that investing in conservation of natural resources was an investment in the future that he was proud he had been able to help make. Earlier he had received, along with Senator William F. Knowland (R-CA), the George Washington

---

[26] For several years, Russell had often acted as de facto chair of the appropriations committee because of Carl Hayden's periodic ill health.

[27] The Richard B. Russell Agricultural Center at the University of Georgia was one such facility. See Afterword.

Award given by the American Good Government Society. He was named Georgian of the Year in 1965 by the Georgia Association of Broadcasters. In 1964 a magazine poll of members of Congress and the Washington press corps named Russell the most effective senator. In 1968 an increasing number of newspaper articles appeared on him and his career, in which he was presented as the Senate's senior statesman, who better than anyone else symbolized the strength and virtues of that legislative body. Harry Truman once defined a statesman as a politician who's been dead twenty years; Dick Russell achieved statesman status in his lifetime.

When several publishing houses in 1969 expressed interest in publishing any book Russell would write about his experiences in the Senate, he replied that he was too busy and did not know if he would ever get around to reviewing his part in "the most thrilling fifty years in the life of the human family." A man of thoughtful philosophy and an avid historian, Dick Russell entirely appreciated the momentous times in which he had lived. Someone else could have written a biography, and this course was suggested, but practically speaking, he was not ready to open his files to researchers. Such action would have signaled that his career was over, and he was not ready to make that kind of announcement. Dick Russell was from long-lived, come-back people. He had not written himself off.

Unfortunately, in 1969, Dick Russell experienced another serious health problem. During a regular examination, doctors found a cancerous spot on his lung. As he had advised his press secretary to do when he was ill in 1965, Russell held a press conference and told all that he knew about the illness. He said he was going to fight it through radioactive cobalt treatment, and he was hopeful about whipping it. He was not a case for surgery, with his reduced lung capacity, but after eight weeks of radiation treatment, the doctors found no trace of the tumor. Dick's sister Ina was in town when he received this report, and both were so happy that they wanted to celebrate. Ina had already made a date for supper with Dick's former fiancée, Pat Collins, now the widowed Mrs. Sal Andretta, and so the three of them went out for an elegant dinner. That the formerly engaged couple had maintained respect and affection for each other seemed evident to others who saw them together that evening. Pat made an effort to speak to Proctor Jones to tell him "to take good care of my dear Dick."

Russell called in reporters to announce the positive results, adding that whether or not he was entirely cured only time would tell, but at least now he could "fall back and worry about the emphysema." Regrettably, these treatments destroyed most of Russell's left lung, so he had even less lung capacity than before. He joked with some of the doctors at Walter Reed that if one of them could find a cure for emphysema, he would make him Surgeon General.

During these last years Russell had numerous check-ups and was frequently in and out of Walter Reed Hospital. In spite of the depressing effects of his illness, he kept up his keen awareness of human nature and his sense of humor. For example, when he was being examined and evaluated by a group of several doctors at Walter Reed, Surgeon General Leonard Dudly Heaton was in the group. Each man in the group made a comment about what he thought the senator's condition was and what they ought to do about it. A young captain was standing a little to the side, and in the usual Russell style of noticing the lesser ranks, once everyone else had finished, the senator asked, "Well, young man, what do you think?"

The captain said straightaway, "I agree with General Heaton."

Dick Russell smiled. "Young man," he said, "I predict a long and brilliant future for you in the Army Medical Corps."

Richard Nixon continued to ask Senator Russell's advice and to honor him as a worthy senator. Nixon favored the Safeguard Anti-Ballistic Missile (ABM) system, and Russell backed the president all the way on this contentious issue. Without this veteran and highly respected defense expert in the Senate on his side, Nixon would not have won this battle. Russell also kept up his call for stronger military action in Vietnam. Nixon called Russell before he ordered the bombing of Cambodia to begin.

Russell was, perhaps surprisingly, a strong supporter of Nixon's China initiative. The senator had consistently criticized giving any recognition to the Chinese communist government and had supported the Chiang Kai-shek regime. Having been friends with Madame Chiang Kai-shek since they were both teenagers, he had a special interest in the situation. In 1965 Madame Chiang had been invited to Wesleyan College, her alma mater, to speak at the fall convocation, and Dick Russell introduced her with lavish compliments. Friendship, however, did not make him blind to what he believed to be in the national interest, and he saw clearly that it was time to develop better relations between the United States and China. His flexibility in these changing times shows that he had not given up thinking about the future.

The harsh truth, however, was that Dick Russell was dying as emphysema destroyed his lungs. He was in and out of Walter Reed Hospital several times during 1969, and by the end of the year he was able to go to his office only a few hours a day. He took a staggering number of medications and needed the almost constant help of Proctor Jones. Jones, while being trusted with keeping up with medicines and diet and other health matters, as well as attending the frail old warrior in his home and at the office, got to know many of the senator's family along with Harriet Orr and Modine Thomas. Jones remembered years later how the senator valued even a telephone conversation with his eldest sister Billie and how he disagreed with his sister Ina sometimes over family matters. Harriet Orr was a faithful companion, though at this stage, Dick Russell refused to saddle her with any of his care. She was spending time caring for her elderly mother in North Carolina and might have retired from government service during these years.

There was speculation that the senator would not be able to finish out his term. He inquired about what kind of retirement income he would have from his thirty-eight years of service. It was estimated at $3,000 a month, a respectable amount for the time. Yet he managed to recover from each new setback and go back to work and meet much of his busy schedule. The report on his retirement income remained stuck in the back of one of his daily schedule books.

To honor the faithful public servant, Cox Broadcasting System filmed a three-part television documentary on Russell's career called "Georgia Giant." It was aired early in 1970. At that time, President and Mrs. Nixon invited Russell's brother Henry Edward Russell, a distinguished Presbyterian minister in the Southern Presbyterian church, to preach at the White House.[28] It surprised the White House staff when a bachelor had so many family members who wanted to attend, and strict limitations had to be set on numbers. This church service preceded a gala banquet for 800 given in the senator's honor by Cox Broadcasting, which the Nixons attended. Addressing the gathering, Nixon praised Russell as a great leader, a man of integrity, and a fine human being. Although usually genuinely embarrassed by this kind of praise, Russell thoroughly enjoyed his evening of honor and declared, in an article in *U.S. News and World Report,* that he had loved the attention.

In the summer he spent time resting at home in Winder, under the care of Modine Thomas. Proctor Jones was also often on hand. For once, the senator had time to watch all the baseball he wanted on television. Sometimes Modine was invited to sit down and watch with him. The black woman, who was nearing sixty at this time, was a no-nonsense person, not given to coddling herself nor anyone else, and it is unlikely that she would have seen much sense in baseball games. If she did not, she certainly would have said so, for the family lore is filled with stories of Modine's caustic comments on various activities and characters in the family. Having come to work for family in the 1930s, Modine could look back on devoted, competent, and utterly loyal care given to Dick's mother, whom she had loved. Now she did the same for the senator, as a matter of course. Both these people were eccentrics, but they appreciated each other.

For several years Dick Russell had been forthright about his regrets at not marrying. He believed he would not be in his current lamentable state of health if he had taken a wife. When Proctor Jones fell in love and was considering marriage, the senator wanted to see the engagement ring. When Proctor brought Virginia to the office for the first time as his fiancée, both of the young people were touched at how choked up the senator became, wishing them happiness.

Charles Campbell, having trouble going to law school at night and holding down his full-time job on the senator's staff, caught Dick Russell going through the office to tell him that he was going to have to drop out

---

[28] Dr. Russell had been recommended to preach at the White House by Postmaster General Winton M. Blount, a former member of one of Jeb Russell's congregations.

of law school. The busy senator looked him straight in the eye and said, "You stay in law school and you get married."

These young office workers were Dick Russell's right-hand men in the last years, and he appreciated their efforts. They, in turn, appreciated him for all his eccentricities. Charles, especially, remembered that the senator had a great sense of humor and was particularly good at laughing at himself. Proctor enjoyed watching how much he loved his numerous family and was ever interested in learning of more kin.

Back at work in Washington in the fall, Dick Russell fell at his apartment and suffered bruises and continued pain and dizziness in October 1970. Either his sister Pat Peterson or Ina Stacy was with him much of the time now, but he was sometimes alone. Once,he entered in his daybook that his weight had registered that morning 130 pounds, a new low. Below that he wrote, "Alone."

Georgia politics was experiencing a "first" since Reconstruction as Hal Suit, who had interviewed Russell for the "Georgia Giant" series, presented a Republican challenge to the Democratic candidate, Jimmy Carter. Because Suit had, in effect, costarred with Russell in "Georgia Giant," and because many felt that Russell was closer to the Republican Party in ideology than the Democratic one by this time, the Georgia senator was questioned about whom he would support for governor. Russell was determined to take his usual pre-election stance. "I never struck a Democratic ticket in all my life," he said, "and it's too late for me to start now." Was that an endorsement of Carter? Apparently it was, and it was duly reported that for the first time, Senator Richard B. Russell had endorsed a candidate for governor. To back the Democrats was Russell's response to the rise of the Republican Party in Georgia.

Russell was able to go home to Winder for Thanksgiving, and he told Modine he'd be home for Christmas. She got the homeplace ready for him, decorating a tree and planning a turkey dinner. Ina had moved into an apartment in Atlanta a few years previously, but she would come home when her brother was there. To the family's regret, late in November Russell was readmitted to Walter Reed, and when Ina joined him there, he told her that he felt he was going to die. She tried to cheer him up by reminding him that he had recovered many times before, but he only said, "Not this time."

In spite of doctors' recommendations that he remain in the hospital, Russell checked himself out on 3 December so that he could be in the Senate to vote against deleting from a pending appropriations bill $390 million in development funds for the supersonic transport plane. This bill was strongly supported by Henry M. "Scoop" Jackson (D-WA), Russell's friend and longtime ally on the Senate Armed Services Committee. To the last, the Georgia senator had his eye on national defense. He worked four days, but had to return to Walter Reed on 7 December.

Although President Nixon offered the use of Air Force One to take Russell to his Georgia home for Christmas, the senator was not well enough to leave the hospital. While there, he received visits from President Nixon and from Secretary of State Henry Kissinger to keep him briefed on the world situation. Some of his family gathered to spend Christmas with him: his sister Ina, his brother Fielding and wife Virginia, and their son Richard Brevard Russell IV. Taking the advice of Ina, who was relaying what her brother had told her, other family members arranged to visit later. A special Christmas dinner was prepared for the senator and his family, and one of his doctors sent a bottle of champagne. At table, Dick Russell offered a special toast to his brother Fielding, "one of the finest and gentlest souls" he'd ever known. Weak and sick, the senator asked to be taken back to his bed after the toast. His sister Ina, knowing how he cherished and loved all his brothers and sisters, how he was pleased to give out silver dollars to all kin who called on Christmas, how he wanted to see all the places of the family dining table filled with family on that day especially, could not hold back her tears. This was the only Christmas Dick Russell had ever spent away from his home in Winder.

On 12 January 1971, Dick Russell had been serving in the US Senate for thirty-eight years. That day, the old statesman did not feel well enough to work on an anniversary press statement that his press secretary, Powell Moore, had drafted. The next day Moore returned and they worked on the statement together, after which Russell told Moore to write a memo to the Senate comptroller raising Moore's salary. Moore thanked Russell and began gathering his papers. The senator advised him to write the memo if he wanted the raise.

"You mean right this minute?" Powell asked.

"Certainly I mean right this minute," the senator returned sharply. "I might not be here fifteen minutes from now."

Powell found a typewriter at a nurses' station, wrote the memo, and Russell signed it.

The dying senator's press release to Georgians thanked them for allowing him the privilege of serving them in the United States Senate for so many years.

Richard Russell's physicians during these last days were Rufus J. Pearson and Andre Ognibene. Both men were amazed at how the senator could be so sick yet perk up when visitors came. Pearson knew that even before Christmas, Russell no longer wanted to live, yet he still fought the disease more than other patients. Russell had the most amazing brain and heart of anyone Pearson had ever known. The doctor realized the old warrior suffered depression, a natural reaction to his illness, but Pearson never felt that his depression arose from affairs of state. The statesman possessed a wise perspective on national affairs that was comforting.

When his nephew Bill Russell visited him during these last days, Dick asked him to read a passage from Corinthians and the Twenty-third Psalm. Bill read from the Revised Standard Version of the Bible. Dick Russell was proud of his minister nephew, who, although as a youngster had never passed the senator's reading challenge, read now with a mellifluous Southern accent and with authority and poetry. Yet when Bill had finished, his uncle said, "That's not right. Here is how it should go." And he recited the King James Version.

By this time, Russell's four living sisters, Billie, Ina, Pat, and Carolyn, had gathered to comfort him in this last struggle. Billie, Ina, and Pat had been his family in Washington, making their homes his. Dick loved and admired Carolyn, the youngest of the thirteen, for her Christian faith that was close to their mother's. To the end, it would be family women on whom he called for comfort.

In a quiet moment, as he lay in bed struggling for breath, he opened his eyes to find his sister Ina sitting beside him. "Ina," he said, "do you think I've done right about my will?"

Ina held his hand. She did not know what was in his will, but she said, "Dick, honey, I'm sure you've done the right thing."

In the organization of the new Senate, a battle had developed for the post of Democratic whip. Well-known liberal senator Edward M. Kennedy had held the job in the previous Congress, but he was being challenged by the conservative Robert Byrd of West Virginia. The vote was to be taken on 21 January. Knowing of this impending caucus, Russell directed a few days before 21 January that his proxy be cast for Robert Byrd. Although Russell's vote would not be the deciding one in numbers, Byrd was strengthened in his resolve to challenge Kennedy, knowing he had Dick Russell's approval.

On 19 January, Russell suffered a stroke, but he seemed to rally the next day. He told his sister Carolyn that he understood now how much her faith must have meant to their mother. Carolyn agreed, but regretted that she did not ask her brother why he felt that way. Jeb Russell was with him also, and when the senator asked his minister brother what he thought dying was like, Jeb did not know what to say. His brother answered for him: "I think it will be like when we were children and we ran to jump into Mother's or Daddy's lap for a hug."

On 21 January 1971, at a morning meeting, Russell's proxy was voted in the election that chose Robert Byrd of West Virginia Democratic whip over the incumbent Edward Kennedy of Massachusetts. Russell's sister Billie was sitting with him that morning, but she was going out to have her hair done. She told her brother she would be back soon and that the other sisters would be with him. He did not speak, but he squeezed her hand. She would feel the actual physical pressure and the love of that response for years afterward. At 2:21 P.M., with his family surrounding him, while resting quietly and without any life-support systems, Dick Russell breathed his last tortured breath. The official cause of death was pulmonary emphysema.

As soon as the senator died, Proctor Jones, obeying instructions, placed a call to give the sad news to Harriet Orr. It would be several hours, however, before the young aide was able to reach Harriet at home in North Carolina. Harriet agonized over whether she should attend the funeral, and she spoke with Dick's sisters about it. They encouraged her to come, but in the end she did not. That love that had been so private would remain so.

Dick Russell had, from his first election to the Senate, considered himself Georgia's man in Washington. Having never truly felt at home anywhere other than Georgia, in spite of having lived more than half his life in Washington, and having carried on a thirty-eight-year love affair with the United States Senate, Dick left instructions that his body be returned to Georgia as soon as possible. Although congressional leaders offered to enact a resolution for the senator's body to lie in state in the rotunda of the US Capitol Building, his family respectfully declined. There would be only scant moments of recognition in Washington of the passing of one of the nation's most powerful and longest-serving legislative officials.

On 22 January at 10:15 A.M., six soldiers carried Russell's casket from the funeral home and placed it in a hearse, which, accompanied by a few cars for family and staff members, followed a sixteen-man motorcycle police escort of District of Columbia police down Constitution Avenue toward Capitol Hill, en route to Andrews Air Force Base. The procession passed near the memorials to Washington, Jefferson, and Lincoln, the White House, and other landmarks of our national heritage. Russell's former places of residence were also included in the route. Ina, who had welcomed him to Washington in 1933, wept when the procession passed by her address on Connecticut Avenue, as did Billie and Pat. Yet their hearts rejoiced in their brother's work and in the long life they had shared in the nation's capital.

When the procession reached the Capitol of the United States, it paused for a few moments at the foot of the long marble steps leading to the chamber of the United States Senate. In the cold January air, more than sixty senators stood respectfully on the steps to the Senate wing, hats off, with hands over their hearts. This simple, silent tribute deeply moved Dick Russell's sisters and other family members. Passing before the great dome of the Capitol, where, by order of the president, the flag flew at half-mast, the procession drove slowly past the steps of the House wing, where the Georgia congressional delegation, the Speaker of the House, and other House members stood in salute. A police honor guard lined the Capitol Plaza, and here many congressional aides, Capitol employees, and members of the press had assembled to pay their last respects to Dick Russell, senator from Georgia.

When the procession reached Andrews Air Force Base, Air Force One, by personal order of the president, was waiting. Full military honors were accorded Richard Brevard Russell, Jr., as his body was placed aboard the aircraft.

In Atlanta, Governor Carter, only days after his inauguration, escorted the body from the airport to the gold-domed capitol building, where a crowd of mourners led by the lieutenant governor, speaker of the House, and members of the Georgia General Assembly waited. Young men representing every branch of military service bore the body of Richard Brevard Russell, Jr. up the granite steps into the rotunda of the capitol. The Third Army Band played in solemn accompaniment. A longtime friend of Dick Russell, Dr. Louie D. Newton, pastor emeritus of the Druid Hills Baptist Church of Atlanta and retired chief of chaplains of the Georgia State Guard, preceded the casket and offered eloquent and grieving words for all Georgians: "From the Savannah to the Chattahoochee, from the cedars to the cypress, from sunset to the evening star, uttered and silent prayers will ascend from broken hearts, praising and thanking God for the good and great man, who 'did justly and loved mercy and walked humbly with his Lord.' Farewell, good and cherished friend, statesman, patriot...."

For the next twenty-four hours an estimated 10,000 Georgians, from every walk of life, of every color and every creed, and of every age, filed by the bier in a last farewell to this man who had lived his adult life in service to the state and its people. From his election to the Georgia Assembly in 1920 to his death marked fifty years of public service.

The State of the Union address was scheduled for Friday evening, 22 January, and some senators thought it should be postponed because of Russell's death, but Nixon declined to do this. He paused in his address, though, for a moment of silent prayer for Russell. The next day President and Mrs. Nixon arrived in Atlanta to lay a wreath of red, white, and blue carnations at the foot of the senator's casket. Speaking to the crowd, Nixon called Russell a leader of the highest ability and character. He had been called frequently "a senator's senator," the president said, but he was also "a president's senator." Nixon described his last visit with the Georgian when, in spite of his dreadful illness, Russell was yet expressing a desire to help with difficult national problems. Russell's last words to him had been "I just wish I could get down there and help out."

President Nixon met briefly with the immediate family in Governor Carter's office. A slight problem emerged because Dick Russell's eight living brothers and sisters, with spouses and thirty-six living nieces and nephews, all considered themselves immediate family. This was too great a crowd for the office, and so the nieces and nephews had to step back. In addition to the siblings and their spouses, Modine Thomas was included. In a well-worn fur coat and a black silk top hat, she stood solemn and stern to be photographed with Dick Russell's family and the president of the United States.[29]

These events were televised so that people unable to be at the capitol could share in the final rites. Dick Russell, eschewing the limelight to the last, had said, when discussing his funeral, that he did not want his passing to be a media event. His press secretary, Powell Moore, had persuaded him that allowing full modern coverage was in the public interest.

A short time after the president's departure, the military casket bearers, accompanied by the United States Air Force Band playing hymns, took the senator's body from the rotunda to a waiting hearse for his last trip from Atlanta to Winder. The casket was preceded at this time by another old pastor friend, the Reverend James Wesberry. All along the route, cars stopped and people got out to salute their statesman. They stood on bridges over the Interstate and watched solemnly as he took his last ride. Parents had given young children American flags to hold, but the grief of the entire state was particularly evident in the lined faces of the generation of Georgians who had been relying on Senator Russell's leadership since the early 1930s when they had elected him their "Boy Governor."

Christine Till, a young woman from New York state who had worked in Richard Russell's office only the last two years of his life, was amazed and moved to see so many different people of all ages, black and white, who turned out to pay their respects as the motorcade passed, not only on I-85 Highway, but in the poorer sections. She saw people standing in front of humble homes, saluting the passing hearse, from

---

[29] When Modine Thomas died some twenty-five years later, a copy of the photo made that day was found in her things and returned to the family. On the back she had written: "If I'd knowed he was a crook, I wouldna done it."

great-grandfathers to babes in arms. For Christine it showed how much Georgians had loved Richard Russell and how much his love of Georgia must have meant to him.

In the small parlor of his beloved homeplace, Dick Russell lay in state another fifteen hours, and over 3,000 Georgians came, continuing all night long, to pay their respects. Some wept beside the casket, remembering a kindness he had shown them, a critical help given at a time of despair. The senator's immediate family, now again including the nieces and nephews, listened with tears in their eyes to these stories and told and retold them to other loved ones who had not been there to hear this witness to a good man's life of service.

The weather the next day was so foggy and stormy that the three planes coming from Washington with fifty-five senators, Dr. L. R. Elson, Senate chaplain, Vice President Agnew, and others, could not land at the Atlanta airport and had to be rerouted to Charleston.[30] More rain, cloud, and fog rolled in until there was no chance that the party would make it to Georgia. J. Leonard Reinch, president of Cox Broadcasting in Atlanta, suggested that television communication be established between Charleston and Winder, so that those in South Carolina could deliver their eulogies. Television monitors were set up at the family cemetery for the crowd. The nineteenth-century man stuck in the twentieth century once again became part of the wave of the future.

Another touching irony occurred when Hubert Humphrey, senator and former vice president, who had not been with the congressional delegation, was put off the bus in a heavy rain shower at the end of the tree-lined drive at the homeplace. He arrived dripping wet on the front porch, determined to pay his last respects to a man whose conduct of life and service to his country he respected deeply in spite of their differences. Some observers commented on the sad irony that John Stennis, one of Russell's closest friends, was unable to deliver his eulogy in person, while his great rival in the civil rights battles, Hubert Humphrey, was on hand. Yet to family and friends, it was a comfort to know that all had respected this dedicated statesman.

---

[30] This was the largest delegation of senators ever to have attended another senator's funeral up to that time.

In the absence of the chaplain, Dr. Henry E. Russell, the senator's brother, was called to direct, and he accepted this task with consummate grace. Ina Stacy could never forget how Jeb recited the scriptures without reading them, both at the podium and at the graveside, his voice assured and comforting. All passages were from the King James Version of the Bible.

The first eulogy was given, as custom dictated, by Spiro Agnew, vice president of the United States and president of the Senate. The second eulogy came from Georgia's Senator Herman Talmadge. Senator Talmadge noted that Dick Russell was a man of all the people but that he was particularly Georgia's own. "He brought unprecedented credit to Georgia," he said, "wherever he went and in everything he did." This credit to Georgia had been Dick Russell's lifelong ambition. John Stennis praised his departed friend for many contributions but chose to emphasize his efforts to guarantee the nation's security.

Following the electronic eulogies, which did, indeed, seem inadequate and out of place for this old-fashioned gentleman, Governor Jimmy Carter gave a disciplined, poetic three-minute eulogy. Hoke Sewell, minister of the Winder First United Methodist Church, where Dick Russell had been a member since he was nine years old, pronounced the benediction. Then the foggy air was graced by the Marine Corps band's playing "Eternal Father Strong to Save," the Navy hymn, and the casket was carried to the graveside.[31]

Nine nephews served as pall bearers, young men, strong and able. Yet they were surprised at how heavy the casket was, how they had to use all the strength of their youth in this last service to their famous uncle. Dick Russell's mortal remains were placed over a hollowed space beside the graves of his parents, and the service of committal was carried out by two of his brothers and one brother-in-law. Jeb Russell recited the scriptures of committal, reminding all that "Blessed are the dead who die in the Lord from henceforth; yea, saith the Spirit, that they may rest from their labors; and their works do follow them." Fielding Russell, Sr. gave the prayer of committal, ending with the ringing assurance that "because

---

[31] Other dignitaries who managed to get to Winder included three cabinet secretaries, General William Westmoreland, Admiral Thomas Moore, chairman of the Joint Chiefs of Staff, and Dean Rusk, former secretary of state.

our faith is fastened in Thee, 'because Thy loving kindness is better than life,' and because Thy mercy is stronger than death, we repose here the body of our beloved brother, his spirit having already entered Thy tabernacle of righteousness. Amen."

The flag was removed from the coffin by the military escort, folded, and presented to Ina Russell Stacy.

Brother-in-law Raymond Nelson, Sr., a Presbyterian minister and husband of Dick's sister Carolyn, pronounced the benediction, using, as had the others, the time-honored and beautiful prose Dick Russell loved: "The peace of God, which passeth all understanding, keep your hearts and minds in the knowledge and love of God, and of His Son Jesus Christ our Lord; and the blessing of God Almighty, the Father, the Son, and the Holy Spirit, be upon you and remain with you always. Amen."

It was still raining. As the crowd drifted away, the numerous family, numbed by this passing of their patriarch, stood grieving. He was where he wished to be, at rest in the red clay of his beloved Georgia, at the place where the family gathered so often. He was no longer struggling to breathe. He had used up his life to the last, he had not outlived himself. These were reasons to rejoice. Yet for those who loved him, standing now forlorn on this side of the Great Divide, his absence created an aching void that underscored how much his powerful and decent presence had meant in their lives.

On Monday, 25 January 1971, the day after the funeral, tributes were paid in Congress to Richard B. Russell, Jr., late a senator from Georgia. In the following days and weeks, his Senate colleagues would pay him tribute again and again, and these comments were collected into a book, as is the custom. While a book of eulogies is certain to contain praise, this volume remains an astonishing memorial for the consistency of its analysis of Richard Brevard Russell, Jr. by his colleagues. They commented on the myriad aspects of his life's work with thoughtful and genuine admiration, affection, sympathy, and respect. Whether Republican or Democrat, liberal or conservative, they believed Richard B. Russell, Jr. a giant in the Senate's history.

In 1972 the United States Senate had, for the first time in its history, the opportunity to name a building in Washington for a senator. What had been the Old Senate Office Building would now be called after a senator chosen by those currently in office. The sitting senators could have chosen anyone in the Senate's long and illustrious history. In eloquent testimony to how those who know the milieu best felt about this man's life and work, they chose Richard Brevard Russell, Jr., the senator's senator.

Afterword

Perhaps his most lasting influence was on matters that were less explosive and less immediately tied to life and death [than civil rights or national defense] *—less immediately newsworthy —bringing electricity to rural America, getting loans for Georgia's farmers, making sure that poor children could eat a decent lunch at school. And there was always that reverence to his life, his Spartan apartment, his utter devotion to the Senate as an institution, his enduring selflessness that inspired even those with whom he disagreed.*
— Vice President Al Gore on Richard Russell, 1996

Early in my work on this book I had been researching at the Russell library in Athens but was taking a break upstairs in the periodicals room of the main library. Browsing the newest magazines, I came across a surprising witness to a positive and historical side of Southern race relations. In the fall 2008 *Southern Cultures* periodical, published by the University of North Carolina Press, there was an interview with Alex Haley, author of the famous novel *Roots*. The interview had been done in 1989 when Haley came to Vicksburg, Mississippi, to support consolidation of schools to prevent the creation of predominantly black city and white county school systems. His coming as a celebrated black author was a major event for the city. The interviewer was William R. Ferris, a distinguished white professor whose specialty was Southern African-American folklore and culture. These two men had worked together when Haley was the featured speaker on North Carolina's Center for the Study of Southern Culture's historic "College on the Mississippi" trip on the *Delta Queen*, and they were friends.

In answering Ferris's questions, Haley was keen to give honor to Southern ancestors, black and white: "[These ancestors] have always struck me as the Foundation Timbers of our South, and I think we who were reared and raised by them, and amongst them, are blessed that we were.... One of the things that drew Bill Ferris and me together as friends so much is our shared feeling of the richness of Southern culture and the heritage and the interdependence of black and white, really...." Haley stated that there had been "some ugly stuff," but also "...then there was a truce and we just decided to 'get on with it' and we did."

Haley had lived up north both as a young man and later in his journalistic career. No one would claim that he was blind to racial injustices. Yet this is what he said about living in the South: "I just feel the South is a place of hands, it's a place of touch, of caress, of less slapping and knocking people down. It's a softer, sweeter culture, on the whole. I wouldn't want to live anywhere else but in the South."

This experience of the South as a place where people care for each other in a deeply personal way, a way that transcends harsh laws and cruel customs, is the South that men like Dick Russell remembered and wanted to see continue. Although memory is a highly selective editor, a South in which black and white individuals lived together in harmony did exist on some level. Its existence has been confirmed by other witnesses. Like Haley, Derrick Alridge, head of the University of Georgia's Institute of African American studies, said in the Winter 2010 *Franklin Chronicle* that his memories of integration in South Carolina—he was a grade-school student in the early 1960s—were of relative calm. This old order of mutual respect within the hierarchy is likely what enabled the South to integrate with, overall, less friction than occurred in many Northern cities.

After two years of research and thought, two years of reading and hearing countless stories about my uncle, I can offer no explanation of his attitude towards civil rights other than that he was a product of his times, in which many decent, God-fearing white people were heirs to a blindness concerning their black neighbors, people they honestly considered their friends. I believe the best on both sides lived with this unjust hierarchy with unusual grace. It is perhaps both the bane and the blessing of being human that we learn to coexist in the thorniest of conditions.

Near the end of his life, Russell's friends realized that his legacy was one they wished to preserve, and they united in 1969 to form the Richard B. Russell Foundation, which, in turn, facilitated establishing the Richard B. Russell Library for Political Research and Studies at the University of Georgia. After nearly forty years, these two organizations remain powerful witnesses to the rich heritage that Richard Russell left to all Americans, both in what he did and what he was.[1]

This vital, two-pronged legacy of library and foundation that honors the life and work of Richard Russell is a powerful one. I have been close to the activities of these organizations for fifteen years as I have researched at the Russell, and I know their work to be outstanding in education, in race relations, and in fostering the thoughtful study of history.[2] However, there are myriad other examples of Russell's legacy of integrity, honesty, and dedication in public service.

Another powerful Russell legacy is incontrovertibly in the field of national defense. In the beginning of my research, I was granted an interview with President Jimmy Carter. Carter had many memories of his early career in the Navy, when he worked under Admiral Hyman Rickover on nuclear submarine development. The young officer sometimes was sent to present aspects of this new work to Russell, who was either chair or ranking minority member of the Armed Services Committee during those years. Carter was proud of his Georgia senator and today still values his unmitigated support of national defense in the postwar years. Whenever he was in Washington, whether on official business or not, young Carter would call on Senator Russell and was always warmly received. As the old Carter spoke, with the witness of his own lifetime of dedicated service to his country and to the world in evidence, his genuine and lasting respect for Richard Russell was unmistakable. He highlighted Russell's wisdom about national defense, his dedication to public service, and his personal integrity. I was humbled that a world-class statesman of Carter's caliber had granted me this interview on the strength of my uncle's record, nearly forty years after his death.

The myriad military bases in Georgia that Richard Russell helped either to establish or to maintain in his home state still contribute heavily

---

[1] In 1984, the United States Postal Service issued a memorial stamp in honor of Richard Brevard Russell, Jr. Its theme was "Not just what he did, but what he was," emphasizing that he was a man of principle, dedication, integrity, and honesty who dealt at high governmental levels with an enormous range of questions throughout forty years of the twentieth century.

[2] See "Note on the Richard B. Russell Library for Political Research and Studies and the Russell Foundation."

to her thriving economy. The senator elected to Dick Russell's seat in Congress was Sam Nunn, great-nephew of Carl Vinson, Georgia's chairman of the House Armed Services Committee for many years. Nunn was even younger than Russell when he went to the Senate, and he chose to put his considerable strengths into national defense. Nunn's outstanding work on the Senate Armed Services Committee for twenty-five years does honor to the records of Russell and Vinson, as does Nunn's current independent think tank to prevent nuclear proliferation.

Numerous federal projects or legislative bills, some of which bear his name, are part of Russell's ongoing legacy in education, medical research, agriculture, and conservation. He was aware that such projects would mean lasting benefits to all Americans, and he was tireless in his efforts to bring their opportunities to Georgia. The school lunch program dating from 1947 is a shining example, but there are others. For example, the Centers for Disease Control and Prevention (CDC) in Atlanta, as well as the Environmental Protection Agency Ecosystems Research Division and the Richard B. Russell Agricultural Research Center in Athens are facilities of global importance. How many of us have enjoyed driving the Richard B. Russell Scenic Highway in north Georgia or boating on lakes Russell, Lanier, Hartwell, or George—all created from hydroelectric projects?

In addition to Richard Russell's public legacy, he also left a strong family, amazing for a man who never married. Nephews and a great-niece and -nephew of Dick Russell's have served in public office: Robert Lee Russell, Jr. served on the Georgia Court of Appeals before his untimely death in 1965, and his brother Richard Brevard Russell III was a Georgia Superior Court judge. Their son and nephew Robert Lee Russell III is a Georgia Superior Court judge at this writing (2010). Nephew Walter Brown Russell, Jr. served as chairman of the DeKalb County Council 1981–1984, and nephew John Davidson Russell served seven terms in the Georgia General Assembly, 1972–1986. Today Dick Russell's great-niece, Jane Vandiver Kidd, who also served in the General Assembly 2005–2006, is chair of the Democratic Party of Georgia (2010). The greatest public service that Russells have given and are still giving is in the field of education. Dick Russell's family entered many professions, but more Russells have become teachers at every level, from kindergarten through graduate-level teaching, than have worked in other fields combined, such as engineering, medicine, law, and business.

When he was writing his final will, Dick Russell wanted to do something that would help his younger nieces and nephews have money for college, and he wanted to help future generations of Russells. Consequently, he left his estate to be divided after certain passages of time, first for his siblings, then for his siblings and nieces and nephews, then adding the great-nieces and -nephews at the final distribution, twenty years after his death. Since most of his estate was in land, it has increased in value over the years. Dick's home was left to the entire family. Valuing all his family equally, he gave another great gift, that of belonging. In 2010, the family met for its sixty-first consecutive reunion at the homeplace, with more than 200 people attending.

Within the first year after Russell's death, his brother Alex had a personal duty to fulfill for his famous brother. Dick Russell had requested in his will that Alex deliver something to Harriet Orr. Harriet was not named in the will, but specific instructions were left for Alex in a sealed envelope for a bequest that Dick Russell gave to her. Alex Russell was troubled at the heartache he heard when Harriet accepted the gift with these words: "This is from the man who gave his life to the United States Senate." It has been frustrating to me that I have not been able to discover much about Harriet Orr, but what I have seen shows that in this woman Dick Russell found someone who loved him so deeply that she was willing to wait for him in a more faithful fashion even than his mother had waited for his father. Harriet waited without benefit of clergy, without titles, without a smidgeon of recognition. Whenever the Senate would release him, she was there, cheerful, affectionate, and faithful. Harriet Orr died at the age of sixty-seven, only a few years after Russell's death.

Conversely, Pat Collins' subsequent career shows her to be a character of a different sort. She continued to have a distinguished career in the Department of Justice. In later years, Proctor Jones, as a young man, met Pat and did not feel that she would have suited his beloved senator. He sensed something hard in her—he was a Southern boy— perhaps the same feeling she inspired in Russell's mother, Ina. Pat married three times and was widowed three times. She had no children. Pat Collins Butler died in 2009 at the age of 101, leaving $1 million to an

Emory University Law School endowment fund. She is considered one of the pioneer women in law in the nation's capital.

It takes no crystal ball to know that those women who loved Richard Russell suffered from his sacrificial work to the Senate. We cannot know if he thought his own sacrifice of a personal life was worth the loneliness at the end.

The *Memorial Tributes to Richard Brevard Russell, Late a Senator from Georgia* provides rich descriptions of this man of contrasts. Yet his Senate colleagues are unequivocal in their assessment of Russell as the quintessential gentleman and public servant. Praise for the Georgia statesman had come earlier, at his twenty-fifth anniversary and his thirty-fifth. It pleased Dick Russell to hear his colleagues voice admiration and respect, to know that they recognized his code of honor. In response to one of the anniversary tributes, Russell said: "When the time comes for me to go out of this Chamber, whether I go out voluntarily, whether my commission is revoked by the electorate of Georgia, or whether I am carried out in a box, I hope it will at least be possible to say of me that I was an honorable man. I do not know of anything that might be said that would better please me."

As the years of his service added up, Richard Russell wanted to be carried out of the United States Senate in a box. His own father had worked at the Georgia Supreme Court on the last day of his life, and his son and namesake wanted to die in harness as well. That is why he rose from a very sick bed to go to the Senate to vote for defense appropriations; why his last words to President Nixon were, "I wish I could get down there and help;" why he gave permission for his proxy to be voted in the Kennedy-Byrd minority leader contest on the day of his death.

I believe that his Senate colleagues recognized and wished to honor this total dedication of self given to the country he loved so much when they named the first Senate Office Building for this statesman. These are the words they inscribed on the wall of that illustrious building:

"This building is dedicated by his colleagues to the memory of Richard Brevard Russell with admiration, affection and respect. His outstanding skills as a parliamentarian and his love of the nation were matched by his wisdom and prudence in foreign policy and defense. A counselor of six presidents, he personified the highest ideals of patriotism. As a man of honor, courage and vision, his greatness will be revered forever in the ranks of those who have served in the Senate."

In the beginning, I remarked on vivid contrasts in the life of Richard Brevard Russell, Jr. At the end, I want to highlight the extraordinary steadfastness that permeates his story. It is steadfastness of high purpose; of wisdom gained from study, work, and a natural gift for thoughtful observation consciously applied; of integrity in relationships; and of impassioned and informed belief in America as the best form of government the world has yet devised. Richard Brevard Russell was a human being, and therefore he had faults. We might judge these faults tragic, but he possessed such a healthy balance of the best that is human—kindness, compassion, tolerance, modesty, courtesy, sense of humor, and self-sacrifice—that it is fair to claim the results of his life indeed show, as his epitaph claims, that "he sought the good of his people and promoted the welfare of all their descendants."

Note on the Richard B. Russell Library for Political
Research and Studies and the Russell Foundation

As Richard Russell's career drew to a close, the University of Georgia was eager to have the Russell papers because they covered such an extended range of modern history. Richard Russell, like many others before him, had trouble deciding how to relinquish this valuable resource. He did not want his papers buried in a traditional Special Collections department of a university library, inaccessible, and essentially lost. The Russell Foundation agreed and set out to raise funds to build a research library in the senator's name. Restricted by Russell from fund-raising during his lifetime, the foundation raised less than they had hoped following his death. Thus, the trustees collaborated with the Georgia General Assembly, the Board of Regents, and the University of Georgia to establish a research library that would have a place apart within the University of Georgia libraries. The Russell Foundation raised nearly $1.5 million to help fund the facility, which was to be called the Richard B. Russell Memorial Library,[1] with the major goal of preserving the senator's papers.[2] Today the Russell library incorporates a vision far beyond that of preserving the senator's papers. The library posted as its motto from the beginning these words of Richard Brevard Russell: "Look to the past as a means of weighing the present and the future," and these words have been followed in a graceful and creative balance. Far from becoming a place where history is buried, the Russell has become a vital point from which to unearth it and seek to understand it in order to affect the present and the future.

Although the Richard Brevard Russell Collection serves as cornerstone, there are today over 300 modern political and public policy-related collections in the Russell library. Consequently, it serves as a

---

[1] In 1992 the library was renamed the Richard B. Russell Library for Political Research and Studies to reflect its growth and evolving development.

[2] This collection never received federal appropriations, as did others, such as those of Hubert Humphrey and Everett Dirksen.

major source for research in a broad area of subjects covering a much longer period of time than most comparable libraries. The holdings demonstrate the breadth, diversity, and full spectrum of Georgia's political life for over a century. Endorsing this change in vision, the Russell Foundation trustees realized the senator's greater legacy was the growth of the library, and that formal collecting did not have to focus exclusively on the senator. The new focus became the comprehensive, interrelated nature of the public policy collections and the ability to support research of politics and policy in the broadest sense. The past is indeed being mined for capital to deal with the present and the future.

As important as is this broader focus, it should also be noted that the Russell houses the papers of numerous other members of the Russell family, including those of the senator's father, mother, his sister Ina, his uncle Lewis, and those of Governor Ernest Vandiver, Congressman Hugh Peterson, and other Russells who have served in public office. This might be the only repository in the country documenting over 150 years of the life of one family. Other families have chosen to leave their papers to the Russell, such as the Dudley Hughes family and the Lamartine Hardman family, creating a valuable primary source for historians on the life and times of earlier Georgians.

It would be impossible here to give a detailed account of the work of the Russell, but two projects of the library well illustrate how the vision of Richard Russell's legacy has evolved. When University of Georgia professors Maurice Daniels (School of Social Work and now dean thereof) and Derrick Alridge (College of Education and now director of the Institute for African American Studies) decided to make a collection highlighting the lives and work in Georgia of common people who participated in the civil rights movement, the Foot Soldier Project was born. The project is not specifically based in any one department, but is a collaborative project with representatives from several departments on campus, including the Russell. According to its founders:

> The Foot Soldier Project partnered with the Russell to develop a permanent archival collection focusing on civil rights, largely comprised of research materials developed through the project. These archival materials include historical papers,

photographs, artifacts, intellectual and social histories, and documentaries with a focus on unsung persons and related events in the movement for civil rights and social justice. By providing a full spectrum of documentation on civil rights experiences, this initiative brings together a vast array of resources in one repository with the aim of fostering interdisciplinary collaboration among scholars, archivists, and the community.

Daniels and Alridge have worked closely with Russell staff members on this project for about ten years. Richard Brevard Russell, Jr. would have appreciated the witness of ongoing partnership in this situation and the strength of historical perspective that it illustrates.

Another project included a program of several months surrounding the activities of the Highlander Folk School of Monteagle, Tennessee, which became a "vital incubator" of the civil rights movement and hosted a series of crucial workshops and training sessions that a number of the movement's most prominent leaders attended, including Rosa Parks and Martin Luther King, Jr. Highlander served to lay the groundwork for the Student Nonviolent Coordinating Committee, the Mississippi Freedom Summer, and Citizenship Schools for African-Americans in South Carolina, Georgia, and elsewhere in the South. It continues to thrive and has adapted its mission to serve Latino immigrants in the South, rural communities in Appalachia and the Deep South, and multiracial and ethnic youth organizations. An exhibit commemorating seventy-five years of the Highlander was on display at the Russell for five months in 2008 and early 2009, and under the direction of Jill Severn, the library sponsored five lectures on the work of this venerable organization. Through such resources, Richard Russell's ideal of allowing all voices to be heard and his view of the importance of broad historical perspective can be seen still hard at work.

While supporting the broadening of the Russell library's mission, the Russell Foundation has continued to carry forward Richard Russell's ideals of education and public service. The foundation has contributed more than $7 million to the University of Georgia since 1973[3] and

---

[3] In 2008 the Russell Foundation pledged a million-dollar endowment upon dedication of the new Special Collections Libraries building to support the Russell Library's public programming.

sponsors yearly scholarships and teaching awards, as well as a biennial symposium on national security, a student leadership program, and other activities that Senator Russell thought important. The symposiums on national security have brought together national and international officials and the university community in order to discuss this increasingly critical arena.

While the foundation was set up mainly by prominent men in business and government[4] and its work has been exemplary, I want to note that the daily working of the Russell library has been carried on primarily by dedicated and capable women. I believe the history of the family shows that it is a mark of most Russell men that they know how to pick a good woman for whatever job needs doing, a woman who will serve with skill and loyalty. Although Dick Russell never married, his thirty-year affair with Harriet Orr shows her to have been such a woman. Amazingly, this tradition of female talent, brains, and loyalty has carried on with the Russell library.

In the beginning, when the senator's papers had to be cleared from his Washington office immediately following his death, there was serious concern over security questions. Barboura G. Raesly, or Babs, the senator's personal secretary for sixteen years, accepted a position with the Russell Estate and the Russell Foundation to review the documents prior to their transfer to the university. Those of us who had known Babs's remarkable prowess as a secretary watched with pride as, in consummate professional fashion, she met the challenge of officially surveying a literal mountain of papers from thirty-eight years of distinguished public service work by a man who never threw out anything.[5] She attended the Georgia Archives Institute to understand archival standards necessary for the proper preservation and management of the papers for research use, and she was a guiding force

---

[4] Richard B. Russell, Jr., wanted the board of trustees of the foundation to reflect society at the time, so there were white men, one woman, and one African-American—and that has always been the make-up with now four women and two African-American males.

[5] That Dick Russell never threw out anything is scarce an exaggeration. I believe this trait is a witness to his utter honesty in public service and in his belief that we can learn from history. Many politicians are quick to destroy a record that might prove embarrassing.

in establishing the operation of the library within the university libraries administrations. When she had finished this Herculean labor, Babs Raesly went back to Washington, completed her federal employment, earned a law degree, and worked as an attorney in Fairfax, Virginia, until her death in 1995. Sheryl B. Vogt, the third director of the Russell, writes in the official guide to the Russell Collection that the guide could be dedicated to no other than Barboura G. Raesly.

Sheryl Vogt is a talented archivist who has served the Russell for thirty-five years with admirable vision. Under Vogt's leadership, the Russell has become the repository for many congressional papers and a national model for their archival management. She went to Washington and persuaded various elected officials and others of the wisdom of leaving their papers to the Russell. A wide variety of other fascinating political documents reside there, such as the papers of Georgia Renaissance man Lamartine G. Hardman, who was a physician and textile manufacturer of the late nineteenth and early twentieth centuries. Active in state government for thirty years, Hardman ultimately became governor. The papers of Dean Rusk, secretary of state under Kennedy and Johnson, and others, such as those of Ambassadors W. Tapley Bennett and Martin Hillenbrand, give the library an enviable strength in foreign affairs and policy. The editorial cartoons of Clifford H. "Baldy" Baldowski provide a delightful snapshot of over thirty-five years of post-World War II local, state, and world history and culture. From the myriad collections at the Russell, a few other notables are those of Michael Thurmond, the first African American in Georgia history to gain statewide elective office without first having been appointed to fill a vacancy in that office by the governor; those of Henry T. "Hank" Myers, presidential pilot from Albany, Georgia, who flew FDR to Yalta and set many flight records, a handsome, dashing, and romantic character; those of Melba R. Williams, Eunice L. Mixon, and Maxine S. Goldstein, women who worked in local civic groups, grassroots activism, and party politics; and those of Iris F. Blitch, Janet S. Merritt, Peg Blitch, Louise McBee, Cathy Cox, and Eva Galambos, who went on to elected office.

People come from all over the world to research at the Russell, particularly in the areas of civil rights and foreign policy, but it is there first for all faculty and students at the University of Georgia. Nothing would have pleased Richard B. Russell more than to see this living library flying high the flag of public education and service. The road the Russell library has taken in its nearly forty-year history well illustrates an evolution of his modest view of his own work as well as his inspiring leadership. The work of the Russell Foundation, a private organization, in partnership with the University of Georgia these forty years, is an ongoing example of Richard Russell's ability to inspire others to public service.

Bibliographical Essay

Intending for this book to be akin to a memoir, I tried not to think of it as an academic exercise. In my view, the academic approach, however "accurate" it might be, too often misses the essential. On the other hand, I did not know Richard Brevard Russell, Jr. long enough as an adult to write a true memoir. Yet it has been my feeling through the years that none of the numerous books in which he features, including Gilbert Fite's thorough biography, have wholly captured, revealed, or understood the man who was Dick Russell and that something ought to be done about that. I wanted to try to find the Dick Russell who had evaded so many others. It is true that he was intensely private. He left scant letters or other papers to help anyone discover his feelings about many of the issues of his day from a personal standpoint. Nevertheless, I felt there were ways to search out the man.

Because I had the pleasure of getting to know Dick Russell's parents and siblings deeply through the academic work I had done on them—work that supported what I have known of them as my family—I started with my own books, *Roots and Ever Green: The Selected Letters of Ina Dillard Russell* and *A Heart for Any Fate*, the biography of Richard B. Russell, Sr. I had worked hard to make the academic reveal the essential in both volumes and am certain that they give an accurate picture of the life Dick Russell, Jr. knew as a young person and an equally accurate description of the characters of his parents. I know of no other books that can tell as much about the formative influences on Dick Russell, Jr., and they are well-documented.

All of the siblings of Dick Russell, Jr. are gone now, and he had no wife who might have left clues to aspects of his personality. There are, however, quite a few nieces and nephews who knew him from his young avuncular days, and they were willing and able to relate some revealing tales. I have consulted with the entire range during the course of my work; there were thirty-nine of us in the beginning, though the ranks have thinned now. These sources are reliable, I know, because of how hard each person strove to tell me stories from an objective standpoint or how he or she frankly admitted that "this is just from my experience." When I put all that together, I was confident I had a faithful picture of the human being that was Dick Russell.

The oral histories in the Russell Collection at the Russell library, which were done soon after Richard B. Russell's death, have been a treasure trove of personal stories. These are interviews with people who had known Dick Russell both personally and professionally. The range of characters in this collection is astonishing, from presidents (Nixon, Ford, and Carter), numerous senators, and even a federal judge, who happened to be the husband of one of his former girlfriends, to Russell's feisty boyhood friend Luke Austin, his lifelong servant, Modine Thomas, and a number of waitresses from the Senate dining room. Again, as I listened to these people, who had had daily experience with Richard Russell or who had been with him through some of the momentous twentieth-century crises of our nation, I learned about a public servant second to none, who was also known and loved as a caring friend. In the text, I try to cite the name or occupation of the person whose history I used in order to indicate where other scholars might want to look. There are 147 oral histories, and although I did not consult every single one, I made a good dent in the pile.

Similar to the oral histories, only briefer, is *Richard Brevard Russell Late a Senator from Georgia Memorial Tributes Delivered in Congress.* The tributes come from the people who knew and worked with him, and even allowing for the word "tribute" as theme, they show a remarkable consistency in their analysis of the character of Richard B. Russell. This volume also contains newspaper articles written at the time of Russell's death and a detailed description of his funeral. The articles illustrate how Russell was respected nationwide at the time of his death, in spite of his opposition to civil rights. A later volume, published twenty-five years after his death, gives witness to the continued respect his life and work earned on the national forum: *Dedication and Unveiling of the Statue of Richard Brevard Russell, Jr. Proceedings in the Rotunda of the Russell Senate Office Building* (Washington, DC, 24 January 1996). This volume contains the entire address that Senator Robert Byrd (D-WV) made to the Senate on 1 February 1988 on Russell's life and work. Byrd's summary gives a balanced view of the career of Richard Brevard Russell, Jr. in all aspects.

I found the Speech File in the Russell Collection useful for opinions or ideas in Russell's own voice. His comments in the *Congressional Record* following tributes to him were also valuable.

For the broad activities associated with Russell's life after 1920, I used Gilbert Fite's biography, *Richard B. Russell, Jr., Senator from Georgia.* Dr. Fite was the first Richard B. Russell Professor at the University of Georgia, and he has done an accurate job of giving the bare facts of Russell's life. I hereby acknowledge my debt to him for these. Another source on which I relied heavily is John A. Goldsmith's *Colleagues: Richard B. Russell and His Apprentice Lyndon B. Johnson.* Goldsmith was a Washington reporter for many years and knew both Russell and Johnson. His book provides valuable insights into the men and the times. I also found helpful Robert Mann's *The Walls of Jericho: Lyndon Johnson, Hubert Humphrey, Richard Russell, and the Struggle for Civil Rights.* Goldberg and Mann, while entirely academic, seem to reveal a lot of the essential, and I recommend their works.

I was fortunate to have interviews with Proctor Jones and Charles Campbell, men from Georgia who worked for Richard Russell in the final years of his life. Proctor Jones spent two hours with me in the spring before his untimely death in summer 2009, and his insights and stories are treasures. Jones was literally Russell's right-hand man in the final five or six years of the statesman's life. Following the death of Richard Russell, Jones chose to continue working in Washington and achieved an outstanding record in government service. Campbell returned to Georgia after the senator died to practice law. He became the fourth chairman of the Russell Foundation and collaborated for seventeen years with Sheryl Vogt of the Russell library. His stories, his witness, and his continued willingness to answer new questions have given my story a depth and breadth I could not have achieved otherwise.

It would not do to list references without listing Sheryl Vogt, who has to be recognized as the world authority on Richard B. Russell, Jr. After thirty-five years with the Richard B. Russell Library for Political Research and Studies, she can point any scholar toward where to find almost anything, if it exists, that he or she would want to know about Russell. In 2004 Sheryl Vogt was chosen Archivist of the Year, by Ina Caro on behalf of the Scone Foundation in New York. I have found her to be the archivist for me of any year. I am especially grateful that she sent the unexpected material from the Patricia Collins Butler estate as soon as it arrived at the Russell so that I was able to include its contents in this narrative. After fifteen years of researching at the Russell, I can only say that my debt to Sheryl Vogt is more than I could ever repay.

I am including at the end of this essay a selected bibliography of other sources that I either consulted or that I think would be helpful to anyone wishing to go deeper into any of the myriad aspects of the career of Richard Brevard Russell, Jr.

Although most of the family papers are now in the Russell library, I did have access to several letters discovered at the homeplace in recent years. As I worked on Ina's letters, I discovered a few that the initial Russell library team had missed, and in 2002, James Millsaps Russell, son of Robert Lee Russell, Jr., found gold when he was cleaning out the smokehouse next to the main house: several years' worth of what was called "the family letter." Starting in 1937, the thirteen siblings wrote to one another, one after the other, in a round robin letter, each one adding his or her letter to the ones before. They wrote thus for about ten years. It took about a year for the letter to get around, and I could frankly wish for more detailed news, but some gems were there with regard to Dick Russell's way of looking at life, particularly one about how early he came to understand the concept of "noblesse oblige."

I used the online *New Georgia Encyclopedia* for information about many Georgia politicians and historical figures. I also used online resources for information on senators, cabinet members, Congress, civil war generals, battles in various wars, and other historical events.

Suggested Bibliography

Barrett, David M. *Uncertain Warriors: Lyndon Johnson and His Vietnam Advisers.* Lawrence KS: University Press of Kansas, 1993.

Caro, Robert A. *The Years of Lyndon Johnson.* Volume 3. *Master of the Senate.* New York: Alfred A. Knopf, 2002.

Fite, Gilbert C. *Richard B. Russell, Jr., Senator from Georgia.* The Fred W. Morrison Series in Southern Studies. Chapel Hill and London: University of North Carolina Press, 1991.

Goldsmith, John A. *Colleagues: Richard B. Russell and His Apprentice Lyndon B. Johnson.* Macon GA: Mercer University Press, 1998.

Horwitz, Tony. *Confederates in the Attic: Dispatches from the Unfinished Civil War.* New York: Vintage Books, 1999.

Logue, Calvin McLeod and Dwight L. Freshley, ed. *Voice of Georgia: Speeches of Richard B. Russell, 1928–1969.* Macon GA: Mercer University Press, 1997.

Mann, Robert. *The Walls of Jericho: Lyndon Johnson, Hubert Humphrey, Richard Russell, and the Struggle for Civil Rights.* San Diego, New York, London: Harcourt Brace, 1996.

Mann, Robert. *When Freedom Would Triumph: The Civil Rights Struggle in Congress, 1954–1968,* Updated and Abridged Edition of *The Walls of Jericho.* Baton Rouge: University Press of Louisiana, 2007.

Russell, Sally. *A Heart for Any Fate: The Biography of Richard Brevard Russell Sr.* Macon GA: Mercer University Press, 2004.

Russell, Sally, ed. *Roots and Ever Green: The Selected Letters of Ina Dillard Russell.* Athens: University of Georgia Press, 1999.

Sitkoff, Harvard. *King: Pilgrimage to the Mountaintop.* New York: Hill & Wang, a Division of Farrar, Straus and Giroux, 2008.

Valeo, Francis R. *Mike Mansfield, Majority Leader: A Different Kind of Senate, 1961–1976. New York: M. E. Sharpe, 1999.*

White, William S. *Citadel: The Story of the U.S. Senate.* New York: Harper & Brothers, 1956.

Index